MARK TWAIN AND ORION CLEMENS

MARK TWAIN AND ORION CLEMENS
Brothers, Partners, Strangers

PHILIP ASHLEY FANNING

Foreword by Alan Gribben

THE UNIVERSITY OF ALABAMA PRESS
Tuscaloosa and London

Typeface is AGaramond

∞

The paper on which this book is printed meets the minimum requirements of American National Standard for Information Science–Permanence of Paper for Printed Library Materials, ANSI Z39.48-1984.

Library of Congress Cataloging-in-Publication Data

Fanning, Philip Ashley, 1935–
Mark Twain and Orion Clemens : brothers, partners, strangers / Philip Ashley Fanning ; foreword by Alan Gribben.

p. cm. — (Studies in American literary realism and naturalism)
Includes bibliographical references and index.

ISBN 0-8173-1310-9 (cloth : alk. paper)
1. Twain, Mark, 1835–1910—Family. 2. Clemens, Orion, 1825–1897.
3. Authors, American—19th century—Biography. 4. Brothers—United States—Biography. I. Title. II. Series.

PS1332 .F26 2003
818'.409—dc21
2002152212

British Library Cataloguing-in-Publication Data available

For Linda
beloved wife, fellow researcher, best friend

Contents

Foreword

Behind the publication of every book typically lies a story of initial discouragement and tribulation. This is especially the case with the notable history of Philip Fanning's dual biography. Mr. Fanning, an independent writer and scholar residing in San Francisco, essentially finished the manuscript for *Mark Twain and Orion Clemens* in the mid-1990s. He had grown fascinated with this fraternal relationship while doing background research for a novel he was contemplating in which Twain and his brother were to appear as minor characters. Soon he found himself deeply absorbed in the story of Samuel and Orion Clemens, and he began to visit the sites of the pair's mutual residency, including Hannibal and St. Louis, Missouri; Muscatine and Keokuk, Iowa; Carson City, Nevada; and Hartford, Connecticut. While touring Carson City, Mr. Fanning and his wife, Linda, actually managed to locate the wooden frame house where Orion once lived with his wife, Mollie, and daughter, Jennie—the same residence in which Sam stayed when he visited them—and the Fannings spoke with an attorney whose office now occupies the property and received an impromptu tour of the structure.

Gradually, upon reading and rereading the brothers' published and unpublished correspondence (much of it in the Mark Twain Papers at Berkeley), Mr. Fanning pieced together a story significantly at odds with much that has been commonly accepted about the Clemenses' brotherly bond. Orion Clemens, it appeared to Mr. Fanning, was not nearly so ludicrously inept and pathetic (particularly in the early and middle stages of his life) as students of Mark Twain have been led to believe, and Samuel Clemens had done a masterful job of concealing from all biographers the depth of his resentment against his elder sibling in his portrayal of Orion as a buffoon and near lunatic.

Perhaps I should concede here that I myself was one of the many scholars taken in by Twain's manipulations. Working for eight years on the Mark Twain Project editorial team assembled by Frederick Anderson at the University of California at Berkeley, I encountered time and again the condescending, dismissive remarks about Orion made by Twain, Albert Bigelow Paine, and subsequent commentators who routinely referred to Orion as hapless and ridiculous, and I accepted their opinions at face value. Then in 1997 I chaired a session for the State of Mark Twain Studies International Conference at Elmira College, to which Philip Fanning submitted one of his chapters—a shocking excerpt speculating about Sam Clemens's one-time intention to murder his brother Orion. I read the paper with utter amazement, but finding its arguments plausible I added it to the program. Mr. Fanning presented his paper to a courteously interested if rather skeptical audience at the conference. He seemed unfazed by the low-key reception, remarking that he could hardly expect wild enthusiasm to greet his sobering version of these events.

Shortly thereafter I asked to look at his entire book manuscript. It was not a pretty story Mr. Fanning told, by any stretch of the imagination: Twain succeeded in hoodwinking generations of biographers (and conceivably even fooling himself) into believing virtually the opposite of what in reality happened during the course of a painful domestic drama stretching from the 1850s to the 1890s. Even Orion's death in 1897 did not entirely free Sam from the grip of the psychological struggle with his brother and his conscience, and evidence exists that his mixed feelings about Orion continued to affect his thoughts and writings.

Although these findings cast a critical light upon an author whom I have personally admired and studied since graduate school, I came to respect Mr. Fanning's calm determination to correct the historical record about Orion Clemens. Yet Mr. Fanning's road to publication was about to get even more taxing than his lengthy and meticulous research. Some twenty publishers turned down his manuscript, university presses as well as trade houses, and most of them cited concerns about its emphasis on the life of a relatively obscure figure while implicitly highlighting the ethical failings of a literary icon. This reaction strikes one as odd, since Hamlin Hill's *Mark Twain: God's Fool* (1973), for instance, which probed searchingly into the foibles and tragedies of Twain's final decade, went on to become a standard work in the field of Mark Twain studies. Guy Cardwell's *The Man Who Was Mark Twain* (1991), a book far more condemnatory of Twain's character and status than anything Mr. Fanning suggests, nonetheless found receptive editors. And Andrew Hoffman's *Inventing Mark Twain* (1997) became a trade-book publication despite the fact that his allegations about Twain's homosexual orientation remain unsubstantiated.

Still, Mr. Fanning's manuscript languished unclaimed, despite his seeking the assistance and endorsement of several leading Mark Twain authorities. Eventually, he approached the University of Alabama Press, which decided that his work warranted publication. I felt the same way about it, and for three distinct reasons. In the first place, his work is well documented and effectively written. In the second place, this is the United States, where unorthodox and even unpopular views can normally find public expression, whether or not they prevail in the long run. Finally, and equally important, any concerns that Mark Twain's literary reputation might be irreparably damaged by revelations that he disliked, sabotaged, and systematically humiliated one of his siblings assuredly sells short both general and academic readers. His stature with them is secure. Besides, numerous other figures of great artistic standing have evinced undesirable and even unsavory traits. Much like the painfully entwined painter Vincent Van Gogh and his brother Theo, Samuel and Orion will in all probability be forgiven for the consequences of their fatefully ill matched temperaments. Indeed, Twain's wretchedly twisted relationship with his older brother will likely endow his complex personality with dark but engaging shadows. He will be seen as even more fascinating as he becomes less flawless.

Sam's character failures regarding Orion can be set against other areas in which his behavior was impeccable. For instance, biographers have long marveled at the unflagging devotion to his wife, Olivia, that kept Sam sexually faithful to her during long periods of separation on lecture tours and writing trips (not to mention her lengthy final illness), when an acclaimed author might easily have found discreet female companionship. He went even further after her death in 1904, choosing to remain celibate as a tribute to their marital love. This strict propriety of untempted fidelity has struck the current generation as, well, perhaps a little too irreproach-able. But now here is a matter—sibling rivalry erupting periodically into raging detestation—that got the better of Samuel Clemens and echoed so deafeningly in his consciousness that he never could grasp its magnitude. Philip Fanning has adroitly traced the outlines and potency of a regrettable series of interactive episodes, and Orion Clemens will at last have his day in the court of world opinion. He merits this opportunity to become better understood, just as twenty-first-century readers deserve to learn the un-mitigated truth about his troubled relationship with one of our literary giants.

Alan Gribben
Auburn University Montgomery, June 2002

Preface

This book tracks Orion Clemens's relationship with his younger brother Samuel from its beginnings in Missouri in the 1830s and 1840s to Orion's death in Iowa in 1897. Orion's influence on the person we know as Mark Twain was profound, pervasive, and prolonged, yet he has been largely ignored by biographers and historians. This was no accident; in his *Autobiography* and elsewhere the great humorist did his best to make sure that if posterity took note of Orion at all it would be as a ludicrous figure. The record shows, however, that while Orion had his quirks, he was not ridiculous. He was a proud, ambitious, intelligent, courageous man who in Nevada Territory acquitted himself with distinction and who throughout his life displayed a humanity and an integrity that were admired by those who knew him. That said, it should be added that during his later years he behaved more and more erratically and was unable to support himself and his wife, becoming obliged to avail himself of his successful brother's ample generosity.

In many ways these two men were alike. Both were writers and lecturers whose outspokenness got them into trouble. Both acquired from their father the dream of great wealth. In the course of a varied career, each tried his hand at printing, newspaper work, editing, mining speculation, and inventing. Each essayed entrepreneurship and failed. Both had youthful thoughts of entering the ministry.[1] Both acted in amateur theatricals. Each had a daughter he named after his mother, Jane Clemens (though neither was called Jane). In 1861 the Clemens brothers went to the new territory of Nevada together, and there each had his first taste of public acclaim. After leaving the West, each separately made his way to the Northeast, lived in Hartford and New York City, and became involved with Elisha Bliss's American Publishing Company and with a newspaper or newspapers. Both Orion and Sam wrote long, revealing autobiographies. Each had an adored daughter who died young, and neither ever fully recovered from the loss, his spirit and his career irreparably harmed.

In other ways Orion and Samuel were dissimilar. Orion was usually patient and easygoing, while Sam's hot temper and short fuse were legendary. Intellectually, Orion was (surprisingly) the more adventurous of the two, constantly challenging the consensus, while socially it was Samuel who was the active one and Orion often the spectator. Politically, Orion was to the left of Sam. In matters of ethics the older brother was for the most part beyond reproach, while the younger was known to cut corners. Orion was self-effacing, while Sam tooted his own horn. If Orion was religious, Sam was materialistic. On the other hand, the younger brother was more sensitive than the older, who once wrote that Sam's "organization is such as to feel the utmost extreme of every feeling. . . . Both his capacity of enjoyment and his capacity of suffering are greater than mine."[2]

Perhaps the most important difference between the Clemens siblings was that Orion believed in free will and personal responsibility, whereas Samuel wasn't so sure. Orion felt that a person could overcome his circumstances and remake himself after a favored model, whereas Sam often expressed the belief that everyone is condemned by temperament and circumstance to follow an unbreakable chain of predetermined acts. On the overarching moral issue of the day, Orion saw the evils of slavery long before Sam did, a fact Sam publicly acknowledged, but only in a misleading way.

In many respects Sam defined himself against Orion's formidable backdrop. He first left home because he thought Orion "hated" him, and once when he felt his elder brother was blocking his progress he challenged him, "By the Lord God! you must clear the track, you know!"[3] At the age of twenty-seven he complained to his mother and sister about "a fearful lecture" Orion had given him on his comportment, protesting, "He will learn after a while, perhaps, that I am not an infant."[4] Sam was probably staying under his brother's roof in Carson City, Nevada, when he first signed the name "Mark Twain," with its connotation of duality, to one of his dispatches to the *Virginia City Territorial Enterprise.*

Orion was Sam's first real editor and mentor. Even though by his own admission Orion was "tyrannical and unjust" to his brother and disciplined Sam when he used the pages of the *Hannibal Journal* to stir up trouble, he was also the first to recognize Sam's writing talent and encourage him to develop it. When it became apparent that the brothers were not going to strike it rich in the silver fields of Nevada, Orion helped Sam take up a career in journalism. He kept scrapbooks of his articles and urged him to write a book. On the other hand, when in 1865 Sam appealed to Orion to form an unusual sort of literary alliance, his brother appears to have turned him down.

This biographical study came about by accident. In 1992 I was researching a novel when I ran across an incident that occurred in San Francisco in 1865 and 1866. It seemed to have culminated when, as Mark Twain wrote, "I put the pistol to my head"—a direct result, evidently, of something his elder brother had done. If this interpretation was right, Orion was—if only at that critical moment—a major factor in Samuel's psychic economy. Why, then, hadn't I (a lifelong Mark Twain fan) heard more about him? Intrigued, I set aside my fiction and tried to reconstruct the happening as accurately as possible, using letters, Twain's *Autobiography,* newspaper items, and other sources. The result was an article called "One Story Mark Twain *Wouldn't* Tell," which appeared in *Californians* in 1995.

Still my curiosity wasn't slaked. I was surprised to learn that of the hundreds of books written about Mark Twain and his milieu, not one was devoted to his elder brother. (In June 1999 the Library of Congress catalog listed 697 titles under the subject category "Mark Twain" and 63 under "Samuel Clemens," while only 1 title, a brief burlesque written by Twain, came up under "Orion Clemens.") I broadened my research and began looking for whatever information I could find in the library, progressively building a chronology in my laptop computer. I read Twain's *Autobiography* and Albert Bigelow Paine's *Mark Twain: A Biography.* I studied the author's correspondence, as published in Paine's two-volume version and in the comprehensive edition issued by the Mark Twain Project, which at this writing has reached its fifth volume (volume 6 is in press). I perused many other primary sources, and secondary ones too—always with the fraternal relationship in mind. Having exhausted the published records, I visited the Mark Twain Papers in Berkeley and spent months reading documents (mostly Orion's and Sam's letters) that had not yet been made public. By now hopelessly caught up in the story, I enlisted my wife's support, and together we traveled to places where Orion lived or spent time—Hannibal, Keokuk, Muscatine, St. Louis, Carson City, Virginia City, Hartford, Rutland—and to institutions where documents he left behind are preserved—libraries and archives in Missouri, Iowa, Nevada, Connecticut, Vermont, and the nation's capital.

There was only one genius in the Clemens family, but Orion is worth scrutinizing in his own right. This book is not, however, a biography of Orion, nor is it a dual life history of the Clemens brothers; rather it is an account of the bond between the two—a biography, if you will, of a fraternal kinship. Throughout I have tried to avoid duplicating information available in other publications and instead to focus on what is less well known. If this strategy seems to favor Orion, it is because he has been so neglected.

Wherever feasible I have used Orion's and Samuel's own words to tell their tale, supplemented by those of their mother, sister, wives, friends, and associates. Unfortunately, despite a wealth of information that survives, key documents—including virtually all of Orion's 2,523-page autobiography—have been lost or destroyed. Consequently, it was sometimes necessary to recover events (as in the case of the pistol-to-the-head incident) on the basis of incomplete evidence. Whenever I have done this, I have tried to make my reasoning clear and to distinguish what is known from what is conjectured. My hope is that points raised herein will be discussed and further investigated by Mark Twain scholars. Many questions remain, and in chapters 2, 5, and 11, I propose specific hypotheses that may be confirmed, disproved, or modified as more information comes to light.

Historians and biographers sometimes face a dilemma. They need to present their subjects accurately, fully, and fairly, yet they may feel obliged to withhold certain facts, lest innocent parties be harmed, reputations ruined, or secrets revealed. Because real, living persons could have been injured, William Dean Howells was probably justified to advise Mark Twain not to let his "love of the naked truth" cause him to publish parts of Orion's ultra-candid autobiography (see chap. 17). Similarly, Twain was within his rights to withhold certain letters from his biographer for the reason that "a man should be dead before his private foolishnesses are risked in print" (see chap. 20).

When all vulnerable parties have long been in their graves, however, the public's right to know becomes paramount. We need to learn all we can about our heroes and icons. To deny them their failings is to rob them of their humanity; blindfolding ourselves to such matters serves no good purpose and diminishes us all. Mark Twain is America's greatest writer; no one has portrayed the human psyche—from its heights of unselfishness to its depths of malice—with greater sensitivity and insight. Twain's reputation will survive the unflattering material in this book, and, if anything, Twain will emerge more compelling—because complex and contradictory—than anyone imagined. Moreover, Orion will be restored to his rightful place in the uniquely American drama of the brothers Clemens.

Acknowledgments

Alan Gribben proved to be a friend of this book from first to last, assisting me in my search for a publisher and improving the drafts with multitudinous recommendations. Shelley Fisher Fishkin read an early version and made valuable suggestions. Robert D. Armstrong perused the Nevada chapters and also provided indispensable guidance in determining what to look for in the Nevada State Archives. During the early stages of research I received words of encouragement and guidance from Thomas A. Tenny, Edgar M. Branch, Kevin Starr, Kevin J. Bochynski, R. Kent Rasmussen, Gladys Hansen, Michael Larsen, and Elizabeth Pomada, for which I am deeply appreciative.

The staff of the University of San Francisco's Gleeson Library should be thanked, especially Hille Novak and Marian Gin. At the Mark Twain Papers everyone was cordial and considerate, but particularly helpful were Kenneth M. Sanderson, Victor Fischer, and Brenda Bailie. In Muscatine, Diane Mayer of the P. M. Musser Public Library and Max Churchill provided friendly and valuable assistance. Emma Lee Lahmeyer of the Keokuk Public Library was extremely helpful, courteous, and professional. Lucille Malone of the State Historical Society of Missouri helped me and my wife navigate the extensive facilities in Columbia. Henry Sweets, director of the Mark Twain Home and Museum in Hannibal, went above and beyond the call of duty in conducting us on a private tour of the new museum, at that time only partly open to the public. Lee Mortinson of the Nevada

Historical Society and Susan Searcy of Library Special Collections at the University of Nevada assisted us with our research in Reno. In Carson City Jeff Kintot was very obliging in giving us access to the Nevada State Archives, and Bob Nylen of the Nevada State Museum showed us historical artifacts associated with Orion Clemens. Joylyn M. Harmer of the Smith and Loomis law firm in Carson City graciously gave us a guided tour of Orion's house, which at that time served as offices for the firm. Jake Sherman of the Rutland, Vermont, Public Library provided information about Orion's stint as editor of the *Rutland Daily Globe.* In Montpelier, Vermont, Marge Zunder helped us find our way around the Vermont Department of Libraries, where files of the *Globe* are maintained. I would like to thank Gretchen Sharlow, at that time director of the Elmira College Center for Mark Twain Studies, for her hospitality while my wife and I were in Elmira. Judy Johnson and Martha Smart assisted us in the Connecticut Historical Society in Hartford. Guenter B. Risse of the University of California, San Francisco, provided important information about medical matters in nineteenth-century America. At the Library of Congress, Margaret Keypepper was very helpful in locating what may be the sole remaining original copy of Orion's sketch "JIM," as published in the *American Publisher.*

I would like to thank my wife, Linda, who acted as my research assistant during trips to the Midwest, Nevada, and the Northeast. She also read the manuscript and was responsible for many essential alterations as it developed.

Permission to quote from the following volumes was granted by the University of California Press: *Mark Twain's Letters,* vol. 1, *1853–1866,* edited by Edgar Marquess Branch, Michael B. Frank, Kenneth M. Sanderson, Harriet Elinor Smith, Lin Salamo, and Richard Bucci, 1988; *Mark Twain's Letters,* vol. 2, *1867–1868,* edited by Harriet Elinor Smith, Richard Bucci, and Lin Salamo, 1990; *Mark Twain's Letters,* vol. 3, *1869,* edited by Victor Fischer, Michael B. Frank, and Dahlia Armon, 1992; *Mark Twain's Letters,* vol. 4, *1870–1871,* edited by Victor Fischer, Michael B. Frank, and Lin Salamo, 1995; and *Mark Twain's Letters,* vol. 5, *1872–1873,* edited by Lin Salamo and Harriet Elinor Smith, 1997.

Permission to quote previously unpublished words of Mark Twain was granted by the General Editor of the Mark Twain Project. Permission to quote from the following volume was granted by Harvard University Press: *Mark Twain–Howells Letters: The Correspondence of Samuel L. Clemens and*

William D. Howells, 1872–1910, edited by Henry Nash Smith and William M. Gibson with Frederick Anderson, Cambridge, Mass.: Belknap Press of Harvard University Press, Copyright © 1962 by the President and Fellows of Harvard College, Copyright © renewed 1990 by Elinor Lucas Smith.

Excerpts from *Sam Clemens of Hannibal* by Dixon Wecter copyright © 1952, and renewed 1980 by Elizabeth Farrar Wecter Pike. Reprinted by permission of Houghton Mifflin Company. All rights reserved.

MARK TWAIN AND ORION CLEMENS

1

Sam Shuns Orion's Role Model

I know that a person that can turn his cheek is higher and holier than
I am. . . . And of course I reverence him; but I despise him, too, and I
wouldn't have him for a doormat.

Oscar Carpenter's "little Presbyterian mother"

One night after young Sam Clemens had gone to bed, the older members
of the family were in the sitting room when Sam—probably seven or eight
years old—returned sleepwalking. Orion had slipped off his boots, and his
little brother found one of them and tried to sit on it. It toppled over of
course, but as the adults shook with laughter, he tried again and again. At
last someone led him back to bed.[1]

The incident is one of the earliest recorded interchanges (if it can be
called that) between the two principals of this book, and it tells us something about their relationship. Orion Clemens, Jane and John Marshall
Clemens's firstborn and ten years older than Sam, was never part of Sam's
childhood world but was always to him a member of the adult circle. Brothers by birth, these two would never be kindred in the sense Sam and his
younger brother, Henry (separated by less than three years), were. Moreover, note that somnambulistic Sam was neither trying to put on Orion's
boot nor attempting to see if he could fill it: he was seeking to seat himself
upon it, and he did so repeatedly. Hindsight allows us to interpret this as a
precocious endeavor to surmount Orion, for that is what Sam continued
to do until he was in his mid-twenties, when at last on April 9, 1859, he
received his Mississippi River pilot's license and took his big brother's place
as head of the Clemens family.

Despite their difference in age Orion and Sam had a few things in common. A belief that someday they would be fabulously wealthy was one of

them. In the 1820s John Clemens had purchased about seventy-five thousand acres of virgin land in Fentress County, Tennessee. In those days land grants could be had for less than a cent an acre, and he was able to acquire the entire tract for no more than five hundred dollars.[2] In his *Autobiography* Mark Twain pictured his father standing in the courthouse door in Jamestown surveying his vast new holdings. "Whatever befalls me," he proclaims, "my heirs are secure; I shall not live to see these acres turn to silver and gold, but my children will." It was not an idle boast; the land contained abundant minerals and thousands of acres of fine timber, and it was, moreover, a natural wine district. "There are no vines elsewhere in America, cultivated or otherwise," Twain had John Marshall Clemens declare, "that yield such grapes as grow wild here."[3]

Orion and Sam also shared a sense of honor in the Clemens name. Their father believed his line could be traced to the first families of Virginia, and beyond that to Gregory Clemens, an English landowner who became a member of Parliament under Cromwell and signed the death warrant of Charles I.[4] Upholding the family repute would bear heavily in the story of Orion and Samuel Clemens.

In addition, the brothers had in common a fear and hatred of abolitionists. Slavery was taken for granted in Missouri in the 1830s and 1840s, and, as Albert Bigelow Paine pointed out, "an abolitionist was something to despise, to stone out of the community. The children held the name in horror, as belonging to something less than human; something with claws, perhaps, and a tail."[5] Though far from wealthy, the Clemenses were slaveholders in a small way, and it was slaves Jenny and Uncle Ned who were really in charge of the children and who entertained them. In the evening everyone would gather around the great open fireplace, and there those two would tell tales—often blood-curdling—derived partly from their African heritage. The children were fond of the slaves and confided in them.[6]

But the institution that held their companions and guardians in bondage was sacrosanct. The children dreaded meeting runaways, who were regarded as worse than wild beasts. Once they saw a fugitive brought into Florida, Missouri, by six men who took the runaway to an empty cabin, threw him to the floor, and bound him with ropes. His groans were loud and frequent.[7] Nor was slave punishment unknown in the children's own home. Jane Clemens once started to discipline Jenny for insolence only to have the young woman snatch the whip out of her hand. When John

Clemens was sent for he came at once, tied Jenny's wrists together with a bridle rein, and administered a cowhide across her shoulders.[8]

Mark Twain asserted in his *Autobiography* that Orion, "born and reared among slaves and slaveholders . . . was yet an abolitionist from his boyhood to his death."[9] Certainly the cruelty of whites toward blacks was not lost on this perceptive youth, but Orion did not take that dangerous political stand until later in life. R. I. Holcomb's *History of Marion County, Missouri* recounts an episode that suggests the charged atmosphere prevailing in Hannibal when the Clemenses moved there in 1839. Three years earlier a number of emigrants from eastern and northern states, many of them abolitionists, had settled in Marion County. When a box of emancipation tracts was discovered in Hannibal, the owners were run out and the booklets burned in a ceremony witnessed by "quite a concourse of the best citizens, who enthusiastically approved what was done." A "sort of crusade" was mounted against the remaining newcomers, and "persons were closely watched. In fact, so intense was the excitement that if it was remembered that any man had, at any time, been heard to say anything on the subject of slavery at all that might, by any possibility, be construed into an opinion against it, even in the abstract, he was marked as a doomed man."[10] The reign of terror was still in effect when the Clemenses came to town.

Nor does Orion appear to have picked up any incipient emancipationist ideas from John Marshall Clemens—despite Mark Twain's assertion in "The Private History of a Campaign That Failed" that their father, though a slave owner, held that "slavery was a great wrong." That claim is unconvincing, for John Clemens seems to have had few compunctions about trading in slaves, lashing a person he owned, or voting to convict abolitionists.[11] Orion contributed to Holcomb's history book, and he probably wrote the passage in it that tells of his father's serving in September 1841 on a jury of twelve men who found three Illinois abolitionists who had come across the river to induce some slaves to escape guilty of grand larceny in "stealing and attempting to carry away certain slaves." The convicted men were sentenced to twelve years at hard labor.[12]

About a year after he married Jane Lampton on May 6, 1823, Kentucky lawyer John Marshall Clemens took his twenty-one-year-old wife and a teenaged slave named Jenny to Gainesborough, a town on the Cumberland River in the rounded hills known as the Knobs of East Tennessee.[13] There, on July 17, 1825, the couple's first child was born, a boy.[14] They named him Orion, after the constellation, though for some reason they placed the accent on the first syllable, pronouncing it *O-ri-on*.[15] John Clemens was a restless man, always looking for greener pastures, and the little family soon moved some fifty miles east. In the log hamlet of Jamestown, Fentress County, Tennessee, Orion spent his early years "among [as Mark Twain would observe many years later] a very sparse population of primitives who were as ignorant of the outside world and as unconscious of it as the other wild animals were that inhabited the forest around."[16] John Clemens joined in the development of the new community, helping to establish the county seat there, personally drawing up the specifications for the courthouse and jail, and becoming the county's first court clerk.[17] He built a fine house, and by and by two more children, Pamela and Margaret, were born.

The Clemenses were soon on the move again, first to a spot nine miles from Jamestown called Three Forks of Wolf and shortly thereafter to the right bank of Wolf River, where a post office called Pall Mall was established, with John Clemens as postmaster. Orion first attended school at Pall Mall, and in 1832 another son, Benjamin, was born there.[18]

John Clemens was not the only one who envisioned a promising future for his elder son. As Orion told Samuel in his last communication to him, "the Tennessee mountaineers" predicted that he would grow up to be "a great man and go to Congress." Orion was willing to accept that dream, he confessed, as long as he could do so on his own terms. "I did not think it worth the trouble to be a common great man like Andy Johnson. I wouldn't . . . be anybody less than Napoleon." And so, whenever new and unfamiliar situations arose he asked himself what Napoleon Bonaparte would do under similar circumstances.[19]

One day a letter arrived from John Quarles, who had married Jane's sister Patsy Ann and settled in Florida, Missouri, where other members of the Lampton family later joined them. Quarles invited John and Jane to do the same.[20] Missouri was still part of America's western frontier. Fewer than half a million persons of European descent lived on the far side of the Mississippi, and St. Louis, with its ten thousand inhabitants, qualified as a virtual metropolis. Florida was a promising village in this new land, just the sort of place John Clemens was drawn to—and Jane no doubt hankered for her people.

Early in the spring of 1835, then, the parents and the three younger children, Pamela, Margaret, and Benjamin, piled into the family's two-horse barouche; nine-year-old Orion and Jenny, the house slave, climbed up on two extra horses; and the long trek west began. Later, Jane Clemens would recall that Jenny always managed to get the pacing horse and leave Orion with the less desirable trotter.[21] Mrs. Clemens was pregnant, and more than fifty years later Orion would tell Sam, "I suppose the trip took over a month, and, if so, you must have left the bank of Wolf river with the rest of us in April or May. I have often thought that the very early age at which you began to travel had something to do with your roving disposition."[22]

When the Clemenses arrived in Florida the outgoing Quarles offered his brother-in-law a partnership in the store he had established, agreed to aid him in the selection of some land, and encouraged him to renew his law practice. John and Jane established their household of seven, including Jenny, in a small frame building near the center of the village, a humble one-story affair with two main rooms and a lean-to kitchen.

One bleak day in November—the thirtieth—Jane gave birth to another son, a puny seven-months child with only a wavering promise of life.[23] Albert Bigelow Paine recorded that "there was no fanfare of welcome at his coming. Perhaps it was even suggested that, in a house so small and so sufficiently filled, there was no real need of his coming at all."[24] Since the biographer drew many of the childhood details of Samuel Clemens's life from Orion's autobiography (now lost), it is likely these sentiments were recalled and shared in that source.[25]

John Clemens's dour manner did not always mesh with John Quarles's easygoing ways, and after two or three years they dissolved their partnership. Clemens opened a store of his own across the street and "hired" his eldest son. By this time twelve or thirteen, Orion was a studious, pensive boy with little taste or aptitude for commerce. Having been repeatedly assured he was heir to riches, he resented having to work.[26]

The father also practiced law whenever there were cases to be obtained, and in 1837 he was elected judge of the Monroe County Court. It was the high-water mark of his professional career, and he was always thereafter known as Judge Clemens.[27] But when he formed a partnership with another man, the venture failed, and the modest tide of success that had come with his establishment in Florida began to ebb. Another boy, Henry, born in July 1838, added still another mouth to feed.

The Judge was finished in Florida. The greener pastures he now saw lay thirty miles to the east, on the banks of the Mississippi, and so in the autumn of 1839 he loaded his family and chattels into a wagon and set out for the little steamboat town of Hannibal, Missouri. The Judge settled his family in the Virginia House, a hotel he had bought along with other frame structures in the quarter-block at the northwest corner of Hill and Main Streets. He saw this real estate as assuring his family a roof and an income from rent as well as a building suitable for a general store. For this he bought groceries and dry goods on credit from St. Louis merchants and commission houses.[28] His oldest son, provided with a new suit of clothes, became clerk. Paine says that "possibly the clothes gave Orion a renewed ambition for mercantile life, but this waned. Business did not begin actively, and he was presently dreaming and reading away the time."[29]

It was not long before John Clemens suggested that Orion become a printer's apprentice in the office of the *Hannibal Journal*. Orion dutifully obeyed, but not without feelings of resentment. Did not the son of a gentleman, prospective heir to the Tennessee land, deserve better—at least a profession, instead of a lowly trade? Orion dreamed of being a public speaker, an orator, "but that had been forbidden by my father, who had placed me at the toil of printing and editing, because his own preference was in that direction."[30] Paine wrote that John Clemens at one time considered buying the *Journal* to give Orion a chance to become a power in western journalism, "and possibly to further his own political ambitions."[31] Some forty years later Orion would write, "Pa was irascible and hasty of speech, but loved his children; could not bear to think of any harm coming to them, and was very ambitious for them."[32] Several years after that, Orion would tell Sam: "It grieves me to think that I was not better to pa while he lived. He had but one fault—the irritibility [*sic*] of disordered nerves. If I had listened to him I might have been of some account. I was *spiteful,* and got even with myself."[33]

Disposed to make the best of a bad situation, Orion adapted to his new job. As Paine tells us, "he remembered that Benjamin Franklin had been a printer and had eaten only an apple and a bunch of grapes for his dinner. Orion decided to emulate Franklin, and for a time he took only a biscuit and a glass of water at a meal, foreseeing the day when he should electrify the world with his eloquence."[34]

Lest we conclude that Orion was a total misfit, consider the words of a schoolmate who claimed to be "quite familiar" with him, written seventy years after the fact. "A more genial character I never met," wrote former Hannibal mayor J. B. Brown, "he was universally loved by the teachers and scholars."[35]

The house of cards John Clemens had contrived began to totter. The store paid little and his law practice not much more. He ran for justice of the peace and was elected, but fees were neither large nor frequent.[36] Within a year of his arrival in Hannibal, everything collapsed about him—a disaster from which he never fully recovered.[37] In 1894 Orion would recall of his father:

When one of the great panics overwhelmed him he surrendered to his creditors his homestead, all his other real estate, and all the dry goods, groceries, boots and shoes and hardware in his store. He even offered to his creditors his cow, and the knives and forks from his table; but they told him to keep these.

At the age of forty-one he began his first acquaintance with poverty. A hard and bitter struggle for the maintenance of his beloved family ended his noble life within seven years.[38]

It became necessary to sell Jenny—to the grief of all, for the Clemenses were fond of her despite her willfulness, and she regarded them as "her family."[39]

Desperate to raise cash on the Tennessee land and to collect some old debts, John Marshall Clemens made a trip that winter, taking with him a slave named Charlie, whom he probably had picked up for a small sum in hopes of making a profit by selling in a better market. After stopping in St. Louis, he continued down the Mississippi to New Orleans. From there he headed back upriver and landed at Vicksburg, where he rode forty miles into the country through rain and sleet to find William Lester, who owed him about $470. When he met him, however, "it seemed so very hard upon him these hard times to pay such a sum that I could not have the conscience to hold him to it." Instead, Judge Clemens consented to take Lester's note for $250, payable March 1, "and let him off at that."

Intending to go to Tennessee to try to sell his tract and then return to see Lester about the time the note fell due, Clemens proceeded north.[40] On January 5, 1842, while on the river below Memphis, he wrote home that "I find steamboat travelling, does not agree with me" and that "this will be an expensive trip, but I suppose I shall be indemnified for it." He told his wife he was very anxious to hear from her. "I still have Charlie," he added. "The highest price I had offered for him in New Orleans was $50, in Vicksburg $40. After performing the journey to Tennessee, I expect to sell him for whatever he will bring."[41] He said he expected to reach home about the middle of March, but as to what he would do then he was in a quandary. "My brain is constantly on the rack with the study, and I can't relieve myself of it. The future taking its complexion from the state of my health, of mind, is alternately beaming in sunshine, or overshadowed with clouds; but mostly cloudy, as you will readily suppose"—the letter is signed "Affectionately John M. Clemens."[42]

Judge Clemens seems to have sold Charlie shortly after writing to his family, for on January 24, 1842, he received a promissory note from one Abner Phillips "for value received" for ten barrels of tar to be delivered in Missouri on or before the following Christmas.[43] He seems subsequently to have traveled to Tennessee and thence to Columbia, Kentucky, where he spent the rest of the winter with his aged mother and half sister. In the spring he went to Louisville to visit friends—evidently a deviation from his original plan—then returned to Vicksburg, and thence to Hannibal.[44]

His long trip had not brought any financial success, but rather a two-hundred-dollar deficit.[45] When Jane Clemens reproached her husband for having used up so much money, he responded softly that he had gone for what he considered good reasons. "I am not able to dig in the streets," he added, and Orion wrote in his autobiography, "I can see yet the hopeless expression of his face."[46] A few months later, in May 1842, nine-year-old Benjamin Clemens became sick and died within a week. Sam long remembered his parents' grief, and Orion recalled that it was the first time he had ever seen them kiss.[47]

By this time seventeen, Orion had finished his apprenticeship and was ready to earn a daily wage to help support the family. He went to St. Louis, one hundred miles downriver, and found work as a journeyman printer in the job office of Thomas Watt Ustick—which brings us to "Villagers of 1840–3." In this sketch (written in 1897) Mark Twain told of how Oscar Carpenter (whose initials matched Orion's) in "about 1842, aged 17, went to St. L to learn to be a printer, in Ustick's job office." Oscar writes to his mother that he is studying the life of Benjamin Franklin and fashioning his own after it. In his boardinghouse he is living on a diet of bread and water, and he is trying to persuade fellow boarders and Ustick's other cubs to give up beer. "They called him Parson Snivel," Twain wrote, "and gave him frank and admirable cursings, and urged him to mind his own business. All of which pleased him, and made him a hero to himself: for he was turning his other cheek, as commanded, he was being reviled and persecuted for righteousness' sake, and all that."

Oscar's "little Presbyterian mother" is not pleased with her son's literal interpretation of the Bible, which he has learned from her, for, "slender and delicately molded as she was, she had a dauntless courage and a high spirit, and was not of the cheek-turning sort." While she believes fervently in her religion and knows it is a Christian's duty to offer that cheek, she would not present her own and will not respect anyone who does.

> "Why, how do you reconcile that with . . ."
> "I don't reconcile it with anything. I am the way I am made. Religion is a jugful; I hold a dipperful. You can't crowd a jugful of anything into a dipper. . . . I know that a person that can turn his cheek is higher and holier than I am. . . . And of course I reverence him; but I despise him, too, and I wouldn't have him for a doormat."[48]

In his next letter Oscar reports that he is getting up at four in the morning and, still emulating Franklin, whose rules he has pinned up in a handy place, dividing his day into allotted segments—"so many minutes for the morning prayer; so many for the Bible chapter; so many for the dumbbells; so many for the bath; so many for what did I do yesterday that was morally and mentally profitable? . . . How shall I order this day to the approval of God, my own spiritual elevation, and the betterment of my fellow beings? And so on, and so on."

He has been to a lecture and is now a vegetarian. He wonders how his intellect survived the gross food he formerly ate; indeed, he wonders if it hasn't already been weakened. When he mentions this to his foreman, the other replies: "Don't worry—nothing can impair your intellect." As the mother reads that her face flushes, "and the foreman was better off where he was than he would have been, here, in reach of her tongue."[49]

No such letters from Orion to his mother are known to exist, but if something like this episode did happen, it suggests that Jane Clemens was at least partly responsible for the ambivalent attitude Samuel would hold toward Orion for the rest of his life—on the one hand recognizing his moral authority while on the other wanting to have nothing to do with his nonconformity. In any case, little Sam Clemens did not embrace his older brother's role model (as might have been expected in some circumstances) but rather took a path that would lead him to become an entirely different person.

If Orion got off on the wrong foot with his fellow workers, eventually he must have overcome that difficulty—and with flying colors—for he was elected president of the St. Louis Apprentices' Association. He held that office when the group was addressed by the distinguished lawyer and prominent Whig politician Edward Bates.[50] This worthy, later Abraham Lincoln's attorney general, was impressed enough by the young man from Hannibal to take him under his wing and encourage him in various studies, including law, oratory, and French. Bates remembered him as "a good boy, anxious to learn, using all means in his power to do so."[51] As part of his education, Orion also surveyed different religions and political parties. In his *Autobiography,* Mark Twain ridiculed his brother for being dilettantish in these pursuits, but Orion seems merely to have been doing what any bright, inquisitive youth would do in the same situation—sampling what must have seemed a veritable feast of broadening experiences.

In Hannibal, the Clemens family enjoyed a modest improvement in their circumstances after Orion went to St. Louis, and John Marshall Clemens was able to build a small house at 206 Hill Street. On a lot behind it stood "an old barn of a place" in which lived the Blankenships—old Ben, the town drunkard; his eldest son, Bence, "a hard case with certain good traits"; a number of sisters; and another son, Tom, "a ruin of rags, a riverrat, an irresponsible bit of human drift, kind of heart and possessing that priceless boon, absolute unaccountability of conduct to any living soul." Paine informs us that Tom Blankenship's society "was prohibited" for Sam, but that the ban only "gave it a vastly added charm." Sam was, in fact, likely to be at his neighbors' house "at any hour of the day," and at night Tom used catcall signals under Sam's window to summon him to join him and five or six other "boon companions."

During one of his trips back to Hannibal, Orion "undertook to improve the Blankenships spiritually." Orion "was concerned with missionary work," the biographer explains, and these derelicts must have seemed prime prospects for reform. Paine hints that Orion's behavior made him the object of the gang's mockery. "They were not vicious boys," he advises, "they were not really bad boys; they were only mischievous, fun-loving boys—thoughtless, and rather disregardful of the comforts and the rights of others."[52] If these scalawags were disregardful of Orion's comforts and rights, Sam probably found himself in a dilemma. He couldn't deny his own brother, yet he no doubt wanted to avoid offending his friends; stand up for Orion, or knuckle under to his peers? If his sentiments toward Orion were conflicted earlier, this new problem (if that is what it was) would have deepened the conflict.

2

John Marshall Clemens's Death

~

The very fact that [an autopsy] was performed suggests that those requesting it believed that this man suffered from another serious disease.

Guenter B. Risse, M.D.

In 1845 John Marshall Clemens was forced to close his law office and take a job as a clerk in a counting room.[1] After that, things got even worse, and 1846 marked the nadir of his fortunes.[2] The family was obliged to sell most of its furniture and accept the offer of Dr. Orville Grant to move across the street and live with his family above his drugstore at the southwest corner of Hill and Main Streets. Grant charged the Clemenses no rent, but Jane Clemens agreed to board his family.

John Clemens sought to recoup his losses by being elected circuit court clerk, and indeed it did seem that at last the Clemenses might be able to live in a style befitting their social position, for he was a popular candidate for that lucrative office. Unfortunately, before the election was held he was caught in a sleet storm while riding the twelve miles from Palmyra to Hannibal.[3] By the time he arrived home, he was half frozen, and, as Paine recorded, "his system was in no condition to resist such a shock." When pneumonia was diagnosed, Orion was summoned from St. Louis.[4]

The dutiful son sat by the bed, encouraging his father and reading to him, but the forty-nine-year-old man grew steadily weaker.[5] Occasionally he would become cheerful and speak of the Tennessee land, and once he said, "I believe if I had stayed in Tennessee I might have been worth twenty thousand dollars today."[6] On the morning of March 24, 1847, he appeared close to death. Among his last words were a whispered, "Cling to the land, cling to the land, and wait. Let nothing beguile it away from you." In

"Villagers of 1840–3" Twain wrote that the dying man motioned his daughter over to his bedside, put his arms around her neck, and kissed her before saying "let me die" and sinking back to his death. "He did not say goodbye to his wife," the son noted, "or to any but his daughter."[7]

Their father's death dazed the children. Judge Clemens had been a distant, reserved man, but they had loved him and respected his uprightness and nobility of purpose. Sam tormented himself with memories of the times he had been wild, disobedient, or indifferent. Seeing his grief, Jane Clemens took him by the hand and led him into the room where the body lay. "It is all right, Sammy," she said. "What's done is done, and it does not matter to him any more; but here by the side of him now I want you to promise me—"

The eleven-year-old boy turned to her, his eyes streaming tears, and flung himself into her arms. "I will promise anything," he sobbed, "if you won't make me go to school! Anything!" His mother held him for a moment, thinking. Then she said, "No, Sammy; you need not go to school any more. Only promise me to be a better boy. Promise not to break my heart." So he pledged to be a faithful, industrious, and upright man, like his father.[8]

The passage in "Villagers of 1840–3" describing "Judge Carpenter's" death is immediately followed by the words "The autopsy," which the author underlined.[9] On October 10, 1903, Mark Twain wrote in his notebook: "*1847.* Witnessed post mortem of my uncle through the keyhole." As Dixon Wecter pointed out, no uncle of Samuel Clemens's died in 1847, and therefore "the true identification is easily made." Wecter, who was custodian of the Mark Twain Papers at the time, described this incident as "one of the more carefully guarded, because shocking, memories of Sam Clemens' boyhood."[10] Orion's lost autobiography told the story in detail. When Twain sent those pages to William Dean Howells in 1880, his friend reacted in horror. "*Don't* let any one else even see those passages about the autopsy," he pleaded. "The light on your father's character is most pathetic."[11]

These references raise two questions: (1) Why was an autopsy performed? and (2) What was it about the results that so unsettled Howells? As to the first, there seems to have been no suspicion of foul play and no involvement of local authorities; therefore the usual explanation of a postmortem can be discounted. Dixon Wecter offered that John Clemens's "lifelong suffering from mysterious maladies" and "the later years of self-dosage" may have "whetted a physician's curiosity in days when dissection of the human cadaver was still a rare and often clandestine privilege."[12] He surmised that Hugh Meredith, the Clemens family doctor, "may have presumed upon his long intimacy with John M. Clemens to ask this boon of the widow." In speaking of Clemens's "self-dosage," Wecter was referring to something Orion Clemens revealed years later. "My father may have hastened the ending of his life by the use of too much medicine," he wrote. "He doctored himself from my earliest remembrance. During the latter part of his life he bought Cook's pills by the box and took one or more daily."[13]

Wecter's interpretation is plausible, but it doesn't account for Howells's shocked reaction. There is an alternative that seems simpler and that can also explain Howells's start: that Jane Clemens suspected her husband of having contracted a venereal disease and requested an autopsy to satisfy her curiosity. John Marshall Clemens was known for his "stern Puritan morality,"[14] but it is conceivable that in a moment of weakness and opportunity—say, for conjecture's sake, during the long trip to the Deep South—he had contracted syphilis. If so, it is possible that even his wife wouldn't have known for sure. The first sign of the disease, typically a single lesion at the infecting organism's site of entry, can appear as soon as ten days after sexual contact and can disappear within a few more days. Symptoms of the secondary stage usually show up several weeks later, when most patients run a low fever and suffer malaise. Syphilis can then enter a latent period of several years, during which no manifestations are present, and in the late stages symptoms can be entirely internal.[15]

Dr. Guenter B. Risse, at this writing professor and chair of the Department of the History of Health Sciences at the University of California, San Francisco, informed this writer that in 1847 it "was not common to solicit an autopsy," and especially not if pneumonia ("a most common ailment") was the suspected cause of death. "The very fact that [an autopsy] was performed" on Clemens, said Dr. Risse, "suggests that those requesting it believed that this man suffered from another serious disease."[16]

When John Marshall Clemens returned from his trip in 1842, his wife criticized him for having spent too much money, and he told her he was not able to do manual labor. These facts, along with Clemens's taking "Cook's pills," may have aroused Jane Clemens's suspicions. A search of Missouri newspapers published during the 1840s turned up no advertisements for "Cook's pills," although notices for other nostrums were much in evidence, suggesting that Orion's reference was not to a commonly available patent medicine. In their book *The Midwest Pioneer: His Ills, Cures, and Doctors,* Pickard and Buley point out that at that time "pills were often as large as cherries and twenty to one hundred grains of calomel were given at a dose. Not many, however, went as far as John Esten Cooke of Lexington, who gave a pound of calomel in one day to a cholera patient."[17]

Cooke (1783–1853) was a physician who in 1828 published *A Treatise of Pathology and Therapeutics* and in 1837 helped found the Louisville Medical Institute in Kentucky, where he taught until his retirement in 1844.[18] John Marshall Clemens, with his close Kentucky ties, may have known, or known of, Dr. Cooke, and it will be recalled that Clemens spent the winter in that state following his trip to New Orleans and Tennessee, making what appears to have been an unplanned trip to Louisville in the spring. If he had obtained a prescription from Dr. Cooke, when he returned to Hannibal his pharmacist friend Dr. Orville Grant could have furnished him with a steady supply of "Cooke's pills" (presumably not of the one-pound variety).

Where would Orion have gotten the idea his father "hastened the ending of his life by the use of too much medicine"? It sounds like something a physician might have told him. Wecter suggested Dr. Meredith carried out the postmortem, but it seems no less likely that Dr. Grant did so, since he lived and had his pharmacy in the building. Dr. Grant seems to have been no stranger to dissection of the human body; two years earlier he had bought Jimmy Finn's body, evidently for just that purpose.[19] He would have needed help in carrying John Marshall Clemens's body downstairs; perhaps Orion lent a hand—and then stayed to witness the procedure. If Grant (or Meredith) gave his friend's son a ringside seat, so to speak, he may also have given him a running commentary. Family records indicate the cause of John Marshall Clemens's death was pneumonia, but mercury poisoning (mercury being the principal ingredient of calomel)—not to mention the debilitating effects of syphilis—could have contributed, and the doctor might have told Orion so.

Again Dr. Risse (to whom I suggested the pills Clemens consumed may have contained mercury): "Since the deceased had been subjected to large doses of calomel, a mercury compound, the question of venereal syphilis and its tertiary manifestations—especially aneurysms—could have prompted the postmortem examination. Another reason for the autopsy could have been a search for evidence of mercurial poisoning, including damage to the kidneys, given the amount of calomel previously ingested." Calomel was used to treat syphilis (as well as other ailments) in the nineteenth century, and the operating physician would (by this thesis) have been looking for vascular sacs as evidence of syphilis and/or kidney damage as a sign of mercury's effect. (Dr. Risse noted that aneurysms can occur in any organ.)

If the autopsy turned up syphilis, that fact would answer our second question, namely, What was it about Orion's account that so horrified Howells and caused him to observe, "The light on your father's character is most pathetic"? Signs of a sexually transmitted disease would have been considered a blight on the Judge's honor, for such afflictions were held to be "just punishment for having sinned."[20]

Samuel wrote in his notebook of witnessing the postmortem "through the keyhole." If the procedure was performed in Dr. Grant's pharmacy he wouldn't even have had to leave the premises to view it; he could have stationed himself in the hall outside the drugstore while his brother and Grant were inside with the body. If Orion was an invited observer and Sam an uninvited one, the former would have been privy to the results while the boy outside wouldn't. It would have been traumatic enough for a twenty-one-year-old to learn that his father was not the paragon of virtue he had seemed; Orion may have shielded his eleven-year-old brother from that mordant knowledge.

What we might call the venereal disease hypothesis, then, goes as follows: Jane Clemens suspected her husband of adultery and of having contracted a venereal disease. When he died she asked a doctor, probably Orville Grant, to perform an autopsy. The physician did so and discovered manifestations of syphilis. Orion Clemens witnessed the procedure and later wrote about it in his autobiography. Samuel Clemens also watched the examination, but surreptitiously, and was not aware of the results until some time later.

The topic of human dissection appears in a passage in the manuscript of *Huckleberry Finn* that was removed before publication. In this episode Jim tells Huck of how his former master, a medical student, ordered him to go to his college and warm up a corpse in front of a fire so that it could be cut open more easily. "What for, Jim?" asks Huck. "I don't know—see if can find sumfin in him, maybe." As the slave heats the cadaver, it falls off the table and lands on him. Jim flees in horror back to his master, who calls him a fool and goes to the institution, finds the body on the floor, "en took en chopped him up. Dod rot him, I wisht I'd a had a hack at him. . . . It warn't no way for a dead man to act no how; it might a scairt some people to death."[21] In the manuscript the scene that immediately follows the deleted one shows Jim and Huck coming upon a house floating down the river. Looking through an upstairs window, they spy the naked corpse of a man. Jim climbs in and recognizes it as Huck's father, but he protects the boy from this knowledge by covering the face and warning him not to look ("It's too gashly"). From the description Twain gives of the room, scholars have concluded the house is a brothel. Among the odds and ends the wayfarers pilfer are "some vials of medicine that didn't have no label on them."[22]

The first time we meet pap Finn in the novel he could almost have come directly from the dissecting table: "There warn't no color in his face . . . it was white; not like another man's white, but a white to make a body sick, a white to make a body's flesh crawl—a tree-toad white, a fish-belly white." Later in the same chapter we learn that, like John Marshall Clemens, who nearly perished in a freezing rainstorm, pap "was most froze to death when somebody found him after sun-up."[23] Pap Finn was directly based on the real-life drunkard Jimmy Finn, who sold his body to Dr. Orville Grant. If Finn and Judge Clemens both ended up under Grant's knife, that bitter irony might have induced Twain to portray his father as pap Finn.

The most telling piece of evidence that pap Finn was inspired by John Clemens, however, may lie in a little detail the author used in describing Huck's faking his own death after breaking out of his cabin prison: To mislead investigators he rips a hole in a bag of meal and carries it away from the house, letting the grain sift out to make a trail.[24] Just as pap had imprisoned Huck in the cabin, John Marshall Clemens had once trapped Sam in his house by securing it and inadvertently leaving him behind. When the mistake was finally discovered and the seven-year-old boy released, it was found that he had "spent most of the day in the locked, deserted house playing with a hole in the meal-sack where the meal ran out, when properly encouraged, in a tiny stream."[25]

Twain seems to have written these passages during the summer of 1876, when his father's remains were moved from the Baptist cemetery on the north side of Hannibal to the newer Mount Olivet Cemetery south of town.[26] The transfer may have reminded the author of the postmortem, and if so, it possibly inspired one of the most loathsome brutes he ever created. Sam had sworn to Jane Clemens at his dead father's side to be faithful and upright, like John Marshall Clemens. If he discovered that this man was neither—that he had, in fact, been untrue to Sam's beloved mother (as that strange woman may have suspected)—he would have had trouble finding a brush black enough to tar him with.

Paine records that "Orion, looking out of his window next morning, saw old Abram Kurtz, and heard him laugh. He wondered how anybody could still laugh."[27] In the unfinished novel "Which Was It?" Mark Twain had George Harrison struggle to understand how his esteemed father could have committed a crime. "He has gone steadily down hill ever since he lost his property," Harrison reflects. "There must be something fearfully disintegrating to character in the loss of money. Men suffer other bereavements and keep up; but when they lose their money, straightway the structure which we call character, and are so proud of, and have such placid confidence in, and think is granite, begins to crumble and waste away, and then . . ."[28] When George's son, Tom, enters the story, George agonizes, "he is entitled to know, and what am I going to say? I can't explain—we have to leave him in the dark,—he were better dead than to know that crime!"[29] The eldest Clemens son was now head of the family. Standing with Sam and Henry at their father's grave, he told them always to remember that brothers should be kind to one another.[30]

Orion had become a fine book and job printer by this time, and according to Paine he returned to his position in St. Louis. Out of his weekly wage of ten dollars (high for that time) he sent home three, which now became the Clemenses' main income.[31] The rest of the family left Dr. Grant's house and moved first to a dwelling that proved too expensive, then apparently back to the frame cottage on Hill Street.[32] In the spring of 1847 a local chapter of the Sons of Temperance was organized and began to hold parades and assemblies. Orion had evidently returned to Hannibal and was occasionally orator of the day. Wecter suggests that on these occasions Sam and his gang were a disruptive presence.[33] Orion may have taken temporary employment in Hannibal, possibly at the job printing office opened by the *Journal* in midsummer 1847.[34] He taught a Sunday school class that summer and made a Fourth of July speech, although his voice, according to the *Gazette* report, was "so low that from where we sat, his remarks were inaudible."[35]

On occasion Orion's behavior struck people as bizarre. "One bitter December night," Twain dictated in 1906, "Orion sat up reading until three o'clock in the morning and then, without looking at a clock, sallied forth to call on a young lady." Instead of that person, her father answered his persistent knocking. Expecting that he would summon his daughter, Orion walked in, sat down, and began talking. Finally realizing this was not going to happen, he rose and said he would go and call again. "That was the old man's chance," narrated Twain, "and he said with fervency 'Why good land, aren't you going to stop to breakfast?'"[36] When Twain first told the story, in 1877, he identified the young lady as the protagonist's fiancée and indicated that the blunder resulted in the breaking-off of the engagement.[37] From these incidentals we may infer that the girl was Jo Smith, for she seems at some point to have been engaged to Orion.[38] In any case, Orion's extraordinary gaffe seems to have carried a high personal price.

Wecter writes that "Orion's ineptitude—as proverbial as Judge Clemens's but without the latter's dignity—had already become a local legend," and he points out that Sam began "to treasure its catalogue of absurdities, which he was later to expand in the mock life story of Orion, the unpublished 'Autobiography of a Damned Fool.'"[39] To be sure, Orion was somewhat inept and indisputably nonconformist, but it seems to have been only after John Marshall Clemens's death that his behavior became patently odd. Several entries in Sam's "catalogue of absurdities" might be attributed to mere absentmindedness, but the 3 A.M. visit seems symptomatic of a profound disorientation. Here was a young man who was trying to set an example to the community—even while he may have been wrestling with private demons.

When Mark Twain wrote "Autobiography of a Damned Fool" (Paine's title), he began it with the death of the narrator's male parent and had him say: "My father's funeral brought me suddenly and violently face to face with the great concerns of the hereafter. During many nights I could not sleep for thinking of my perilous situation. I resolved at last upon an immediate and thorough reform of all my ways."[40] That Twain had the year 1847 in mind is supported by the fact that he shows "Bolivar," as his antihero is called, teaching a Sunday school class, working in a job printing office, and joining a temperance society, in which he takes a leadership role.[41] The author even has him staying up late reading devotional literature.[42] Twain's purpose was burlesque, but behind the comic scenes of Bolivar flitting from Methodism to atheism to Mohammedanism can be discerned a man caught in a spiritual maelstrom, casting about for something, anything, to believe in.

3

Sam Leaves Home

Orion, exasperated by desperate circumstances, fell into a passion and rated him. . . . Soon afterward Sam confided to his mother that he was going away; that he believed Orion hated him; that there was no longer a place for him at home.

Albert Bigelow Paine

How long Orion remained in Hannibal is unknown, but as late as March 1848 he seems to have still been there. He had sent Edward Bates a copy of a temperance speech he had given and apparently asked his mentor for advice about a career in journalism or politics. Bates awarded Orion's address a "high eulogy" and characterized it as "sensible."[1]

Eventually, Orion returned to St. Louis, and in January 1850 Pamela wrote to him that the newspaper at which he had apprenticed had changed hands. Jane Clemens added that "I think about the time you come up they will be through and you can get it at your own way [sic]."[2] The assumption seems to have been that John Marshall Clemens's ambition to own the *Journal* had naturally fallen to his eldest son—and, indeed, Paine informs us that "a periodical ambition of Orion's was to own and conduct a paper in Hannibal."[3]

Whatever his feelings in the matter, the following summer Orion threw over his well-paying job and stimulating life in St. Louis and returned to Hannibal. At twenty-five, Orion Clemens had grown to be a tall, handsome, serious-faced man whose hair and beard would soon begin to turn gray. Twain later recalled his brother's "grave mien and big earnest eyes that seemed to be always searching, seeking, weighing, considering," as well as his "voracious appetite for books and study."[4]

Orion did not buy the *Journal* right away but instead purchased a press and some type—probably out of savings or the fifty dollars paid for a fragment of the Tennessee land sold on May 3, 1850—and around the first week of September he started a new weekly he called the *Western Union*.[5] "The editor is a thorough Whig," he announced in an early issue, "and, of course, his political articles will bear the genuine Whig stamp throughout, but no effort will be spared to obtain for the public, the very latest news, on all subjects, and to impart to his paper a high degree of interest and usefulness to every class of readers."[6]

The new publisher was filled with enthusiasm. "He worked like a slave to save help," reported Paine, "wrote his own editorials, and made his literary selections at night." Those opinion pieces were, we are told, so brilliant it was not believed Orion could have written them.[7] In one such he castigated members of his own party in New York for associating themselves with the Free-Soilers, who opposed the spread of slavery into the territories. "We scarcely know which we are most inclined to do," Orion wrote, "denounce the shameless prostitution of such conduct, or laugh at the amusing facility with which these fellows accommodate themselves to circumstances."[8] In the following issue he rebuked alike Northern radicals who obstructed the enforcement of the Fugitive Slave Law and their counterparts in the South who openly called for secession, saying that such agitations indicated "a gathering storm, which must, soon . . . convulse the nation." The young editor opined that the country looked to the conservative elements of both regions for the antidote and that "only from the two great parties, Whig and Democrat, can salvation come."[9]

The paper was excellently turned out, and it seemed to be on the high road to success. In January 1851 Orion announced that (in the pattern of many newspapers of that era) he would publish a triweekly as well as a weekly. "This is an enterprise that requires additional labor," he observed, "and we eventually hope we shall have a liberal share of patronage to sustain us."[10] He seems already to have taken eleven-year-old Henry out of school to learn typesetting and to help, and now he induced Sam to leave the rival *Courier*. Sam seems to have been apprenticed to printer Henry La Cossett sometime in 1847 and subsequently, probably in May or June of 1848, to Joseph P. Ament, who owned the weekly Democratic newspaper, the *Missouri Courier*. At that time Sam had left his family to go live in Ament's house.[11] The bashful apprentice Jim Wolfe and Dr. Meredith's son Charles may also have come to work for Orion at this time.[12] Although the triweekly lasted only two weeks (Hannibal was still more nearly a village than a town), the augmented staff was retained; there seems to have been plenty of work for all.[13]

If, as Albert Bigelow Paine says, Samuel Clemens's Tom Sawyer days began in 1844, they seem to have ended when he went to work in his brother's printshop seven years later.[14] At his previous employer's, he had been given a daily task, after which his time was his own; by three in the afternoon he was with his gang down by the river or in the cave immortalized in *Tom Sawyer,* or perhaps with Laura Hawkins up on Lover's Leap gathering columbine.[15] But under the new arrangement he had to work long, hard hours. It was probably at this time that he moved back into the Clemens house, which was now, of course, ruled by Orion. As head of the family, Orion had evidently freed himself of the mythos of the Tennessee land, for he no longer took the Clemenses' future prosperity for granted. On the contrary, everything, it seemed to him, was riding on the new venture, and each family member must labor without stint.

Sam didn't see it that way. He considered the new arrangement temporary, as he later recalled, and "it was not worth while to go at anything in serious earnest until the land was disposed of and we could embark intelligently in something."[16] Orion must have bridled at such impudence on the part of this young tyro, even though he was his brother. By Orion's own testimony, "I was tyrannical and unjust to Sam. He was as swift and as clean as a good journeyman. I gave him tasks, and if he got through well I begrudged him the time and made him work more. He set a clean proof, and Henry a very dirty one. The correcting was left to be done in the form the day before publication. Once we were kept late, and Sam complained with tears of bitterness that he was held till midnight on Henry's dirty proofs."[17]

Bitter indeed must have been that proud fifteen-year-old's tears, for they signaled the end of the only part of his life that would afterward seem worthwhile. "I should like to call back Will Bowen and John Garth and the others," he wrote to Bowen's widow in 1900, "and live the life, and be as we were, and make holiday until 15, and then all drown together."[18] To add insult to injury, Orion had promised Sam the generous wage of $3.50 a week, but he was unable to furnish him anything more than "poor, shabby clothes," as Orion described them, and board, with Jane doing the cooking with groceries bought by her eldest son.[19]

Eventually the strain of overwork took a toll on Orion, and his enthusiasm flagged. "I grew more despondent," he recalled in a surviving fragment of his autobiography. "My prospect was gloomy." Despite Paine's claim to the contrary, "It had never been my ambition to become an editor or printer." That occupation had been forced on him, he recalled with acrimony, by his father. "His pleasure in knowing that I was so engaged, must have been slight, compared with the happiness I might have enjoyed if I had been permitted to pursue a course warmed by the fervor and illuminated by the light of my childish dreams [of being a public speaker]." He tried to reconcile himself to his fate by reasoning that his hardship was for the good. "I felt as if my business had been forced upon me [so] that my character might receive the elevating and chastening influence of daily and hourly affliction." But such rationalization was of little avail, and soon "I began to yearn for a chance to get away from the office, and rest and breathe fresh air."[20]

A story Pamela and Jane often told afterward may date from this time. There was an election for mayor, and one of the candidates was furnishing free whiskey. "[P]ractically every man in town was drunk. . . . Orion came home and the family were all gathered around. He was very foolish. Sam would exclaim, 'Why Orion! Why Orion!' He enjoyed it at first, but after a while he said, 'Orion, don't be such a fool.'" If Orion found temporary surcease in breaking his own rule regarding alcohol, the following day "he went out and signed the pledge, and with his natural conscientiousness he took it seriously."[21]

Unlike Sam, Henry (three years younger) was a willing, if untidy, assistant. "If I commanded him to do something," wrote Orion, "without a word he was off instantly, probably in a run. . . . If a stray kitten was to be fed and taken care of Henry was expected to attend to it, and he would faithfully do so."[22] On the other hand, if "a cat was to be drowned or shot Sam (though unwilling yet firm) was selected for the work." That was what Orion wrote in 1858; years later he gave a slightly different account. "We had too many kittens," he stated in his autobiography. "Sam was . . . the only one of the family who could nerve himself to the point of doing a very disagreeable thing. He enclosed them in a bag which he swung over his shoulder and took to the river, where he sunk to the bottom the little creatures, whose only offense was that they lived."[23]

From his earliest days Sam had had a special place in his heart for cats. Whether Orion "selected" him or he volunteered for this onerous task, the experience made an enduring impression. At the time it seems to have been a sort of rite of passage, indicative of a changed Sam Clemens. A year earlier he probably couldn't have done it; now he could. Gone were the romantic days of pirate raids with the boys, derring-do on Glascock's Island, going on the warpath with Indians. In their stead was a new adjustment to the world and its ways—pragmatic, realistic, more mature, more somber. When Sam went to work in Orion's shop Tom Sawyer died and someone else—someone more like Huck Finn—was born.

A year after he started the *Western Union,* Orion finally realized his father's ambition and bought the *Hannibal Journal,* apparently having borrowed five hundred dollars from an old farmer.[24] The first issue of the consolidated *Journal and Western Union* appeared on September 4, 1851 (five months later the title was shortened to the *Journal*). Orion remembered the date because around that time he saw the former Jo Smith in her wedding procession on the way to the boat that would carry her to her new life. "I was pleased to observe that there were not many carriages and it was a small affair," he later allowed, "while there was a pitiful attempt to put on style." In his sour grapes he no doubt imagined himself on the threshold of a career that would make his former fiancée sorry she had rejected him.[25]

By November the augmented paper was doing well enough that the owner could boast, "we have a larger circulation, by *over one hundred,* than any other paper published in this section."[26] To his subscribers, Orion continued to advocate a pro-Southern but moderate position on national issues, stoutly opposing the "hair brained Fanatics" of the North, who by their "impudent interference" and "hypocritical cant" had, in his opinion, crushed all feeling in the South for gradual emancipation. To him the twin evils of the day were nullification (the refusal of a state to recognize or enforce any federal law held to be an infringement on its sovereignty) and immediate abolition. He called for a firm but constitutional opposition to the Wilmot proviso, which forbade slavery in any area acquired from Mexico and its extension to other territories.[27] Surveying his situation at the new year, Orion reflected editorially that "the circumstances under which we took the Journal were anything but flattering," but through consolidation the circulation now compared "favorably with any paper out of St. Louis."[28]

Sam had begun to contribute occasional pieces to the *Journal,* but when Orion was obliged to go to Tennessee to deal with a potential land buyer, he engaged as editor pro tem not his brother but Dr. Hugh Meredith. "He

was a man of steady habits, advanced in life, and would preserve the solemnity of the editorial columns"—evidently something Orion did not trust Sam to do. Sam got the appointment of foreman.[29]

That summer Orion used his editorial columns to condemn a city ordinance requiring every free black man to post a one-hundred-dollar bond and pay a ten-dollar tax for the privilege of living in Hannibal. "A negro," Orion wrote, "capable of honor and gratitude has principle enough under his sooty hide to behave himself without security." Thieving white men, he pointed out, posed a greater menace to the community than free Negroes.[30]

The next time the editor was called out of town, in the fall of 1852, he did ask his younger brother if he thought he could edit judiciously one issue of the weekly. Sam replied eagerly in the affirmative, and so Orion (no doubt with trepidation) left him in charge. The resulting issue of the *Journal* was memorable. Dated September 16, 1852, it contained, among other "spicy" items (Paine's term), a story headed "'Local' Resolves to Commit Suicide." Illustrated with a crude woodcut of a dog-faced man wading into a stream with a lantern in one hand and a cane in the other, it reported that the man had decided to "'extinguish his chunk' by feeding his carcass to the fishes of Bear Creek, while friend and foe are wrapt in sleep. Fearing, however, that he may get out of his depth, he sounds the stream with his walking-stick."

As Twain explained later, a man named Higgins, the editor of a rival paper, "had lately been jilted, and one night a friend found an open note on the poor fellow's bed, in which he stated that he could no longer endure life and had drowned himself in Bear Creek. The friend ran down there and discovered Higgins wading back to shore. He had concluded he wouldn't. The village was full of it for several days, but Higgins did not suspect it." The story and woodcut were Sam's clumsy and callous attempts to exploit the editor's misery. "I thought it was desperately funny and was densely unconscious that there was any moral obliquity about such a publication."[31] The victim, editor of the *Tri-Weekly Messenger,* was not amused. He responded with fighting words, calling his attacker "a writer who has not the decency of a gentleman nor the honor of a blackguard."[32]

When Orion returned, he was "very angry." Paine reported that he "remonstrated" and "reduced Sam to the ranks."[33] The next issue of the *Journal* seemed to indicate tension in the newspaper office. There were two more woodcuts further ridiculing a "local," but in the adjacent column an

editorial attempted to mollify the rival editor: "The jokes of our correspondent have been rather rough; but originating and perpetrated in a spirit
of fun, and without a serious thought, no attention was expected to be paid
to them, beyond a smile at the local editor's expense."[34]

A note below the illustrations, signed "W. EPAMINONDAS ADRASTUS BLAB,"
while hardly an apology, seemed to be Sam's face-saving retreat:

I believe it is customary, nowadays, for a man, as soon as he gets his
name up, to take a "furrin" tour, for the benefit of his health; or, if his
health is good, he goes without any excuse at all. Now, I think my
health was sufficiently injured by last week's efforts, to justify me in
starting on my tour; and, ere your hebdomadal is published, I shall
be on my way to another country—yes, Mr. Editor, I have retired
from public life to the shades of Glascock's Island!—and I shall gratify
such of your readers as have never been so far from home, with an
account of this great island, and my voyage thither.[35]

Since Glascock's Island was just across the Mississippi, no real journey
was contemplated, and in any case, the competing editor was not placated.
In that afternoon's issue of the *Messenger,* he commented on the "picture
gallery furnished in the Journal this morning," calling the woodcuts "the
feeble eminations [*sic*] of a puppy's brain."[36] According to Twain's later jocular
account, the editor "dropped in with a double-barreled shotgun early in
the forenoon. When he found that it was an infant (as he called me) that
had done him the damage, he simply pulled my ears and went away."[37]

Mark Twain took many liberties with the facts when he told the story of
"My First Literary Venture" in the *Galaxy* of April 1871, one of which was
that it occurred while he was working on his "uncle's" newspaper. This
fictionalizing may have been more than just a literary device; it may have
reflected the confusion he felt in his relationship with Orion. Too old for a
brother yet too young to be a father, he seemed to occupy some netherworld
of kinships.

Orion was surely aware of Sam's growing discontent at the *Journal,* and
eventually he awarded him his own space. But that linage, pointedly named
"Our Assistant's Column," appeared three times only, on May 23, 25, and
26—and on the 25th an urgent appeal also ran in the *Journal:* "Wanted!
An Apprentice to the Printing business. Apply Soon."[38] What had hap-

pened? According to Paine, Sam asked Orion for a few dollars to buy a secondhand gun, and "Orion, exasperated by desperate circumstances, fell into a passion and rated him for thinking of such extravagance. Soon afterward Sam confided to his mother that he was going away; that he believed Orion hated him; that there was no longer a place for him at home."[39]

Why did Sam want a gun? His close brush with a duel (if that is what it was) may have planted the idea, but the weapon was probably less important to him for protection than for what it symbolized. Many years later he would write, in "No. 44, The Mysterious Stranger," that when the title character was raised "to the honorable rank of apprentice to the printer's art" by the master of the printshop in which he worked, he "should have been invested with a dagger, for he was now privileged to bear minor arms— foretaste and reminder of the future still prouder day when as a journeyman he would take the rank of a gentleman and be entitled to wear a sword. . . . [But t]hese courtesies were denied him, and omitted."[40] When Sam asked Orion for the privilege of bearing a firearm, the frustrated adolescent brought to a boil the simmering rivalry with the older sibling who had substantially terminated his boyhood. He had forced the issue. The Clemens household, as in effect he told his mother, was no longer big enough for both him and Orion.

Before Sam left, Jane Clemens asked him to swear on a Testament not to "throw a card or drink a drop of liquor while I am gone." He did so, and she kissed him. "Remember that, Sam," she admonished, "and write to us."[41] Two years earlier, Pamela had married a man named Will Moffett and gone with him to live in St. Louis, where he became a partner in a firm of commission merchants. Sam took the evening packet downriver and went to visit his sister and brother-in-law and to see their new baby Annie.[42] He then found a job in the same printing office Orion had worked for, Thomas Watt Ustick's.[43]

After Sam left Hannibal, Orion was unable to find a replacement for him, and for a month, from June 11 to July 11, he failed to get out the *Daily Journal*. He explained to his readers in the *Weekly* of June 30, "We shall recommence the publication of the Daily Journal in the course of a week or two—so soon as we can gather our hands together, who have gone off on a sort of 'bust.'"[44] Did he expect Sam to return soon from St. Louis? Perhaps, but in any case he seems to have harbored no resentment. In fact, in his autobiography he took all the blame himself: "And so [Sam] went

wandering in search of that comfort and that advancement and those re-
wards of industry which he had failed to find where I was—gloomy, taci-
turn, and selfish. I not only missed his labor; we all missed his bounding
activity and merriment."[45]

The venture that had started with such promise was foundering; it may,
in fact, have been in trouble even before Sam left. Such "gleams of liberal-
ism" (Wecter's phrase) as Orion evinced in his condemnation of the bond
and tax on free black men seem not to have gone over well in Hannibal,
and circulation may have dwindled. Even Jane Clemens no longer read her
son's editorials but turned to the general news instead.[46]

Orion tried everything he could think of to keep the *Journal* afloat. The
idea of a serial story having occurred to him, he wrote to a number of well-
known authors in the East, but none of them would supply material at a
price he could pay. He bought a translation of a French novel for five dollars, but when it ran, it did little to help.[47] By August 11 he must have
realized Sam was not coming back from St. Louis anytime soon, for he
urgently advertised for two compositors.[48]

The responsibility of supporting the family weighed heavier than ever.
"I sat down in the dark," he wrote later, "the moon glinting in at the open
door. I sat with one leg over the chair and let my mind float." The owner of
the rival Whig paper, the *Tri-Weekly Messenger,* had offered five hundred
dollars for the office—the amount of the mortgage. Slouching there in the
moonlight, Orion resolved to accept the offer.[49]

In late August, Jane Clemens received a letter from Sam—postmarked
New York City. He wrote, "MY DEAR MOTHER: you will doubtless be a little
surprised, and somewhat angry when you receive this, and find me so far
from home; but you must bear a little with me, for you know I was always
the best boy you had, and perhaps you remember the people used to say to
their children—'Now don't do like Orion and Henry Clemens but take
Samuel for your guide.'"[50]

If Orion harbored no grudge against Sam, Jane Clemens seems to have.
The *Journal* was, after all, the family's bread and butter, and Sam had se-
verely hampered Orion's ability to get it out. When she received this communication, she allowed Orion to run it in the paper, after deleting all
personal references ("The free and easy impudence of the writer of the
following letter will be appreciated by those who recognize him," prefaced
the editor), but she did not answer it—and she seems to have forbidden

Orion and Henry to do so. "Oscar Carpenter's" mother had answered his letters from St. Louis—had, in fact, "poured out her affection upon" her son—but for the time being, neither Jane nor Orion nor Henry would respond to Sam's.[51]

On September 7 Orion notified his subscribers that because of "a large amount of business demanding undivided attention . . . for three or four weeks to come," he was placing the editorship of the *Journal* in the hands of the Reverend Daniel Emerson. It is likely that business involved a trip to Muscatine, Iowa, and negotiations to form a partnership with John Mahin to edit the *Muscatine Journal.*[52] Two weeks later the *Hannibal Journal* ran a "Notice to the Public. Notice is hereby given that I have this day sold the 'Journal' office, with its patronage to Wm T. League, Esq. Proprietor of the 'Whig Messenger.' The 'Hannibal Journal' will therefore after this date cease to be published."[53] Someone sent a copy to Sam in New York but included no letter of explanation.[54] Conceivably that someone was Jane Clemens, and if so, the implied message may have been "See what you have done?" On the twenty-seventh the *Messenger* bid Orion adieu: "Whither he will go is unknown to us. Kind and obliging to all, Mr. Clemens did not deserve to have a single enemy. . . . His talents as a writer will command the respect of the community, and his integrity will win for him the confidence of the people wherever he goes."[55]

On September 30, 1853, Orion published his first issue in Iowa.[56] Muscatine was a thriving town of 5,500 inhabitants some two hundred miles up the Mississippi from Hannibal, and the *Journal's* business had grown so much it required additional help.[57] The Clemenses found a house at 109 Walnut Street, a one-story frame structure adjacent to a grassy slope that stretched to the riverbank. At the rear of the house was a latticed porch and a little grape arbor. There Jane Clemens was often seen performing household chores.[58] Henry found a job as a clerk in Burnett's bookstore.[59]

Orion's move to Iowa was no doubt prompted by economic consider-ations, but it also reflected a growing disenchantment with the underpin-nings of the society he had grown up in, specifically the institution of sla-very. We have seen how in Hannibal he took a stand against abolition and even against the exclusion of slavery from the territories, while also con-demning the secessionists. In 1851 he had written, "We are entirely con-servative, and while our contempt for the Abolitionists of the North knows no bounds, we are loath to claim brotherhood with the 'Fire-eaters' of the

South."[60] By the time he arrived in Muscatine, however, he seemed almost apologetic about being "an old slave State resident," telling *Journal* readers that "the main difference between Missouri and Iowa consists in the presence and absence of slavery." In his former state, he admitted, the institution's influence "permeates and depresses all interests. Many of the people of Missouri observe the superior growth of Iowa, and understand this to be the reason."

He nevertheless denounced Northern radicals and partially defended his former home by asserting that "it is Free State interference which will hold the negro in slavery in . . . Missouri, for twenty or more years to come—perhaps a half or whole century. Not exactly Free State interference, either, but . . . that small portion who violently insist upon abrupt, unconditional emancipation."[61] These were hardly the words of a firebrand, but clearly Orion was having second thoughts about the South's peculiar institution.

Two months later a piece appeared under the title "Freedom of the Press." "Conflicting opinions there always must be in society," it declared, "where great interests and great ideas occupy men's minds. It is from opposition, it is from clashing interests, it is from conflicts of minds, that truth is frequently brought to light and error made to disappear. How can any man be certain of the correctness of his views," it asked, "until he has carefully examined a question on all sides?"[62] That too sounded like Orion, and it suggested he was struggling with his received beliefs.

Six months later, on July 17, 1854, Orion Clemens was appointed one of the three members of the Whig central committee of Muscatine County.[63] Three weeks subsequent that body published in the *Journal* a proclamation declaring, "wherever slavery exists now, or has existed, in this country, it was established without law, and legalized afterwards. . . . slavery never asks to be established. It establishes itself by usurpation where it is not excluded, and waits to be legalized and recognized by law. Its place in our country was usurped at first, and its existence only tolerated by the Constitution as a result of a compromise."[64] Orion affixed his name to the declaration, along with his two fellow Whigs, and very likely he wrote it. The following day another piece appeared in the *Muscatine Journal* stating that "the 'inevitable hour' for slavery has come. . . . Slavery has culminated, and from the present, now, its decay may be dated. . . . The South itself will find some safe and gradual means of getting rid of the institution."[65] Those words were probably also written by Orion.

These opinion pieces documented a striking moral journey. If Orion hadn't yet embraced "abrupt, unconditional emancipation," he had moved a considerable distance toward that position. Made in contravention of his childhood society, the Southern pulpit, and his kindred, this odyssey must have been a difficult and lonely one. The rest of the Clemenses evidently remained loyal to their origins, and they seem to have developed doubts about the head of the family. As Mark Twain would write many years later, "for a man to speak out openly and proclaim himself an enemy of negro slavery was simply to proclaim himself a madman. For he was blaspheming against the holiest thing known to a Missourian, and could *not* be in his right mind."[66] Orion retained his domestic status, but it may have been at this time he also became something of the family butt. His niece Annie Moffett remembered hearing him referred to as a "Black Republican"; to her it was equivalent to being one of the devil's angels.[67]

4

Sam Returns

You wouldn't let me buy a gun, so I bought one myself, and I am
going to use it, now, in self-defense.

Sam to Orion

About a month after moving to Muscatine, Orion received a letter from
Sam, now in Philadelphia, which had been mailed to St. Louis and forwarded by Pamela. Sam had been wanting to send Jane Clemens some
money, he complained, "but devil take me if I knew where she was." He
enclosed a gold dollar for Orion to give to their mother ("I know it's a
small amount, but then it will buy her a handkerchief"). He informed his
brother he had found work as a temporary substitute at the *Inquirer* and
had been engaged until the first of April, at which time he intended to
come back and take Jane to visit her girlhood home in Kentucky.

He told Orion of having visited the grave of Benjamin Franklin, and he
drew a diagram of its inscription. Several times he deferred to his former
editor's superior knowledge ("darned if I know . . . but you, know, for you
are a better scholar than I am"; "is that proper?"; and "I don't know what
else to call it"). By the end of the letter his irritation had eased. "You must
write often," he appealed. "You see I have nothing to write interesting to
you, while you can write nothing that will not interest me."[1]

When Paine quoted from this letter in *Mark Twain: A Biography,* he
commented, "one is sharply reminded of the similarity between the early
careers of Benjamin Franklin and Samuel Clemens. Each learned the printer's
trade; each worked in his brother's printing-office and wrote for the paper;
each left quietly and went to New York, and from New York to Philadelphia, as a journeyman printer."[2] Paine even titled that chapter "In the Foot-

steps of Franklin." He would hardly have drawn those parallels without the approval of his subject—but even the authorized biographer may not have understood their full import. Franklin was (along with Napoleon Bonaparte) Orion's chosen hero.[3] In "Villagers of 1840–3" Oscar Carpenter's mother, even though she despised her son's cheek-turning humility, praised him "for his resolution to be a Franklin and become great and good and renowned."[4]

That Samuel was emulating Orion's champion suggests he was trying to outdo his big brother; in fact, the striking similarities between his behavior and Franklin's hint that Sam adopted Franklin's *Autobiography* as his personal guide. "I concluded, therefore," wrote Franklin, "to remove to New York; but . . . I was sensible that, if I attempted to go openly, means would be used to prevent me."[5] Sam also went to New York on the sly. Franklin: "I . . . found myself in New York . . . at the age of seventeen, without the least recommendation, or knowledge of any person in the place, and very little money in my pocket. . . . I offered my services to a printer of the place."[6] Clemens (who was also without contacts and was just seventeen): "I arrived in New York with two or three dollars in pocket change and a ten-dollar bill concealed in the lining of my coat. I got work at villainous wages in the establishment of John A. Gray and Green."[7] True to his pledge to his mother, Sam was abstemious while away from home, spending much of his free time at the library. Franklin: "Reading was the only amusement I allowed myself. I spent no time in taverns, games, or frolics of any kind."[8] Franklin also spoke regretfully of "the service I had deprived [my brother] of by leaving him so early."[9]

Instead of the spontaneous act it seemed, then, Sam's "running away" might more reasonably be viewed as a deliberate step. Before bringing the smoldering tension between himself and Orion to a flashpoint, he seems to have made up his mind that he would go his brother one better. After pointedly getting work in St. Louis at the very printshop Orion had worked for, he followed the lead of his brother's model (but not his brother) and traveled on to New York. When he made a pilgrimage in Philadelphia to the founding father's grave (a man who was the icon of American printers) and diagrammed its inscription for Orion, he could hardly have made his point more explicitly. The competitiveness that had caused little Sam Clemens to try to sit on his brother's boot was as strong as ever.

About the only thing Sam didn't do to emulate Franklin was embark on "the bold and arduous project of arriving at moral perfection."[10] It was, perhaps, one thing to top Orion; it was another to ape him. But if Sam hoped that, like Franklin, he would soon receive a letter from home "mentioning the grief of my relations and friends . . . at my abrupt departure, assuring me of their good will to me, and that everything would be accommodated to my mind, if I would return," he was disappointed.[11] The closing sentiment in his letter to Orion ("you can write nothing that will not interest me") now takes on new significance; he may have been fishing for an apology, but it became apparent that he had miscalculated. He had received no letters from his mother or either brother since he arrived in New York, and now even Pamela's missives had stopped.

When Orion received Samuel's forwarded letter he published it in the *Journal*, but another two weeks passed before he answered it—at which time he informed his brother at last of the family's whereabouts. Nearly two months had passed since their arrival in Muscatine and almost three since Sam had first written from the East. Evidently Orion liked Sam's description of his travels, for he encouraged him to send more letters for publication.

Sam seems to have been shocked that Orion had moved the family to the North. He answered his brother's letter the day he received it, carping, "I think Ma ought to spend the winter in St. Louis. I don't believe in that climate—it's too cold for her." Probably it was not just meteorological conditions he had in mind; although adventurous, Sam carried with him all the conventional baggage of a white Southerner. In his first letter from New York he had written of "the infernal abolitionists" and joked that "I reckon I had better black my face, for in these Eastern States niggers are considerably better than white people."[12] Now he asked his brother, "How do you like 'free-soil?[']" and added pointedly, "I would like amazingly to see a good, old-fashioned negro."[13] In his next dispatch to Pamela he complained: "I have received one or two letters from home, but they are not written as they should be; and know no more about what is going on there, than the man in the moon."[14]

How aware Sam was of his brother's movement toward the camp of the "infernal abolitionists" we don't know, but it is possible that some of Orion's editorials were sent to him or that Orion conveyed his views in letters now lost, or both. If so, Sam must have seen these opinions as nothing short of sacrilege. Even so, he responded to Orion's request for more letters for the paper, sending at least four during the winter of 1853–54. In publishing them the elder brother deleted personal remarks; corrected lapses; altered sentence breaks, paragraphing, and hyphenation of compound words and other punctuation; changed language to suit his taste; and omitted words he may have found offensive, such as "infernal."[15]

On March 10, 1854, and again on March 17, there were unclaimed letters for Samuel Clemens at the Philadelphia post office.[16] There is no way of knowing who wrote them, but it is not unlikely they were from Muscatine. Sam had left Philadelphia and returned to New York, evidently without telling his family. Forty-five years later, writing in the third person, he declared that he was "obliged by financial stress to reveal his whereabouts to the family. He returned to the west."[17] Conceivably his default of telling his family was an intentional snub, revenge for their long delay in revealing *their* whereabouts. According to Paine "his second experience in New York appears not to have been recorded, and in later years was only vaguely remembered."[18] Unemployment among the city's printers was high at the time, at least in part as a result of the destruction by fire of two major publishing houses in December 1853.[19] According to the official biographer, "It was late in the summer of 1854 when he finally set out on his return to the west." As the editors of the University of California edition of Twain's letters have pointed out, however: "In fact, given the hard times in New York, it is reasonable to speculate that Clemens' return to the west came as early as April 1854."[20]

Paine, probably relying on Orion's autobiography, tells us that Orion, Jane, and Henry were seated at breakfast when suddenly Sam appeared at their door.

> He came in carrying a gun. They had not been expecting him, and there was a general outcry, and a rush in his direction. He warded them off, holding the . . . gun in front of him.
>
> "You wouldn't let me buy a gun," he said, "so I bought one myself, and I am going to use it, now, in self-defense."
>
> "You, Sam! You, Sam!" cried Jane Clemens. "Behave yourself," for she was wary of a gun.
>
> Then he had had his joke and gave himself into his mother's arms.[21]

Paine treated the strange incident as a prank, and apparently the family took it as such—but was it? In 1901 Mark Twain wrote to Joseph H. Twichell: "I bought a revolver once and travelled twelve hundred miles to kill a man."[22] When Paine included this letter in the collected correspondence, published five years after the *Biography*, he introduced it with the statement: "At what period of his own life, or under what circumstances, he made the long journey with tragic intent there is no means of knowing now. There is no other mention of it elsewhere in the records that survive him."[23] Had Paine remembered writing the passage just quoted he might not have been so sure.

Consider these points: First, when he arrived at Muscatine, Clemens had a gun he said he had bought. Presumably he had done so before he began his journey, for even though he stopped briefly in St. Louis, the time he had there was spent at his sister's.[24] Given his monetary circumstances, it seems unlikely he would have made such a purchase merely for the sake of a "joke." Second, it is roughly nine hundred miles from New York to St. Louis and three hundred from there to Muscatine, a total of about twelve hundred miles. Third, before his mother called out his name, Sam announced his intent to use the weapon. Henry was a mere boy of fifteen, whereas Orion was twenty-eight. Was he the man Sam said he had traveled twelve hundred miles to kill? A year earlier Orion had fallen "into a passion" and denied his younger brother a gun, a symbol of manhood. It was manifest proof to Sam that the head of the family abominated him and that the Clemens domicile was no longer big enough for both of them. Since then nothing had happened to change his mind; in fact, just the opposite.

The grueling trip from New York to Muscatine took the better part of a week. "During a whole week," Twain told Twichell, "my head was in a turmoil night and day fierce enough and exhausting enough to upset a stronger reason than mine." In his account in the *Autobiography*, Twain stated: "When I reached St. Louis I was exhausted. I went to bed on board a steamboat that was bound for Muscatine. I fell asleep at once, with my clothes on, and didn't wake again for thirty-six hours."[25]

"Among the animals," Mark Twain wrote in *Letters from the Earth*, "man is the only one that harbors insults and injuries, broods over them, waits till a chance offers, then takes revenge."[26] Kept in the dark as to his family's whereabouts for three months, then receiving letters that were "not written as they should be," Samuel Clemens might have considered himself wronged—"I . . . know no more about what is going on there, than the man in the moon." Later, if word of Orion's apostasy regarding slavery reached him, he may have learned more than he cared to know. And still later, obliged to abandon his long-cherished dream of returning to take his mother to Kentucky, he instead came home humiliated, broke, and spent. And, perhaps worst of all, that home was no longer his beloved Hannibal but—thanks to Orion—an alien community, a cold Yankee town that did not share the sacred certitudes of Sam's boyhood village but rather dishonored them. Samuel Clemens's mission may have been driven by the same passions that would, seven years later, turn brother against brother on a national scale.

As nicely as these two happenings jibe—the 1854 trip to Muscatine and the 1901 reference to a journey of deadly intent—there are some pieces that don't seem to fit. First, in his letter to Twichell, Clemens followed his startling admission with "He [meaning his intended victim] was away. He was gone a day." Obviously this does not describe what reportedly happened when Sam entered Orion's house and found him, together with Jane and Henry Clemens, seated at breakfast. Second, when Paine compiled *Mark Twain's Letters*, he gave a different version of Sam's entrance into Muscatine: "It was early when he arrived—too early to arouse the family. In the office of the little hotel where he waited for daylight he found a small book. It contained portraits of the English rulers, with the brief facts of their reigns. Young Clemens entertained himself by learning this information by heart. He had a fine memory for such things, and in an hour or two had the printed data perfectly and permanently committed."[27] This doesn't sound like the behavior of a man with blood in his eye. Such a person would hardly have compunctions about rousing the family; or, even if he had, it seems unlikely he would "entertain himself" by memorizing a book while he waited.

Third, the description of Sam's entrance into Orion's house given in Paine's *Biography* contains three words I omitted when quoting it. Paine wrote: "He warded them off, holding *the butt of* the gun in front of him." If this murky phrase is interpreted to mean he was grasping the revolver so that the handle was pointing away from him, then the idea that the whole thing was a joke becomes more believable. (At least one biographer has made that interpretation.)

Turning to the second point first, it is possible Sam spent time in a hotel that morning. He had never been to Muscatine, and he was arriving unannounced. He must have needed directions to his brother's residence. The Ogilvy House was on the riverfront. If he stepped inside and found no one on duty, he would have had little choice but to wait. In explaining to Twichell why most men who contemplate murder don't go through with it, Clemens wrote, "but new and strong interests have intervened and diverted their over-excited minds long enough to give them a chance to settle, and tranquilize, and get back upon a healthy level again." Had he found that little book a sufficiently "new and strong" interest to give him a chance to cool down? Did it somehow divert his overexcited mind into memorizing the monarchs of England? He told Twichell that "within an hour—within half of it—I was ashamed of myself—and felt unspeakably ridiculous."[28] If this is what happened, by the time he entered Orion's house his mood might have lightened; he might even have held the revolver in the Keystone Kops manner described. This doesn't rule out the trip's having begun with lethal purpose, but it does suggest that that determination was blunted before the traveler reached his final destination.

Let us return to the first point—the assertion that his victim "was away. He was gone a day." It is the most crucial of the anomalies, for, if true, it rules out the possibility that the 1901 confession refers to the Muscatine trip. Occasioned by the shooting of President McKinley a few days earlier, the long, rambling letter to Twichell is more an outpouring than a communication. After excoriating the newspapers for "saying wild things, crazy things," Clemens declares that the journalists were as temporarily insane as the assassin—even as "with one voice they declare the assassin *sane*." He then broadens the frame of reference to take in everyone, pointing out that "an immense upheaval of feeling can at any time topple us distinctly over the sanity-line." He speaks of how the recent killing of the king of Italy had probably set the assassin off. "*Every* extraordinary occurrence unsettles the heads of hundreds of thousands of men for a few moments or hours or days." Then Mark Twain springs his stunner: "I bought a revolver once and travelled twelve hundred miles to kill a man."

One pictures his pen stopping there. "He was away," Twain writes next. "He was gone a day." Only he knows whether it is a statement of fact or a red herring. The extraordinary letter continues for several paragraphs, but in all its specifics and generalities except that one it is consistent with what seems to have happened in 1854. In reviewing Clemens's travels I have found no likelier candidate for "the long journey with tragic intent" that Paine spoke of than the trip to Muscatine—indeed, there seems to be no other candidate at all. For that reason, as well as others, I believe the statement that "He was away; he was gone a day" should be read as an attempt to mislead rather than inform.

In 1877 Mark Twain worked on a novel he called "Simon Wheeler, Detective." In it he told of how Hale Dexter, "a fine manly creature" of about eighteen, makes a three-day horseback journey from Kentucky to "Guilford," Missouri.[29] The author informs us that the trek "was becoming wearisome work, and tedious," and that Hale "ceased to take interest in the scenery or anything else, and fell to drifting off into dreams and thinkings." When he arrives at his destination and is reminded of the purpose of his journey, "He was dazed, confused—like a sleeper roused suddenly out of a gracious dream and confronted with some vague and formless horror."[30] He has come to kill his cousin, Hugh Burnside; Dexter has made a deathbed promise to his father to carry out the imperatives of a long-standing family feud.

That night, after much soul-searching, Dexter dozes off into "a dream-ridden, unrefreshing sleep."[31] Next morning he takes his gun and goes out into the street, where his intended victim is pointed out to him in front of his house.[32] Twenty-year-old Hugh is described as "an innocent," as "giddy and thoughtless, when he was not sappy and sentimental," and as "the butt of the town and the apple of his mother's eye."[33] As Dexter crosses the street the thought flashes through his mind, "It is no dream, then! and to think that this thing must be done, not tomorrow, next month, next year, but *now!*—it seems hideously sudden."[34]

Hugh's back is turned. Dexter stands waiting a moment, then says "in a voice that seemed not his own, so dreary and hollow it sounded—'I will not take you at a disadvantage, sir, but—'"

Before he can finish, Hugh turns around and Hale recognizes him as a stranger who helped him on the road. Hugh seizes his hand with a cordial grasp and exclaims, "Hello! Why it's you! This is splendid! Come right in!—don't stand on ceremony." Ushering Hale into the house, he calls, "Hi! mother! Clara!"

Hale's mind is reeling. "Only one thought took form and shape in this confusion. It was, 'Thank God, the time has come and gone, and I shall never be a murderer, now.'" When the women enter, he introduces himself and announces he is "proud to be your relative." Twain informs us at this point that "the hand-shaking that immediately followed was hearty and general."[35]

In his working notes the author wrote that "Mrs Hugh is Ma." He put these words into her mouth:

> You come now with that innocent gun, and nothing is thought of it; but if it were in the old days I should drop lifeless, because I would know you had come to kill my Hugh! . . . And I could imagine . . . one or both of you stretched dead and bleeding on my threshold, and I standing there dumbly trying to realize the truth that my daughter's life and mine were blighted, wasted, ruined past help, by that wicked and useless act, when we had done no harm to any one— for . . . the long misery, the real suffering, falls upon the innocent.[36]

Assuming that Hale will join them at table, "The old lady patted him on the shoulder and said—'It was so good of you to be so impatient to come and see us' and she accompanied this with a smile of such sweet approval and endearment that it fairly blistered the young man's remorseful heart."[37]

Although the cousins agree to become "brothers in misfortune," constantly hanging over their relationship is the cloud of Dexter's duplicity, or what Twain called his "devastating secret": "it rung him with such anguish, and it made him so hate himself and loathe the shackles that bound him to his double-dealing office, that all his vigilance and all his strength of will were required to keep the devastating secret from leaping from his lips."[38] Dexter agonizes, "O, one needs the shoulders of Hercules to carry burdens like these, one needs the double-faced guile of the devil to play my part!"[39]

Here, then, is the homicidal intent hypothesis: (1) in 1854 Samuel Clemens bought a revolver in New York and traveled to Muscatine to kill Orion; (2) the mission was aborted either by his mother's last-minute intervention or by his cooling down before reaching Orion's house; and (3) this egregious chain of events became Samuel's "devastating secret," which profoundly affected his future relations with Orion and the rest of the family.

In 1882, at the age of forty-seven, Samuel Clemens returned to the Mississippi Valley to prepare for expanding into a book a series of articles he had written for the *Atlantic Monthly*. From St. Louis he traveled by steamboat to New Orleans, then back up to Hannibal, where he spent "three delightful days" visiting with old friends. Then, as he continued upriver, his mood changed. He wrote to his wife of being "desperately homesick" and of dreading "this hideous trip." If he hadn't promised to meet an associate in Minneapolis, he complained, "I would take the train at once and break for home."[40] When the steamer stopped at Muscatine the *Daily Journal* reported:

> Yesterday evening at about 5 o'clock the steamer Minneapolis landed at our levee, having on board as a passenger Mr. Samuel Clemens of Hartford, Conn., known the world over as "Mark Twain." Quite a number of our citizens, most of them from the younger portion, were at the landing to get a look at the great humorist. He was not at first visible, having retired to his stateroom, as he afterwards admitted, to avoid being made a public spectacle. The senior editor of the JOURNAL, however, with whom Mr. C. was employed as a printer in this place 28 years ago, sought him out and was at once recognized. Mr. C. accepted his invitation to walk out [on deck] and take a look at the city.[41]

This trip was the first Clemens had made to Muscatine since the journey from St. Louis in 1854. Although he had begun his Mississippi River trip traveling incognito, once his identity was discovered he had shown no reluctance to making "a public spectacle" of himself in any of the other towns he had stopped in. Having been flushed from his hideaway, Twain "was exceedingly cordial in greeting old friends," but when one of them invited him to ride around the city in his buggy, the visitor begged off on the grounds that the boat wouldn't remain long enough.[42]

5

Sam Displaces Orion

~

What was the greatest feature in Napoleon's character? His unconquerable energy! . . . I want a man to—I want *you* to—take up a line of action and *follow* it out, in spite of the very devil.

Sam to Orion

Paine tells us Sam turned down Orion's offer of a job on the *Journal* and instead went back to St. Louis, but local tradition has it that he remained in Muscatine several months and worked at the *Journal* office. If Samuel hadn't gotten wind of Orion's changing views toward slavery while in the East, he surely did now. Almost certainly the brothers clashed. Two years later Sam wrote Henry, "But you know what Orion is. When he gets a notion into his head, and more especially if it is an erroneous one, the Devil can't get it out again."[1] The reference was to a different matter, but the observation is consistent with the possibility the three brothers disputed in Muscatine over Orion's antislavery views.

Which may account for the fact that by August Sam *was* back in St. Louis, where he once again took a job at Ustick's and wrote occasional letters to the *Muscatine Journal*.[2] He also seems to have written to a radical antislavery organization in New England representing himself as an abolitionist who had just been released from the Missouri Penitentiary after serving a two-year sentence "for aiding Fugitives to escape." Robert Sattlemeyer has discovered evidence that in September 1854 Samuel Clemens of Missouri hoodwinked this group into paying him $24.50 for "passage from Missouri Penitentiary to Boston" under such a pretext.[3] "Clemens, who already had some experience as a writer, skill at literary impersonation, and a penchant for hoaxes going back to his days writing for the *Hannibal Journal*," observed Sattlemeyer, "found it a simple matter to write a letter to the Boston Vigilance Committee representing himself as an abolitionist recently released from the Missouri pen in dire need of funds to return to the more hospitable climate of Boston." Sattlemeyer speculated that Clemens may have been in arrears for his railroad passage from the East back to Missouri "and had hit upon a neat scheme to secure the exact amount owed."[4]

To all appearances Sam and Orion in 1854 could hardly have been more at odds concerning the question that was looming portentously over the nation. By 1890 Sam's views had changed. At that time he referred to slavery as "a bald, grotesque and unwarrantable usurpation."[5] His use of "usurpation" is interesting, for it was the same somewhat unusual term Orion employed (in a somewhat different way) in 1854.

The record doesn't show whether Sam was present or not, but on December 19, 1854, Mary Eleanor (Mollie) Stotts and Orion Clemens were married in the Westminster Presbyterian Church in Keokuk, Iowa. The groom was twenty-nine, the bride twenty. Since the Mississippi was closed by winter ice, the newlyweds had to return to Orion's home in Muscatine by stagecoach.

Mollie did not take well to Muscatine. In April she fell so ill that her mother was sent for and stayed ten days. Paine writes that "in those early days of marriage she may have found life with [Orion] rather trying, and it was her homesickness that brought them to Keokuk."[6] In any event, on June 9, 1855, after Orion had sold his share in the *Muscatine Journal*, the couple, accompanied by Jane and Henry Clemens, moved to Keokuk. There Orion bought on credit the Ben Franklin Book and Job Office.[7] Henry, now seventeen, went to work there, along with another young man named Dick Higham.

Paine tells us that "Brother Sam came up from St. Louis, by and by, to visit them, and Orion offered him five dollars a week and board to remain. He accepted."[8] In fact, Sam seems to have lost little time in moving to Keokuk, for his name appeared in a "List of Letters" unclaimed at the St. Louis post office as early as June 16.[9] Perhaps he was caught up in Keokuk's boomtown spirit; otherwise it is hard to understand why he would once again voluntarily place himself under Orion's sway. (The move was one example of several during the brothers' lifetimes in which they were drawn or thrown together when they would probably have been better off staying apart.)

On January 17, 1856, the printers of Keokuk held a celebration commemorating the 150th anniversary of the birth of Benjamin Franklin. The banquet hall in the Ivins House, Keokuk's finest hotel, was elaborately decorated, and around the tables sat not only the employees of the various printing offices but a larger company of invited guests. After everyone had partaken of the lavish bill of fare, speeches began. Various dignitaries, including Orion Clemens, who had been unanimously elected secretary for the occasion, rose and addressed the assembly.

Finally, after all the grandees had finished their remarks, Orion's younger brother Sam was loudly and repeatedly called for.[10] "Seated next to him," a witness recalled years later, "I detected his embarrassment as his tormentors still kept up their clamour for a speech. Blushing and slowly getting upon his feet, stammering in the start, he finally rallied his powers, and when he sat down, his speech was pronounced by all present a remarkable production of pathos and wit, the latter, however, predominating."[11] In Orion's formal report, published two days later in the *Keokuk Gate City,* he described the speech as "replete with wit and humor, being interrupted by long and continued bursts of applause."[12] It was Samuel's first effort at public speaking. He had joined his brother on the platform and, if not beating him at his own game, had more than held his own.

Orion was now a father, as Mollie had given birth to a girl on September 14, 1855. They named her Jane, after Orion's mother, but called her Jennie. Despite the flush times, Orion was having trouble supporting his family. In December he, Mollie, and Jennie moved in with Mollie's parents in their brick cottage on Timea Street ("ostensibly as boarders," according to Twain, "but it is not likely that Orion was ever able to pay the board").[13] It may have been at this time that Jane Clemens went to live with her daughter and son-in-law in St. Louis, where Will Moffett's mercantile business was prospering.

When Orion found it difficult to pay Sam's wages, he made him a junior partner—which meant that Sam got no wages at all and barely a living. Orion seems to have put Sam in charge of job printing, with Henry and Dick Higham as his assistants, while he himself continued to prepare the Keokuk city *Directory,* which he had begun assembling immediately after he arrived in town.[14]

Sam took his new responsibilities seriously enough, but he chafed under his senior partner's indifferent managerial skills. In June 1856 he wrote to his mother and sister in St. Louis that "the Directory is coming on finely. I have to work on it occasionally, which I don't like a particle." And, he complained, "They take Henry and Dick away from me too. . . . They throw all my plans into disorder by taking my hands away from their work." "They," of course, could mean only Orion. "I am not getting along well with the job work," Sam continued. "I can't work blindly—without system."[15]

Once again it seemed the premises were growing too small for both brothers, but despite all the difficulties Orion faced he managed to publish the *Directory* and put it on sale, for one dollar, on July 12, 1856. In addition to its listings, it contained Mayor Samuel R. Curtis's inaugural address and a "Sketch of the Black Hawk War and History of the Half Breed Tract" prepared by Orion Clemens.[16] Compact, clear, and well written, the piece testified to Orion's literary craftsmanship.[17]

One day Sam came across a copy of *Exploration of the Valley of the Amazon, Made under Direction of the Navy Department* by William Lewis Herndon, and while reading it nights he came up with the idea of going to the headwaters of the South American river and making a fortune by collecting coca. He enlisted two other adventurers, Joseph S. Martin, M.D., and a young man named Ward. The plan was for Sam and Ward to go to Brazil via New York in September, to reconnoiter, and then to report back to Dr. Martin in time for him to follow in the spring.[18]

But the specifics of the plan are less important for our purposes than the way Sam used it. When he broached his intentions to his senior partner, Orion agreed to let him go and even promised him fifty or a hundred dollars, but he argued that Sam should proceed only as far as New York or New Orleans and wait there until Ward sent back word from Brazil. Sam was unwilling to do that, but rather than quarrel he let his brother believe he would. He wrote to his mother and took her into his confidence, however, and she gave her permission for the full trip. For some reason, Jane Clemens also felt Orion should be kept in the dark. This, of course, was a reversal of her position of three years earlier when she had apparently conspired with her eldest son to keep Samuel in ignorance of the family's whereabouts.

But if Sam saw this as a form of revenge, he was not satisfied, for he next wrote to Henry, who was out of town. After bringing his younger brother and assistant up to date, he cautioned, "Now, between you and I and the fence you must say nothing about this to Orion, for he thinks that Ward is to go clear through alone." He then subtly contrasted his own powers of discrimination with those of Orion. "I want to see with my own eyes, and form my own opinion," he said, adding the remark already quoted about Orion's obstinacy once he got an idea into his head. Then he played his trump card. "Ma knows my determination, but even *she* counsels me to keep it from Orion. She says I can treat him as I did her when I started to St. Louis and went to New York."[19]

It was an endeavor not only to exclude Orion but to undermine his authority as head of the Clemens family and manager of the Ben Franklin Book and Job Office. Samuel was going away soon and would not be around to see the fruits of his labors, but Henry, if he could be won over, would be there to vex Orion.

By October Martin and Ward had dropped out of the venture, but Sam was determined to carry on anyway.[20] Spending the winter in Cincinnati, Ohio, he found work to earn money for passage.[21] In April 1857 he set out for New Orleans on the packet *Paul Jones,* but soon an old ambition reawakened. Beguiled by the river, he abandoned his trip to Brazil and went into training under Horace E. Bixby to become a Mississippi River pilot.[22]

When the Moffetts and Jane Clemens received the news in St. Louis, they moved into a larger house so that Sam could come live with them. In all the towns along the river it was considered a great honor to have a pilot in the family. Years later, Annie Moffett remembered what a stir there was when the family learned her Uncle Sam had decided to become one. "It seemed to me as if everyone was running up and down stairs and sitting on the steps to talk over the news."[23]

Meanwhile, Orion's printshop was in trouble. Even though he managed to bring out a bigger and better version of the city directory in 1857, there was little outside work to be had.[24] In his *Autobiography,* Twain blamed his brother's difficulties on his poor business skills, but that year the whole city economy suffered a slump that came, as Fred Lorch reported, "when the boom utterly collapsed and left Keokuk gasping at the suddenness and extent of the catastrophe."[25]

In June Orion sold his printing office, and three months later he and his little family set out for Tennessee "to spend the winter," as Mollie entered in her notebook.[26] It seems that once again John Marshall Clemens's

influence was at work, for not only did the Tennessee land beckon, but
Orion had decided to follow his father into the law; he wanted to be trained
where Judge Clemens had begun his practice.[27] (That wish seems to argue
against the venereal disease hypothesis [see page 16], but it may in fact only
signal Orion's inconsistent feelings toward the memory of his father.)

In Tennessee, Orion busied himself with reading Blackstone and surveying the huge tract of real estate. He must have expressed his hopes for a
sale in a letter to Sam, for his brother replied from St. Louis in March
1858, "I am glad to see you in such high spirits about the land, and I hope
[you] will remain so, if you never get richer. I seldom venture to think
about our landed wealth, for 'hope deferred maketh the heart sick.'"[28] The
sale did not materialize, but Orion's studies culminated in his being examined by a Judge Goodall in Jamestown and gaining admission to the bar.[29]

In June 1858 Orion received word from Sam that Henry, for whom
Sam had obtained a job as "mud clerk" on a riverboat, had been seriously
injured when the boat's boilers blew up. Orion set out for Memphis, Tennessee, where Sam was taking care of his injured brother, but before he
arrived he saw a newspaper announcing Henry's death; in a later letter to
his wife he described the "stopping and stillness of the heart" he felt at that
moment.[30] He didn't catch up with Sam until he reached St. Louis, where
Sam had taken Henry's body.[31] Some sympathetic citizens of Memphis had
sent a young man with Sam, "who was so overcome with grief that they
were afraid he would go insane."[32] From St. Louis the family took the remains to Hannibal, where Henry was buried in the Baptist cemetery beside
his father.[33] He was the third sibling Orion and Sam had lost; Margaret had
died in 1839 and Benjamin in 1842.[34]

After the funeral the family returned to Pamela's home in St. Louis.
Paine reports that "there one night Orion heard his brother moaning and
grieving and walking the floor of his room. By and by Sam came in to
where Orion was. He could endure it no longer, he said; he must 'tell somebody.'"[35] What he confessed was this: Just as Henry seemed near death, he
rallied. That day and the next he improved slowly. About eleven o'clock
that night, the doctor in charge came and made a careful examination. "I
believe he is out of danger," he told Sam, "and will get well. He is likely to
be restless during the night; the groans and fretting of the others will dis-
turb him. If he cannot rest without it, tell the physician in charge to give
him one-eighth of a grain of morphine."[36]

Henry did wake during the night and became fidgety. Sam told the young medical student who was in attendance what the physician had said. But morphine was a new drug, and the student demurred. "I have no way of measuring," he said. "I don't know how much an eighth of a grain would be."

Henry grew more and more disturbed. Half beside himself, Sam went to the student again. "If you have studied drugs," he insisted, "you ought to be able to judge an eighth of a grain of morphine." This time the young man yielded. Portioning out what he believed to be the right amount in the old-fashioned way, on the point of a knife-blade, he administered the drug. Henry immediately sank into a heavy sleep. Before morning he was dead.[37]

How Orion reacted to this unburdening we don't know. Henry's reported injuries seem so severe as to have made his recovery unlikely in an era that lacked modern burn-treatment techniques, and Sam would manifest a lifelong habit of heaping blame upon himself for his supposed carelessness. In any case, a few months later Orion expressed his feelings about the death in a letter to a Miss Wood of Memphis, who had been one of Henry's nurses:

> How I could have sat by him, hung over him, watched day and night every change of expression, and ministered to every want in my power that I could discover. This was denied to me, but Sam, whose organization is such as to feel the utmost extreme of every feeling, was there. Both his capacity of enjoyment and his capacity of suffering are greater than mine; and knowing how it would have affected me to see so sad a scene, I can somewhat appreciate Sam's sufferings. In this time of great trouble, when my two brothers, whose heartstrings have always been a part of my own, were suffering the utmost stretch of mortal endurance, you were there, like a good angel, to aid and console, and I bless and thank you for it with my whole heart.[38]

After Henry's death Orion went for a time to Memphis, Missouri, a small county seat some forty miles west of Keokuk, and then returned to Keokuk to continue his legal studies in the office of S. T. Marshall and a Colonel Worthington. Using Keokuk as his home base, he practiced law both there and in Memphis.[39]

Sam returned to his apprenticeship on the river, and the following spring, on April 9, 1859, he received a coveted license as a Mississippi River steamboat pilot.[40] At the age of twenty-three, he had acquired a profession that surpassed virtually all others for absolute sovereignty and, as Paine informs us, "yielded an income equal to that then earned by the Vice-President of the United States."[41] Suddenly the Clemenses' domestic relations were turned upside-down, for, as the biographer matter-of-factly reports, "At once, of course, he became the head of the Clemens family."[42] By virtue of his two years' training and his newfound affluence, Sam now stepped out of Orion's shadow—which had fallen on him when he first went to work in his brother's Hannibal printshop eight years earlier—and into the leadership of the Clemens clan. Paine elaborates: "His brother Orion was ten years older, but he had not the gift of success. By common consent the younger brother assumed permanently the position of family counselor and financier."[43]

"By common consent"—in other words, Orion made no objection. We can even imagine he was gracious in defeat; indeed, he may have been glad to pass the mantle to his brother. Only the untimely death of John Marshall Clemens had thrust it upon him in the first place, and a sense of duty seems to have made him forego a promising future in St. Louis to return to the river hamlet and provide support for his mother and employment for his brothers. If Orion was a good loser, however, had he felt no resentment he would have been something other than human. Admittedly, he hadn't evinced "the gift of success"—anyone could see that—but for more than a decade he had somehow managed to keep the wolf from the Clemenses' door—this despite Sam's sudden departure from Hannibal, which had thrown the *Journal* into disarray, and Sam's divisive tactics in the Ben Franklin Book and Job Office.

As for Sam, Paine tells us he became at this time "well dressed—even dandified—given to patent leathers, blue serge, white duck, and fancy striped shirts."[44] A contemporary photograph shows him sporting an imposing set of muttonchop whiskers that was not in evidence in an earlier picture.[45] Ruggedly good-looking, he had thick, curly chestnut hair that some called red (though now it was streaked with gray).

In May 1860 Orion moved from Keokuk to Memphis, Missouri, to practice law, leaving Mollie and Jennie to join him later.[46] Why he chose at the age of thirty-three to move from the free state of Iowa back to the slave state of Missouri is not clear, but we know he had long-range plans to run for Congress.[47] That being the case, we may surmise that his feeling of mission overcame his common sense. His St. Louis mentor Edward Bates would write of him the following year: "His success as a lawyer was not great, chiefly, I am told, because his politics did not suit his locality—He *was* a Whig, but joined the Republicans, and that, while it was honest and manly, subjected him to an opposition amounting almost to persecution."[48]

The pressure seems to have worn Orion down. He had been living in Memphis only a month when he wrote a letter to St. Louis that so upset Jane Clemens she "never slept a wink" the night of the day she received it and was still distressed the following morning. We don't know the letter's specific contents, but in it Orion seems to have spoken of having second thoughts about his career choice, of feeling sapped of strength, and of turning outside the family for support.

Sam, exercising his new authority (and invoking a name from Orion's pantheon), penned a stern reply.

> And what is a *man* without energy? Nothing—nothing at all. . . . What was the greatest feature in Napoleon's character? His unconquerable energy! . . .
>
> I want a man to—I want *you* to—take up a line of action and *follow* it out, in spite of the very devil. . . .
>
> I am not talking nonsense, now—I am in earnest. I want you to keep your troubles and your plans out of the reach of meddlers,—until the latter are consummated—so that, in case you fail, no one will know it but yourself.[49]

A year earlier he wouldn't have dreamt of addressing his elder brother in such a voice.

6

The Brothers Go West

As we lay and smoked the pipe of peace and compared all this luxury
with the years of tiresome city life that had gone before it, we felt that
there was only one complete and satisfying happiness in the world,
and we had found it.

Mark Twain

The year 1860 brought a presidential election, a momentous time of decision for the eighty-four-year-old Republic, and the very month Orion
moved to Memphis, Missouri, the Republican Party met in Chicago to
nominate a candidate. Edward C. Bates, Orion's counselor, was among
those being considered, for some delegates felt the election of a Southern-
born candidate from a border state who held free-soil opinions might prevent secession. Early in the proceedings, however, Bates threw his support
to the then little-known Abraham Lincoln of Illinois. The contest was then
between Lincoln and William H. Seward, who was a former governor of
New York, a United States senator from that state, and an antislavery leader.
Much to the surprise and chagrin of the Seward forces, Lincoln was nominated on the third ballot.[1]

In the fall of that year, having brought Mollie and Jennie to live in Memphis, Orion closed his law office and stumped the northern part of the state
for the Republican ticket.[2] If his politics "subjected him to an opposition
amounting almost to persecution" before he began campaigning for Lincoln and the antislavery party, one can only imagine the hostility he encountered afterward. Contemporary records have not survived, but according to a sketch published in the *Keokuk Gate City* at the time of Orion's
death, he "took an energetic and active part in Lincoln's first campaign[,]
going on the stump and espousing the candidacy of the great emancipator
in northern Missouri."[3] He must have conducted himself well, for the

Memphis People's Messenger recalled that when he lived there "he was a very prominent Republican and an able man."[4] Perhaps Orion was heeding his brother's directive to "take up a line of action, and follow it out," but if so, he was keeping his own counsel, for Sam, who according to his grand-nephew was a Democrat at this time, would hardly have approved of that particular course.[5]

In the national election Lincoln polled a clear plurality of votes in a field of four candidates, and although he failed to gain a majority of the popular ballots, which split along regional lines, he was later chosen by the Electoral College to be the sixteenth president of the United States. To William Seward went the number-one position in Lincoln's cabinet, secretary of state; to Edward Bates the office of attorney general.

Orion, at least partly because of the unpopularity of his views, was having trouble supporting his family, and he had run up some debts. He now wrote to Bates and requested a government appointment.[6] "In Jan. 1861 [as Mollie recorded in her journal], he went to St. Louis to see Judge Edward Bates"—no doubt to press his case in person. On March 12 Bates wrote to Secretary of State Seward on Orion's behalf, saying that he had asked for "the post of Secretary of a Territory—any Territory except *Utah.*" (Orion's antipathy for Utah may have been due to his dislike of Brigham Young.) The new attorney general allowed that "I consider him an honest man of fair mediocrity of talents & learning—more indeed of both, than I have seen in several Territorial secretaries." He concluded his half-hearted recommendation: "Without being very urgent with you, I commend Mr Clemens to you, as a worthy & competent man, who will be grateful for a favor."[7]

Lincoln was inaugurated on March 4, 1861. On the twenty-seventh Orion received news he had been appointed secretary of the new territory of Nevada.[8] It was a position of considerable responsibility. Mark Twain did not exaggerate when he wrote, in *Roughing It,* that it was "an office of such majesty that it concentrated in itself the duties and dignities of Treasurer, Comptroller, Secretary of State, and Acting Governor in the Governor's absence." Although Orion's yearly salary of $1,800 would be considerably less than Sam's $3,000, the brothers found themselves for the first time on a comparable footing. In describing his reaction in *Roughing It,* Twain, though obviously exaggerating for comic effect, may have revealed something of his true sentiments: "I envied my brother. . . . What I suffered in contemplating his happiness, pen cannot describe."[9] Sam may have sensed that his own highly valued occupation was in jeopardy. As he wrote many years later in *Life on the Mississippi*, "I loved the profession far better than any I have followed since, and I took a measureless pride in it. The reason is plain: a pilot, in those days, was the only unfettered and entirely independent human being that lived in the earth."[10]

On April 12, 1861, the tension that had been building for years between the North and South broke as the Charleston, South Carolina, harbor batteries fired on Fort Sumter. Shortly afterward Orion came down to St. Louis, where he met with the rest of the family. Surely the Clemenses wanted to confer about Orion's plans to move to the West, and perhaps he showed them the certificate he had just received from Washington. While not as ornate as Sam's pilot's license, there was about it a certain dignity— and it bore the presidential seal and the signature of Honest Abe himself.[11] No doubt the war was discussed, and the Clemenses found that they, like many American families, were divided. Jane Clemens, born and reared in Kentucky, a former slaveholder who hated Yankees, was sympathetic to the Confederacy.[12] Orion had made a firm commitment to the Union.[13] Sam found himself somewhere in the middle.

Whatever the upshot of that family council, differences remained when the brothers went their separate ways, Orion returning to Keokuk to prepare for his trip and Sam rejoining the *Alonzo Child* on its May 2 departure. Even though the war had been raging for more than two weeks, he was loath to tear himself away from the river. When the *Child* arrived in New Orleans six days later, its captain chose not to return to St. Louis.[14] Sam left the *Child* and went north on another boat, probably the *Nebraska,* as a passenger.[15]

The war had now reached the Mississippi Valley. Because Missouri had allied with the South, Union forces from Illinois invaded and took possession of St. Louis, Jefferson Barracks, and other strategic points. Governor "Claib" Jackson issued a proclamation calling out a militia of fifty thousand to repel the invaders.[16] The *Nebraska* thus became the last boat from New Orleans to gain free passage through the Union blockade at Memphis, Tennessee, which put a virtual end to commercial traffic on the river.[17] In his autobiographical dictation, Twain described his perilous journey. "Every day on the trip a blockade was closed by the boat, and the batteries at Jefferson Barracks (below St. Louis) fired two shots through the chimneys the last night of the voyage."[18]

Annie Moffett later recalled that in St. Louis her uncle was obsessed with the fear he might be arrested by federal agents and forced to act as a pilot on a Union gunboat "while a man stood by with a pistol ready to shoot him if he showed the least sign of a false move." She added: "He was almost afraid of leaving the house." George Schroeter, Will Moffett's partner and next-door neighbor, who was in Hannibal with his family for the summer, offered Sam the use of his residence so that he could stay in hiding there. Meanwhile, Jane Clemens gave strict orders that if anyone called at the Moffett house and asked for her son she was to be summoned first so she could ascertain whether the visitor was friend or foe.[19]

Apparently Sam didn't stay out of sight all the time, for his niece told of how one day she and he were standing on the front steps when eight or ten boys appeared carrying a Confederate flag and shouting "Hurrah for Jeff Davis!" Sam called to them and asked if they wanted badges. When they answered yes, he sent Annie up to his room to bring down the ribbons she would find there. She located two bolts, one red and one white, and carried them down. Sam made cockades of red, white, and red and gave them to the boys, who were delighted and marched off proudly.

A short while later, Sam, Jane, and Pamela were in the parlor when they heard shouting. It was Frank Pomeroy, a neighborhood boy of eight or nine, who was having his own one-person procession by the hitching post in front of the house, waving a Union flag. Suddenly a gang of older boys, probably the same ones who had received Sam's decorations, appeared and fell on him. They captured the flag and, putting the stick through the mouth of the horse's head that topped the post, set it afire.

Sam rushed out, rescued the flag, put out the fire, and chased the boys away. Annie Moffett remembered that he then "came in furiously angry; strangely enough not with the hoodlums, but with Frank because he did not fight."

"But Sam," said his mother, "probably he has been taught that he must not fight."

Sam turned to her and let out: "Not fight? He should have guarded his flag with his life!" Annie recalled that "he walked the floor in a rage, while we sat amazed." It was only years later that she realized it was not Frank

Pomeroy Sam was angry with, but himself: "He loved his country's flag and all that it symbolized, and it hurt him to see even this cheap little flag insulted. I know he would gladly have given his life for his country, but he was a Southerner, his friends were all Southern, his sympathies were with the South."[20]

One day a man called and gave his name as Smith. Jane Clemens recognized him as a friend of Sam's from Hannibal. "He had come with the wild project of forming a company to join General Price," reported Annie. "Uncle Sam accepted at once."[21] It was mid-June when Samuel went to Hannibal and joined the Marion (County) Rangers, a desultory band of would-be Confederate volunteers.[22] His rainy, abortive two-week "campaign" for the Southern cause bore less resemblance to a military operation than to the exploits of Tom Sawyer's gang (a good many of whose real-life counterparts were in the rangers), with their comical raids on peach orchards and melon patches. According to Paine, Sam's hitch ended after he fell out of a hay window and sprained his ankle. The unit disbanded soon afterward, and some of its members returned to their civilian occupations while others went on to real combat.[23]

Meanwhile, sixty miles upriver in Keokuk, Orion received from Elisha Whittlesey, first comptroller of the U.S. Treasury, fourteen pages of handwritten instructions for his new office, and he and Mollie began to prepare for his departure.[24] Orion had hoped to take his wife and daughter with him to Nevada, but when the government ignored his request for an advance of his salary that expectancy was dashed.[25] Into a large portmanteau they packed the administrative tools and personal gear they thought he might need—an unabridged Webster's dictionary, books of Iowa statutes, assorted rules of order, formal clothes, tobacco, pipes.[26] By the fourth of July they were ready. There was only one thing lacking—money for passage. Perhaps Orion hoped to borrow from Will Moffett, for after bidding Mollie and Jennie good-bye, he went down the river to St. Louis and stayed with his sister and brother-in-law.[27]

As it happened, Sam was there too. It turned out to be an important meeting, and the appearance of thirty-five-year-old Orion must have made a lasting impression on Sam, for many years later he would describe a character based on his big brother in lifelike detail: "George was about thirty-five. He was tall and thin, with bristly black hair which stood up unparted; intellectual sharp features; eager, restless, unstable black eyes; quick of movement, carriage not without a certain grace and dignity when with his familiars."[28] Sam had saved several hundred dollars out of his pilot's salary, and, according to both him and Paine, he and Orion struck a deal: If Orion would take Sam on as his secretary, Sam would pay passage for both of them.

Paine says that Sam "had had enough of war and the Confederacy. He decided to visit Orion. . . . Orion was a Union abolitionist and might lead him to mend his doctrines."[29] Two pages later he writes, "He agreed that if Orion would overlook his recent brief defection from the Union and appoint him now as his secretary, he would supply the funds for both overland passages," adding that Orion "was always eager to forgive, and the money was vitally necessary."[30] The clear implication is that Sam sought out Orion and accepted not only his employment but his political guidance as well, and that he was willing to provide the travel money in return.[31] In *Roughing It* Twain echoed this story.[32]

The problem is that Orion was in no position to offer his brother or anyone else the position of private secretary under him. In the letter that accompanied his orders, Whittlesey had written, "It is held that, as a general thing, the Secretary can, *in person*, perform *all* the duties pertaining to his office."[33] The directive left open the possibility that once Orion had arrived in Nevada he might hire "additional help" if needed, but only when the legislature was in session. Contrary to both Paine and Twain, then, Sam did not receive a quid pro quo for his monetary aid to Orion, only the possibility that he might be hired at some future date on a temporary basis.

To further complicate matters, several years later the authorized biographer contradicted his earlier account and wrote that by the end of his brief stint in the Marion Rangers, Sam had already "discovered that he was more of a Union abolitionist than a slave-holding secessionist, as he had at first supposed."[34] Whatever his position on the grave issues dividing the nation, Sam was no doubt more than willing to buy passage to a place where those questions would seem less urgent than they did in Missouri.

On July 11, 1861, Orion swore before U.S. Supreme Court justice John Catron in St. Louis to "support the Constitution of the United States, and faithfully discharge the duties of the office of Secretary."[35] Seven days later he and Sam boarded the Missouri River packet *Sioux City* and set out for St. Joseph, Missouri, on the opposite side of the state.[36] The trip upriver took six days. In St. Joseph, Orion purchased tickets on the overland stage to Carson City, Nevada, seventeen hundred miles to the west.[37] When he did so, however, he learned that the baggage allowance for each passenger was only twenty-five pounds, far less than their trunks weighed.[38] Hurriedly selecting what they thought they would need most, they stuffed it into one valise and shipped the portmanteaus back to St. Louis with their swallowtail coats, white kid gloves, stovepipe hats, patent-leather boots, and other nonessentials inside. Orion kept his six-pound dictionary, his statute books, and the small Colt revolver he wore strapped around him, while Sam held on to his Smith & Wesson seven-shooter and what was left of his savings, which he carried as silver coins in a little shot bag.[39]

When the brothers were finally under way, they felt (by Twain's account) "an exhilarating sense of emancipation from all sorts of cares and responsibilities, that almost made us feel that the years we had spent in the close, hot city, toiling and slaving, had been wasted and thrown away."[40] After the coach's thoroughbrace broke and was repaired, the conductor folded the seat backs down and filled the interior half full of mailbags, thereby leaving the passengers with no seats but with a lumpy common bed. "We objected loudly to this," Twain wrote, "but the conductor was wiser than we, and said a bed was better than seats, and moreover, this plan would protect his thoroughbraces." As the passengers stretched out on the mail sacks and gazed at the passing countryside, "our perfect enjoyment took the form of a tranquil and contented ecstasy. . . . the cradle swayed and swung luxuriously. . . . As we lay and smoked the pipe of peace and compared all this luxury with the years of tiresome city life that had gone before it, we felt that there was only one complete and satisfying happiness in the world, and we had found it."[41]

On Monday, August 4, the coach pulled into Salt Lake City. Spending the night at the Salt Lake House, the travelers rose the next day to explore the fifteen-thousand-strong polygamous Mormon enclave, which they found a "fairyland."[42] The U.S. Department of State had given Orion, in his capacity as a federal official, an important assignment: to interview Mormon leaders and try to discover what they intended to do in the wake of the secession of the Southern states.[43] Accordingly, on their second day the brothers, accompanied by three territorial officials, paid a call on principals of the Mormon Church.

Seven years earlier Orion's *Muscatine Journal* had reported that "Brigham Young's time is out as Governor of Utah, but he declares he will not leave the office until the Lord removes him; that neither President Pierce nor any other President can do it, and that if anybody else is sent there as Governor, he is liable to be killed." The newspaper commented: "The government would be disgraced by yielding to such insolence."[44] Now it was Orion's task to represent the United States to the Mormon leaders. He described the meeting in a letter to the *St. Louis Missouri Democrat.* As Franklin R. Rogers pointed out, just below the surface of this report are evident "the heated passions and violent controversies" of the occasion.[45]

Evidently, Young was out of town, for Orion's interview took place with Second President of the Church Heber C. Kimball. "I'd like to see the South give the North a grubbing," began the Mormon leader, "and I'd like to see the North give the South a grubbing, but I want the South to grub a little the hardest for we were run out of both North and South; but Douglas, a Northern man [Stephen A. Douglas, Democratic candidate for President in 1860, who had died on June 3] said that about 'twin relics of barbarism;' but he's gone to hell, and old Buchanan [James Buchanan, Lincoln's Democratic predecessor in the presidency] will follow after him."

"Will Lincoln go that way, too?" inquired Orion.

"Well," said Kimball, turning to another in the company, "he's trying to draw me out."

"I am," replied Orion. "I want to know your sentiments."

"Well," answered the Mormon, "if Lincoln hadn't got his hands so full with the South, he would have pitched into us."

"Not unless you pitched into him first."

"He was going to pitch into us—and now mind, we are considered to be great on prophecy, but I ain't prophesying; it's my opinion you won't see peace any more; the United States will go all to pieces, and the Mormons will take charge of and rule all the country; republicanism will be overthrown, but I won't say what will take its place, nor when, nor at what time the Mormons will commence their rule." Having delivered himself of this remarkable declaration, he went on to give Orion a personal warning: "You are going to have trouble in Nevada."

Orion did not record how he took this, but his reaction must have registered with Kimball, for at that point the Mormon backed off. "But mind, I am a Union man, we are Union men, we are going to stand by the country. Now," he added, "tell it just as I say it."[46]

The brothers' stay in Salt Lake lasted only two days, but it allowed them to stock up on food for the remaining six hundred miles of their journey. Their little "snuggery" among the mail sacks was now complete. "Ham and [hard-boiled] eggs and scenery, a 'downgrade,' a flying coach, a fragrant pipe and a contented heart—these make happiness. It is what all the ages have struggled for."[47] In the desert west of Salt Lake, however, with its ovenlike heat and alkali dust, romance quickly faded into harsh reality—"a thirsty, sweltering, longing, hateful reality!"[48]

Yet when they finally reached their destination on August 14, 1861, twenty-six days out of St. Louis, the brothers (at least according to Twain) were not relieved but sorry: "It had been a fine pleasure trip; we had fed fat on wonders every day; and we were now well accustomed to stage life, and very fond of it; so the idea of coming to a standstill and settling down to a humdrum existence in a village was not agreeable, but on the contrary depressing."[49]

7

Sam Confronts Orion's Ascendancy

~

I am at the helm, now. I have convinced Orion that he hasn't business
talent enough to carry on a peanut stand.

Sam to his mother and sister

Carson City sat in the shadow of a sheer range of mountains, its main
street lined with white frame buildings packed close together, "as if room
were scarce in that mighty plain."[1] The lure of silver had attracted a population of some two thousand, and the board sidewalks, dusty streets, and
central plaza bustled with emigrants from all corners of the globe.

After checking into the Ormsby House and cleaning themselves up, the
brothers hastened to see Governor James Warren Nye.[2] Nye was a white-
haired, genial-faced man in his forties and in good physical condition. His
deep, lustrous brown eyes "could outtalk his tongue," Twain stated in his
autobiographical dictation, "and this is saying a good deal, for he was a
very remarkable talker, both in private and on the stump."[3] Nye, former
president of the Metropolitan Board of Police in New York City, had been
in Carson City since July 11, during which time he had announced the
names of the officials of the territory, set up courts, provided for the taking
of a census, and arranged the electoral districts to choose members of the
territorial legislature and a delegate to Congress. Further than that he had
found he could not go, for Orion had the official instructions for setting
up the new government.[4]

Nye was apparently duly impressed by his secretary, for shortly after
their meeting he went to Sacramento, California, for several weeks, leaving
the territory in Orion's hands. Nye wanted to study California mining statutes and also to confer with authorities about a festering border dispute

between his territory and their state—all in preparation for his inaugural address to the Nevada legislature.[5]

If the month-long journey west had been one of indolent regression for Sam, for Orion it was just the opposite. The day before the brothers left St. Louis he had turned thirty-six, and the occasion surely gave him cause to reflect that if ever he was to make something of his life the time was now; the solemnity of the moment was reinforced by his taking the oath of office. While Sam luxuriated in the "cradle" of the stagecoach, Orion, mindful of the hour, was carefully noting their progress in a journal, and soon after he arrived in Carson he began keeping a scrapbook.[6] On August 29, 1861, he wrote to the *St. Louis Missouri Democrat:* "Heretofore we have had no law . . . but now that we have a Territorial organization we shall have law."[7] It turned out to be both a prediction and a personal commitment.

His resolve must have redoubled when, three weeks after reaching Carson, he received from Keokuk what he called "the most fearful letter I ever read." Six-year-old Jennie had taken seriously ill and gone into convulsions, Mollie reported, and she herself had been in such constant attendance that she had managed only three hours' sleep in three days. Only when Orion reached the end of Mollie's communication did he discover that the physician thought Jennie was out of danger. "You have indeed passed through a ter-rible trial," he commiserated. "How could we spare her?" He went on to speak of his longing for his family. "Nothing keeps me from depression on account of your absence, but being busy from the time I get up till I go to bed. . . . I shall look for a letter every day, until Jennie gets entirely well."[8]

Fortunately, the secretary had plenty to keep him busy, for it was his responsibility to set up the machinery for the first territorial legislature.[9] One of the things he had to do was find a meeting place. Although there were several large and handsome homes in Carson City, there was no pub-lic building spacious enough to accommodate a body of twenty-five law-makers together with their assistants and other officers. There had to be at least four rooms—one for the council, one for the house of representatives, and a committee room for each.[10]

Abraham V. S. Curry, owner of the Warm Springs Hotel, came to the rescue and offered, rent free, the barnlike second floor of his large stone building. It was situated nearly two miles east of town, but that was not considered a problem for Curry also offered free transportation for the legislators on the wooden-track horse railroad he had built to carry cut stone from his quarry.[11]

Since the quarters were unfurnished Orion tried to order desks and chairs from the one furniture store in town, but the owner was not willing to give credit, so the secretary ordered plain pine desks and wooden benches made. When he discovered that the space was unheated, he borrowed stoves from government officials he had met in Salt Lake City and had them shipped by overland freight. He installed partitions to separate the two houses and their committee rooms, and he got two large American flags to place on the wall behind the presiding officers' chairs.[12] Congress had appropriated only twenty thousand dollars for running the government during its first year.[13] Out of that sum all salaries, the printing of the journals of both houses, office rent, writing paper, envelopes, pens, penknives, and anything else that was necessary was to be paid. Orion had to make out vouchers for everything and forward them to Washington, where the comptroller would decide whether the congressional appropriation could be drawn upon.

There was one more thing to be taken care of. The new territory needed an official seal, and so Orion designed one himself—a miner holding a pick and an American flag, at his feet a miner's pan and in the background a mill wheel turned by a mountain stream, a man pushing an ore car out of a mine tunnel, and a five-stamp quartz mill in action.[14] There was no uncertainty in the secretary's mind about what made Nevada important to the Union: mining and more mining. He took special satisfaction in the device, calling it his "buntling" (perhaps "bantling" + "bunting") and instructing the engravers "to see that it is skillfully executed" for "my pride will be to have the prettiest seal in the Union."[15]

Sam cracked to his mother that he had suggested using a buzzard in the layout but that Orion found the idea "disgusting." "I understand it though—he wanted the glory of discovering and inventing and designing the coat-of-arms of this great Territory—savvy?—with a lot of barbarous latin about 'Volens and Potens'—(able and willing, you know,) which would have done just as well for my buzzard as it does for his quartz-mills."[16] In later years the seal seems to have assumed symbolic importance for its designer's brother. One of the depredations Tom Sawyer heaps on Jim while he is being held captive in the final chapters of *Huckleberry Finn* is to design for him a travesty of a coat-of-arms (chap. 39), and the resolution of *The Prince and the Pauper* comes when Tom Canty prompts Edward to recall where he hid the great seal the night they switched places, thus enabling the forsaken prince to prove his identity and regain his lost throne (chap. 32).

Sam was often seen lounging at the corner of King and Carson Streets, smoking a clay pipe and gazing languidly at the human kaleidoscope in the plaza. On the river he had cut a fine figure in his fancy percales and patent leathers, but in Carson he went to the opposite extreme, affecting a broken-down slouch hat, a blue woolen shirt, and coarse trousers crammed into his heavy cowskin boots. Paine tells us that "the more energetic citizens of Carson did not prophesy much for his future among them."[17]

At noon on October 1, 1861, having surmounted many difficulties, delays, and frustrations, Orion called to order the first meeting of the legislative assembly of Nevada, presiding over it until officers had been elected and sworn in.[18] It then became his duty to record the activities of the lawmakers, to receive all papers from them, to pay their salaries, and to carry on all correspondence with the national government.[19] It was a heavy responsibility, the weightiest he had ever shouldered, but all his experience up to that point—his public speaking, his legal studies, his political campaigning, his printing businesses, even clerking in his father's store—had prepared him for this key role in state building. He took Sam on as his clerk. Sam wanted fourteen dollars a day, but Orion made him settle for eight.[20] During the proceedings the former riverboat pilot recorded, copied, delivered messages, and rendered general assistance to his brother.

The legislature had been in session only a few days when friction developed between it and the secretary. In order to settle a contested seat, the upper house needed Orion's testimony and certain papers he held, but when the sergeant-at-arms went to get him, he was sent back with a message that the secretary "would come tomorrow morning." Nettled, the lawmakers voted unanimously to compel Orion to appear before them "forthwith," the president of the council instructing the sergeant to bring him even if he had to call out a posse comitatus. When the secretary finally arrived, he was wearing, as the reporter for the *Sacramento Union* put it, "a smiling exterior, though evidently a little anxious in regard to final results." The journalist added that the whole affair had "created a little excitement, and a great deal of fun." Orion explained that he had not come immediately because he supposed the council had other business to attend to and because no conveyance was at hand. It was a tactical error, for Orion's selection of a venue was not popular among the legislators. Some of them suggested that if he chose to provide a place of meeting two miles out of town he ought to be willing to walk out there at least once. The secretary and other witnesses were examined, and the council adjourned for the day.[21] The following morning Orion was on hand to offer his humble apologies for putting the council to the trouble of arresting him. If he had been aware that the body was waiting for him, he assured them, he would have come immediately. The apology was accepted and no contempt citation brought.[22]

But a month later Orion once again found himself at odds with the lawmakers. On examining the printed journals of the council, the secretary of that body found that all references to the "President of the Council" and the "Secretary of the Council" had been struck out. On inquiry he discovered that the changes had been made by order of the secretary of the territory. This, the solons felt, was a serious matter. If the territorial secretary could "exercise a general supervision over legislation, and direct what should or should not be done," they would be "shorn of all power." A resolution was offered to the effect that "the Secretary of the Territory, from the commencement of the present legislative session, has, by an assumption of dictatorial power in various ways, continued to annoy and perplex the operations of the Legislature, in matters pertaining solely to their own business" and that, consequently, the leaders of the two houses be authorized to write a letter to Washington to ascertain whether "the Legislative Assembly of the Territory have any rights whatever, or are compelled to submit to the dictation of the Secretary." The resolution was adopted with only one dissenting vote.[23]

It matters little that the whole thing was a misunderstanding, that Orion was merely following federal orders in altering the journal, and that the resolution was soon rescinded. What interests us is that the legislators found Orion, "from the commencement of the present legislative session" and "in various ways," to have assumed "dictatorial power." Saintlike though he may have been, there was something imperious in Orion's makeup—something Napoleonic, if you will. Anxious to make the most of his opportunity, upset over his separation from wife and daughter, driven by a sense of mission, Orion Clemens was very likely capable of acting the martinet.

What Sam's role in these affairs may have been, if any, we don't know, but despite his facetious reference to "His Majesty the Secretary" in *Rough-*

ing It, he seems to have been genuinely impressed by Orion's new incarnation.[24] After he had had a few years to reflect on it, he told his brother that he "got acquainted with" him during this period and "thought . . . how you would tower head and shoulders above any of the small-fry preachers of my experience!"[25] It seems hardly happenstance that Sam's letters at this time took on the tone that would eventually become his hallmark—brash, irreverent, puckish. Pamela's daughter, Annie, related that when Sam read one of these letters to Orion, his brother persuaded him to send it to the *Keokuk Gate City,* where "it created quite a furore [*sic*] and may be said to have been the real beginning of his literary work. He had written squibs and short articles, but this was his first writing that attracted attention."[26] (It is worth noting that Orion himself wrote letters to the *Gate City.*)

The brothers were now sharing a room and eating at Mrs. Margret Murphy's boardinghouse on the main plaza, living off Sam's little shot bag of silver coins. Since their landlady charged them only ten dollars a week apiece, the money held out well.[27] Orion kept his office in the room and charged the United States no rent, even though, as Twain pointed out in *Roughing It,* "his 'instructions' provided for that item and he could have justly taken advantage of it (a thing which I would have done with more than lightning promptness if I had been secretary myself)."[28] Orion, by contrast, used to "lie awake . . . planning economies for the government, or how to make up excess charges out of his salary."[29]

Just as the legislature was about to adjourn, Orion finally received the first installment of those earnings from Washington—$925 for the period March 27 through September 30. He then rented an office for fifty dollars a month and furnished it with tables, chairs, desks, and spittoons from the legislative hall—nothing fancy, although it did have a little bedroom in back. "The wind had blown in a large quantity of dust which had settled on the cloth ceiling," he wrote, "and was always sifting down. . . . The snow sometimes blew in and settled on the ceiling, and was always sifting down."[30] The government directive allowed for a more liberal rent than he was paying, but, as Orion wrote to Treasury Comptroller Whittlesey, "I have studied economy in every way on account of the war."[31]

Sam's job as Orion's temporary clerk had ended, and he found himself smitten by the highly contagious silver fever. With three other hopeful prospectors he set out on an expedition to the Humboldt mining district.

Jennie had recovered from her ailment, and now that Orion had received his salary Mollie was eager to join her husband. "I want to be with you not caring where you are," she had written in November, and apparently she suggested making the trip overland.[32] The idea didn't appeal to Orion at all. On January 16, 1862, he wrote her that

Traveling across the plains sometimes develops the d——l in people. But of all ways of traveling for a woman, the very last I have ever tried is a stage. Half the time for three weeks it will be so dark in the stage you can't see your hand before you. The stage is rolling and tumbling, you may be asleep, your man company awake, but pretending to be asleep. His hand wanders over you. If you catch him he snores or yawns sleepily, and you don't know whether he was asleep or awake. They say the worst enemy a woman has is opportunity, and if I didn't know you to be incorruptible, I would be almost doubtful whether to sleep with you or not, if you came three weeks of dark nights, through a wilderness, with only a man acquaintance.[33]

By January 30 Sam was back in Carson City. That day he added his words to a letter Orion wrote to his wife. "Well, Mollie, I think July will be soon enough, because I think that by that time some of our claims will be paying handsomely. . . . And we could have a house fit to live in—and servants to do your work."[34]

Sam wrote to his mother describing his excursion. His mention of fourteen decks of cards, one small keg of lager beer, a book of church music, and a balky horse that could have been "a blood relation of our family—he is so infernally lazy" seemed calculated to raise her hackles. The member of the family he had in mind is suggested by his description of the horse as "standing, solitary and alone, away up on the highest peak of a mountain, where no horse ever ventured before."[35]

Orion might have climbed a summit where no member of the Clemens family had gone before, but he was not solitary and alone—as he discovered when he told Sam that relations between him and the governor had become strained. These two men had utterly different backgrounds and personalities. Orion's only experiences with politics were of the rural and small-town variety—when his father ran for surrogate judge, when he associated with Edward Bates in St. Louis, and when he campaigned for Lincoln in Missouri. Orion, moreover, was scrupulously honest. James Nye, several years older, was a graduate of New York's Tammany Hall and a professional politician.[36] To him Nevada's chief importance lay in providing a stepping stone to the U.S. Senate; in the meantime, he and his entourage were determined to enjoy all the perquisites and emoluments their positions afforded.[37]

The difference was manifest in the respective choices of office space. Nye set himself up in gubernatorial splendor in the best obtainable quarters on the main street of Carson, while the secretary took a room on the southwest corner of Curry and Telegraph, far on the outskirts of town. Nye conceived that the federal government was not so much interested in economy as in the appearance thereof and knew how to juggle accounts accordingly.[38] To such trickery Orion Clemens was a formidable impediment, and he could not be brought to a proper political understanding.[39]

Sam was fond of the governor, but he had a higher regard for the family name. When he heard Orion's troubled story, he called on Governor Nye and delivered himself in his best pilothouse fashion. Paine wrote that "we may regret that no stenographic report was made of the interview. It would be priceless now."[40] The episode seems to have fixed the manner for an agreement the brothers entered into regarding their business dealings, wherein Orion was to remain above the fray while Sam attended to troublesome details. "I am at the helm, now," Sam wrote to his mother and sister on February 8, 1862, invoking his piloting days. "I have convinced Orion that he hasn't business talent enough to carry on a peanut stand, and he has solemnly promised me that he will meddle no more with mining, or other matters not connected with the Secretary's office."[41] In *Life on the Mississippi* Twain wrote of the relationship between the captain and the pilot of a riverboat:

The captain could stand on the hurricane deck, in the pomp of a very brief authority and give five or six orders while the vessel backed into the stream, and then that skipper's reign was over. The moment the boat was under way in the river, she was under the sole and unquestioned control of the pilot. . . . I have seen a boy of eighteen taking a great steamer serenely into what seemed almost certain destruction, and the aged captain standing mutely by, filled with apprehension but powerless to interfere.[42]

This, then, was how Sam had decided to deal with his brother's ascendancy: As long as he himself could remain "at the helm," he was willing to begrudge Orion the hurricane deck. Years later he would write of the Connecticut Yankee Hank Morgan dictating a similar arrangement to King Arthur. "You shall remain king over your dominions," he declares as the famous eclipse blackens the sun, "and receive all the glories and honors that belong to the kingship; but you shall appoint me your perpetual minister and executive."[43] Later Hank remarks that "I was the substance; the king himself was the shadow."[44]

Years later, Mark Twain would find another metaphor for the strained bond between two men. Invoking the famous Siamese twins Chang and Eng, he stated, "while Mr. Chang . . . had a high—in fact, an abnormally high and fine—moral sense, he had no machinery to work it with; whereas, Mr. Eng . . . who hadn't any moral sense at all, and hasn't yet, was equipped with all the necessary plant for putting a noble deed through, if he could only get the inspiration. . . . Thus, working together, they made a strong team; laboring together, they could do miracles; but break the circuit, and both were impotent."[45] The Civil War changed many American lives, not the least of which was that of Samuel Langhorne Clemens. But for that terrible upheaval, he would probably have remained on the river and followed a more or less conventional path to maturity. As it was, he not only lost his valued occupation but was once again thrown in with his elder brother. By wedding Orion's high-mindedness with his own scrappiness and craftiness, he hoped to make the most of a bad situation; he hoped they could become "a strong team."

A few paragraphs later in the letter Samuel added, "Pa wouldn't allow us to fight, and next month Orion will be governor, in the governor's absence, and then he'll be sorry that his education was so much neglected." As he closed, he playfully scolded his mother, "you ought to have raised me first, *ma mere,* so that Orion could have had the benefit of my example."[46]

In early April 1862, Sam went to Aurora in the Esmeralda mining district, some one hundred miles southeast of Carson City.[47] As Paine put it, "He had about exhausted his own funds by this time, and it was necessary that Orion should become his financier. The brothers owned their Esmeralda claims in partnership, and it was agreed that Orion, out of his modest depleted pay, should furnish the means, while the other would go actively into the field and develop their riches. Neither had the slightest doubt but that they would be millionaires presently, and both were willing to struggle and starve for the few intervening weeks."[48]

Sam's letters to Orion of this period were businesslike and humorless. Often he asked for money—forty, fifty, a hundred dollars, or more. "Stint yourself as much as possible," he wrote on April 13, "I go to work to-morrow, with pick and shovel. Something's got to come, by G——, before I let go, here."[49]

Stint himself Orion must have done, for he was also sending money home. Indeed, his contributions to Jane Clemens were now her main source of income.[50] He also had his hands full looking after Governor Nye's work as well as his own, for Nye spent most of the hard winter and long, cold spring in San Francisco.[51]

"Col. Young's [sic] says you must rent Kinkead's room by all means," Sam's letter continued. "Says you are playing your hand very badly, for either the Government's good opinion or anybody's else, in keeping your office in a shanty." He and Orion knew Colonel Samuel Youngs, owner of a quartz mill in Aurora, from his days as a member of the first territorial legislature.[52] "When old Col. Youngs talks this way," continued Sam, "I think it time to get a fine office. I wish you would take that office, and fit it up handsomely, so that I can quit telling people that by this time you are handsomely located, when I know it is no such thing." He closed with, "Don't buy *anything* while I am here—but save up some money for me. Don't send any money home. I shall have your next quarter's salary spent before you get it, I think. I mean to make or break here within the next 2 or 3 months."[53] In his next letter he repeated his admonition not to buy any mining stock. "The pick and shovel are the only claims I have any confidence in now. My back is sore and my hands blistered with handling them to-day." He went on to tell Orion not to pay De Witt Harroun, a Humboldt miner, any money.[54]

But it was too late. In a communication written the same day, Orion apologetically informed his brother that he had given Harroun fifty dollars and agreed to pay part of the expenses of a man named Perry, who was trying to locate a mill site. As soon as he had done so, he admitted, he had cursed himself for being so easily persuaded.

When he received this letter, Sam proceeded to read his brother the riot act. After reminding him of their solemn agreement and that they had specifically discussed Harroun and "*decided,* then, that he was not to receive a cent of money," he went on to charge that "you knew, at that very moment, that you were breaking your word with me." Spleen vented, he calmed down a little. "Now, Orion, I have given you a piece of my mind—you have it in full, and you deserved it—for you would be ashamed to acknowledge that you ever broke faith with another man as you have with me." By that time a new wave of emotion—homesickness and frustration, mainly—had swept over Sam, and he declared: "I shall never look upon Ma's face again, or Pamela's, or get married, or revisit the 'Banner State,' until I am a rich man—so you can easily see that when you stand between me and my fortune (the one which I shall make, as surely as Fate itself,) you stand between me and *home,* friends, and all that I care for—and by the Lord God! you must clear the track, you know!"[55]

If in a moment of weakness Orion had broken faith with Sam, he was still looking out for his brother's best interests. After he showed some of Sam's *Keokuk Gate City* letters to William H. Barstow of the *Virginia City Territorial Enterprise,* that paper reprinted at least one of them, or portions of it. When Sam learned of this he was encouraged enough to send occasional contributions directly to the *Enterprise,* using the pen name "Josh." He was not paid for these, and, as Paine pointed out, "he did not care to sign his own name. He was a miner who was soon to be a magnate; he had no desire to be known as a camp scribbler."[56]

By July that attitude had changed. Sam was in debt and none of the claims was producing. "The fact is," he told Orion, "I must have something to do, and that *shortly,* too."[57] He asked his brother to inform the *Sacramento Union* he would write as many letters as they wanted for ten dollars a week. "If they want letters from here, who'll run from morning till night collecting materials cheaper[?]"[58]

In his next dispatch he informed Orion that Barstow had offered him the job of local reporter for the *Enterprise* at twenty-five dollars a week. "I have written him that I will let him know next mail if possible."[59] To accept the job, of course, meant giving up on the mines. In *Roughing It* Twain wrote of his divided feelings about the *Enterprise*'s offer. "Yet if I refused this place I must presently become dependent upon somebody for my bread, a thing necessarily distasteful to a man who had never experienced such a humiliation since he was thirteen years old. . . . So I was scared into being city editor."[60] Since he had been totally dependent on Orion for three months this statement was disingenuous, but it may have expressed his wish to free himself from "such a humiliation." At last, toward the end of August, Sam slung his heavy pack on his shoulders and, apparently so poor he couldn't afford a horse, walked to Virginia City, a distance of more than one hundred miles through hilly terrain.

Meanwhile, Orion was busy in Carson City preparing for the arrival of his family. He had bought a plot of land on the northwest corner of Spear and Division Streets, and he now proceeded to have a house built there. It was a two-story, three-bedroom frame affair with a curved porch and a bow window, and when it was done it was one of the finest in town; Twain later said no other house in the capital could approach it in style and cost.[61] The price was twelve thousand dollars, and the furnishings—handsome walnut Victorian pieces and a large square grand piano—added several thousand more.[62]

Where did Orion get the money? In April he had had but a "modest depleted pay" out of which to finance Sam; the house was mortgaged, but nonetheless a considerable outlay of cash must have been required. The answer may lie in a bill the territorial legislature had passed in its first session entitling the secretary to collect fees for certain public services—certifying documents, providing copies of laws and other instruments, filing certificates of incorporation.[63] At first these fees didn't amount to much, but after a while they probably became a significant source of income. Twain claimed in his *Autobiography* that "I got the legislature to pass" this bill, although he mistakenly attributed it to the second session. He also claimed that Orion's fees accounted for an average of one thousand dollars a month, in gold.[64]

In September Mollie and Jennie, accompanied by a woman acquaintance, set out on the long trek west by first going east to New York, then by steamer to the Isthmus of Panama, overland by primitive conveyances, and then on another steamship to San Francisco. On October 2 Orion went down to meet them. The reunited family arrived in Carson City ten days later.[65] Since James Nye had no family in Nevada, the Orion Clemens's home was now the de facto governor's mansion. Mollie became active in church, school, and charitable affairs and was often the chair of committees. With a servant to help her she entertained often, and soon the house was the social center of the capital, with Mollie in effect First Lady of Nevada Territory.[66]

The second legislature convened on November 11, 1862. Sam had by that time become prominent among the *Enterprise* journalists, and it was he who went down to Carson City to cover the proceedings.[67] He stayed in Orion's guest room, and every day the brothers walked the few blocks to Abraham Curry's new Great Basin Hotel, where the legislature now met and where Orion had his office.[68]

During the second session of the territorial legislature Orion was no longer responsible for keeping a record of its deliberations, but he made periodic reports to the lawmakers.[69] Twain noted in his *Autobiography* that Orion was very popular with the solons "because they found that whereas they couldn't usually trust each other, nor anybody else, they could trust him. He easily held the belt for honesty in that country." He pointed out, however, that Orion's popularity didn't benefit him because he "had no talent for either persuading or scaring legislators. But I was differently situated. I was there every day in the legislature to distribute compliment and censure with evenly balanced justice and spread the same over half a page of the *Enterprise* every morning; consequently I was an influence."[70]

Paine observes that it must have been gratifying to Sam to come back and command respect in a town where less than a year earlier he had been regarded as "no more than an amusing indolent fellow, a figure to smile at."[71] In place of his miner's rude outfit, he began sporting a long broadcloth cloak, a starched shirt, and polished boots. "Once more," Paine noted, "he had become the glass of fashion that he had been on the river."[72] His jokes, his songs, and his general exuberance made him a favorite at Mollie Clemens's get-togethers. Indeed, Sam and "Sister Mollie" seem both to have taken to the social whirl. Twain later wrote that "Mrs. Governor Clemens enjoyed being a Governor's wife. No one on this planet ever enjoyed a distinction more than she enjoyed that one. Her delight in being the head of society was so frank that it disarmed criticism, and even envy."[73]

When the legislature adjourned on December 20, Sam returned to Virginia City. Ready for a vacation, he wanted to spend a few days in San Francisco, but the *Enterprise* had no replacement for him, so once again he returned to Carson. From there he sent off at least three letters to the paper. One of these was the first article he is known to have signed "Mark Twain," and it was probably written on January 31 and printed on February 3, 1863.[74] Up to that time, his dispatches from Carson had been unsigned; afterward the nom de plume would be attached to most of Samuel

Clemens's work. His friends even began calling him "Mark" instead of "Sam."[75]

Much has been written about the famous pen name—which was a riverboat leadsman's call meaning two fathoms, or twelve feet. Paine tells us that Sam gave the matter a good deal of thought and tried many possibilities before settling on that particular one. For our purposes it is sufficient to note that the appellation, with its connotation of duality and its similarity to the word "twin" (not to mention its evocation of the mark of Cain), was first used by Sam shortly after two months of close association with his brother and at a time when he was living under Orion's roof.

8

Orion Faces a Challenge

Governor Clemens moves slow but very sure, and when he resolves to
do a thing he does it.

Virginia City Union

Orion was extremely busy. Governor Nye had gone on yet another extended trip, and as secretary of the territory, Orion was left in charge. As
acting governor he appointed and removed officials, granted passports, sol-
emnized marriages, issued proclamations, and extradited and pardoned
prisoners.[1] He also found himself responsible for all Indian affairs in the
territory. When a Washoe chief complained to him that white men were
cutting down the pine nut trees on which his tribe depended for food,
Orion promised to write to "the great chief at Washington, eastward over
the mountains, three thousand miles away, and hear in two moons, or may
be three moons." On February 3, 1863, he rather plaintively requested of
Washington: "Please send me general instructions as to my duty as Superintendent of Indian Affairs. I have done the best I could since I commenced
acting as such."[2]

After Sam returned to Virginia City, Orion found himself embroiled in
a dangerous conflict between Nevada and California. Before he left, Nye
had issued commissions to newly elected officials in Roop County, and the
legislature had ordered a judge to go to Susanville in that county and hold
court. These seemingly innocuous acts were actually provocative, for the
young territory was behaving contrary to both the federal act that created
it and the sentiment of the California legislature.[3]

When Congress carved Nevada out of Utah it gave it a more liberal
western boundary than the mother territory had had, along the summit of

the Sierra Nevada instead of on the 120th meridian. It added the proviso, however, that "so much of the said territory as is within the present limits of California shall not be included until California assents to the same." In other words, it was up to territorial officials somehow to wheedle that land away from their neighbor.[4] Governor Nye and two other emissaries had spent six weeks in 1862 in San Francisco, where the California legislature was meeting, trying to do just that—but to no avail.[5] Nevada was, therefore, extending its jurisdiction into an area that had not been transferred to it.[6]

Naturally there was a reaction. Plumas, the California county that exercised authority in the region, brought a number of legal maneuvers. When these failed, the sheriff raised a posse comitatus of 115 men, who armed themselves (they even had a cannon) and went to Susanville, where a pitched battle with a force of 35 local residents, who were pro-Nevada, followed. After several hours of brisk gunfire, during which 6 men were wounded (2 seriously), the adversaries agreed to an armistice and held a parley. Noting that a "state of war" existed between the California and Nevada counties, they appealed to their respective governors to settle the matter. Tempers ran high, and the emergency threatened to spread.[7]

When word reached Orion, he telegraphed Governor Leland Stanford of California that "action of the late Legislature renders it necessary for me to sustain the action of the Roop County officers" and inquired, "What course do you propose to pursue?" He also dispatched J. K. Lovejoy to Susanville to investigate and report back to him.[8]

Governor Stanford wired back: "I regret much there should have arisen this serious difficulty—But we will meet it in the spirit of kind neighbors and adjust it as speedily as possible."[9] He then sent Judge Robert Robinson to Susanville and thence to Carson City to meet with Orion.[10]

Lovejoy reported back to Orion that a state of lawlessness obtained in Roop County. Government and courts were not functioning, and even the schools were closed. "Unless most decisive and prompt measures are taken," he warned, "trouble of a terrible character, as between California and our Territory will most certainly ensue." But the danger didn't stop there. "This state of affairs must not continue in that region, as it will induce . . . a similar state of affairs all along the border."[11]

Orion urged the sheriff of Roop County to "abide faithfully and patiently" by the temporary peace agreement, lest "the evils widen and strengthen till they pass beyond control."[12] Even though the residents of Roop addressed a petition to him that "it is their express wish and desire to be within said Territory and be governed by its jurisdiction," Orion cautioned them that they "had better be very careful," because if they were in California, Nevada laws could not protect them.[13]

Orion then drafted an eight-page letter to Governor Stanford in which he pointed out that since the California legislature was in session it could readily solve the difficulties by making the eastern boundary of Plumas County the summit of the Sierra Nevada. Barring that, the matter could be submitted to the people of California or the line jointly surveyed and established without doubt, for as it was, nobody was sure where it lay ("You doubtless have your opinions, as we have ours").

He drafted the letter on March 4, but instead of dispatching it he decided to sleep on the matter. The following day he carefully crossed out each page from corner to corner and composed an entirely new message. Although he copied some of the passages from the first draft into the fresh one, he made one significant change: He subtly suggested that if a survey were to be made it should include not only the northern part of the California-Nevada line, where Roop County lay, but the southern as well.[14]

It was a clever stroke—indeed, a brilliant one. As long as the difficulty was confined to Roop, Nevada didn't have a leg to stand on; drafting the first letter must have made Orion painfully aware that the best he could do was appeal to the California officials' sense of altruism and concern about the threatening violence. If, on the other hand, the compass could be broadened to include Aurora to the south, the territory gained important leverage. Despite Sam's lack of success there, the area around Aurora (known as the Esmeralda district) was rich in mineral wealth and was therefore a much more important prize than Roop County. Moreover, in 1862 Nevada had run a survey that showed Aurora to lie within its borders. California refused to recognize the Kidder-Ives line and had, in fact, made Aurora the seat of its Mono County. A state of disorder thus existed in Esmeralda, where two jurisdictions claimed authority.[15] By broadening the scope of the high-stakes poker game, Orion was in effect saying to California: "Very well, if you are determined to control Roop, you will have to abandon your illegitimate claim to Esmeralda."

When Judge Robinson arrived in Carson City, he told Orion unequivocally that California would not even consider the "dividing ridge" boundary in the north.[16] At first Orion was conciliatory. He admitted that Nevada had perhaps acted hastily in organizing Roop County and for that reason was the aggressor in the Sagebrush War.[17] But when Robinson agreed that a joint survey should be run to establish permanently the entire boundary, Orion won his point. Surely the judge recognized then that he had been outmaneuvered—or perhaps he was simply hoping that a new survey would somehow produce different results.

In order to prevent further bloodshed in the meantime, the negotiators wanted to settle on a tentative boundary. The California representative proposed that it run north of Lake Bigler (now Tahoe) through the eastern end of Honey Lake, thus placing Roop County under California's jurisdiction. To this Orion acceded, but only on condition that south of Bigler the line established by Kidder and Ives be recognized as the temporary boundary and that administration of Aurora accordingly pass from California to Nevada.[18] Here Orion got tough. He knew the California legislature had shown a tendency to procrastinate on the border question and that unless it could be forced to act, the opportunity might not return before a full-scale war broke out. He therefore specified that in order

to give the California Legislature time enough to act, the Governor of Nevada Territory will not organize Esmeralda County until the 8th of April 1863, but that from and after that date and until the permanent line shall be run and established, the officers of the State of California and especially of Mono County will exercise no authority east of said line as run by Kidder, and that east of said line the officers of the Territory of Nevada shall exercise full jurisdiction according to the Laws of said Territory and the Citizens will be governed thereby, the town of Aurora being recognized as the County Seat of Esmeralda County and within the Territory of Nevada.[19]

Diplomatically worded though it was, it was a clear ultimatum: Act by April 8 or face the consequences. Judge Robinson "did not feel authorized to consent" to Orion's demands. He agreed only to carry the unsigned document back to Governor Stanford.[20]

How aware of these machinations the *Virginia City Territorial Enterprise* was we don't know, but two days after this instrument was dated the paper editorialized that it would be "content" to have Orion Clemens permanently installed in the office of governor of Nevada. "He does his business punctually and thoroughly, and has disclosed so little of the politician since he has been in the Territory that we are sometimes surprised that he ever received a Federal appointment."[21]

When Robinson reported to Governor Stanford what Orion had in mind, the executive was not pleased. In presenting the matter to the California legislature, he dropped the conciliatory tone of his telegram to Orion and stated that "to do this in so populous and important a district is at once to complicate matters and pave the way for serious difficulties. With the prospect of an early settlement of the boundary line by a Joint Commission, I trust his Excellency Governor Clemens will think better of his determination to organize the county of Esmeralda."[22]

Feelings ran high on both sides. On April 3 the *Virginia City Enterprise* printed a long editorial that read in part:

> Governor Clemens, if he consults the feelings of the people of this Territory, will not recede one inch from the position he has taken. . . . If the California Legislature, through neglect or obstinacy, fail to make a satisfactory settlement, and invite a collision of jurisdiction, let us accept the issue. We have used quite enough supplication and conciliatory means. . . . We have submitted to enough insolence. Our people are tired of this aggression, and before yielding another foot of ground will raise the standard of The Summit Boundary or Blood.[23]

The impending conflict was more than a disagreement between Nevada and California. In Aurora the pro-California faction was not only vocal in its Southern sympathies, it had already clashed with Unionists, confiscating their weapons and defiantly holding violent secessionist demonstrations. When Brigadier General George Wright, commandant of the Department of the Pacific, headquartered in San Francisco, rearmed the Esmeralda Rifles the time seemed ripe for hostilities on a heightened level.[24] In April of the previous year Sam had written Orion from Aurora that "the Secessionists have declared that in case Cal. accedes to the new boundaries, Gov. Nye shall not assume jurisdiction here."[25] What was in the offing, then, was nothing short of the opening of a western front in the Civil War, with Nevada's vast mineral wealth at stake.

On April 2, 1863, General Wright wrote to Orion suggesting he raise companies of federal troops in Nevada, ostensibly for Indian fighting. Orion replied that he thought from one to four companies could be mustered and that "it will afford me pleasure to have them organized," adding ominously that "I observe from the public prints, that enemies of the Government are apparently plotting to bring on civil war in California; and I have heard a suspicion expressed of similar designs in this Territory. I would be pleased to have your advice as to the propriety and best forms and extent of measures of preparation, and as to what my reliance should be placed upon in case of any military emergency."[26]

General Wright's response seems to have been to order Major C. McDermit, commander of Fort Churchill, to write to Orion putting his forces at the acting governor's disposal. In any case McDermit did that, informing Orion that mountain howitzers and Springfield rifle muskets were on their way from Washington. He also invited Orion to visit the fort, which was thirty miles east of Carson City and was the command center of all federal troops in Nevada Territory. The large installation was strategically located on the route of the overland mail and the telegraph line.[27]

A powerful faction in Virginia City wanted Orion to call a special session of the legislature to address the crisis. Orion opposed that, perhaps feeling that to do so would signal irresolution to California, but on April 7, 1863, he traveled from the capital to confer informally with the group. The *Union* reported that he came "at the earnest request of prominent citizens, and to hold grave consultation concerning matters of great public importance," adding that "the responsibility of Chief Executive seems to rest light on his shoulders, judging from his personal appearance."[28]

Orion was not moved by the arguments presented by the dissidents but rather brought them around to his way of thinking, assuring them that he could preserve the jurisdiction of the territory without a special session. He then reiterated to the *Union* what he had told Governor Stanford: If the California legislature failed to take action before adjourning, he would organize Esmeralda County. The newspaper duly published this warning and editorialized that "if the California authorities think he will not, it is because they don't know the man. Governor Clemens moves slow but very sure, and when he resolves to do a thing he does it."[29]

The day this piece ran in the *Union,* Orion wrote to his friend Colonel

Samuel Youngs in Aurora asking him to select men to apply for the various offices of Esmeralda County. He stipulated that he wanted candidates of "character, popularity and influence; honest and capable, and Union men, supporters of the Administration, including the Emancipation Proclamation."[30] The long spiritual trek that had begun in Hannibal at the beginning of the 1850s with a young newspaper editor affirming "our contempt for the Abolitionists of the North" had culminated in Nevada Territory some thirteen years later with the acting governor explicitly invoking the decree that abolished slavery in the rebelling Confederate states. Pointedly, Orion sent a copy of his letter to Judge Robinson.[31]

Orion's message seems to have gotten through to the California legislature, where one member told his fellow lawmakers that it was "vain to say that Nevada was only threatening . . . and it was no difficult matter to bring on a collision destroying a great many lives."[32] When the lawmakers postponed their adjournment to April 20, Orion accordingly deferred organizing Esmeralda until after that date.[33]

On April 10 the *Virginia City Union* published an open letter to Orion Clemens criticizing him for refusing to call an extra legislative session and, while it conceded his honesty and patriotism, suggesting that he was a pawn of conspirators. "You are placed there as a sentinel upon the watchtower," lectured the anonymous correspondent, "and if, by your inattention, civil war is brought upon us, will not the people and posterity hold you, in some degree, responsible?"[34]

The *Enterprise* came to Orion's defense, asserting that he had acted entirely on his own. "He could see no necessity for such a course. The arguments in favor of it did not shake his resolution, and when those who advocated an extra session acquiesced in his views, it confirmed but did not alter his determination."[35]

"I suppose we are on the verge of war now," Sam wrote to his mother and sister that day. "If Orion assumes jurisdiction over Esmeralda county, California . . ." Unfortunately, we do not have Sam's further thoughts on the emergency, for two pages of his letter are missing at this critical point.[36] How he might have counseled his brother had he been at his side, however, is suggested by this later passage: "How I *hate* everything that looks, or tastes, or smells like California!—and how I hate everybody that loves the cursed State! . . . We *hang* one of these scabby, putrefied Californians every now and then."[37]

The two governments did indeed stand on the brink of war. On April 20 Orion wrote to Major McDermit at Fort Churchill asking how many troops were subject to his order "and of what description, and if accouterments are complete, and how many rounds of ammunition?" He also wanted to know when the fieldpieces and other arms were expected from Washington. He said that because he was "very busy" he could not at the moment visit the fort, but if there was an "immediate urgent need" and the major wanted him, he would come.[38]

Apparently the commander perceived such a need, for on April 27, when Orion sent General Wright a copy of his proclamation calling for two companies of cavalry and two of infantry to be raised, he mentioned having visited Fort Churchill. While there, he told the general, he had asked the lieutenant in charge of drawing up the officer candidate examination to include a question about whether the applicant was a supporter of the Union, the Lincoln administration, and the Emancipation Proclamation—adding, "and make the interrogatory pointed" as to the last.[39]

On April 27 the California Legislature passed an act "to survey and to establish the eastern boundary of the state of California and to request the governor of Nevada to join in the survey."[40] Governor Stanford soon signed the act, and in May he and Clemens appointed a joint commission of California and Nevada surveyors to run a final boundary line. Since the two men chosen to head it were the very ones who had conducted the earlier survey, Butler Ives and John F. Kidder, it was not surprising that the results were the same—Aurora belonged in Nevada.[41]

It was Orion Clemens's finest hour. By linking the crisis in Susanville to the higher-stakes conflict in Aurora, and then holding the California legislators' feet to the fire until they capitulated, "his Excellency Governor Clemens" forced that state to abandon its illegal occupation of Nevada's territory, giving up little in return. Not only did he bring the rule of law to an important and particularly unstable corner of the West, but at a time when America could ill afford to open a new front in the Civil War, he enforced the peace. The acting governor was no Abraham Lincoln, but like that other obscure country lawyer who had known nothing but failure early in life, when his country desperately needed the qualities of diplomacy, humility, shrewdness, and iron will, he displayed them—and to a degree worthy of the Great Emancipator himself. Orion may have lacked youthful experience in fighting, as Sam pointed out, but he made up for it in strength of character. A photograph taken about this time shows a handsome man with thick, wavy black hair, a full beard, and dark, piercing eyes. He wears the look of someone who knows what he is about. An observer who didn't know him and Sam probably wouldn't have guessed they were brothers.

How did Orion's younger brother react to his moment of greatness? As soon as it became clear that war had been averted, Sam—who had expressed such bitterly anti-California sentiments a scant three weeks earlier—left Virginia City and, with his friend Clement T. Rice, went across the Sierra Nevada and down into the "cursed state." The departure was abrupt and—from the sound of the announcement in the *Territorial Enterprise*—permanent: "Mark Twain has abdicated the local column of the Enterprise. . . . He assigned no adequate reason for this sudden step."[42] Publisher Joe Goodman speculated facetiously on his friend's motives. "We thought him the pitiable victim of self-conceit. . . . The poor fellow actually thought he possessed some breeding—that Virginia was too narrow a field for his graces and accomplishments." Or perhaps, Goodman suggested, Twain had left town because he was running away from a girl. "Who ever thought beneath that ingenuous face was concealed a heart that could wrong confiding innocence?"[43]

Goodman's first guess seems to have been closer to the truth. In his letters from San Francisco to his mother and sister, Sam made no mention of Orion's triumph but bragged about his own ability to manipulate the price of mining stock by writing about it in the newspaper ("if I don't know how to levy black-mail on the mining companies—who *does . . .* ?") and about his popularity in San Francisco ("I suppose I know at least a thousand people here").[44] Sam apparently hoped to make a killing in the stock market in San Francisco, but his aspirations were not realized, and eventually he had to face reality. "My visit to San F is gradually drawing to a close," he wrote on June 4, "and it seems like going back to prison to go back to the snows and the deserts of Washoe, after living in this Paradise."[45] When he got back to Virginia City he wrote of his employers that "I believe they thought I wasn't coming back any more," for they had stopped sending the *Enterprise* to St. Louis—but he corrected that.[46]

Orion's problems had not disappeared with California's yielding. Insurrection was still a danger in Nevada, especially in Lander and Humboldt Counties. When the commander of the Buena Vista Guards in Humboldt asked Governor Clemens for a shipment of arms, Orion refused to release them until he could be satisfied the officers in charge supported the Union, the Lincoln administration, and the Emancipation Proclamation—it had become almost a litany.[47] Governor Nye had not helped matters when, before he left for the East, he had unwittingly appointed as territorial officials a number of Southern sympathizers. Orion had to remove at least two of these in June, and he also asked General Wright to station a company of soldiers at Reese River. "From the number and boldness of the secessionists there," he explained to the commandant, "I fear trouble unless they are overawed."[48] The following month the acting governor removed from office the probate judge of Lander County, citing as the reason "his disloyalty."[49]

For these actions Orion won the praise of the *Virginia City Union:* "Governor Clemens seems to be the right man in the right place. He has acted bravely, patriotically, promptly, and to the extent of his power in aiding to oust treasonable officials. He will be gratefully remembered for it by all the loyal citizens of this Territory."[50]

Later that month Orion wrote to Jonathan Williams in Lander County that "complaint is made to me that in you I have been so unlucky as to appoint a loud mouthed Copperhead as Notary Public. Please explain."[51] Williams responded by calling Orion a "Black Republican" and stating that "your slang does not affect my nervous system a particle. . . . You are but an accidental Governor at best. I respect the office, but not its present incumbent." Despite this bluster he returned his commission and resigned his position.[52]

About this time, Governor Nye returned from his seven-month absence and once again took up the reins of territorial leadership, while Orion—no doubt with a sigh of relief—reverted to the more banal role of territorial secretary.[53]

9

Sam Lashes Out

If I have been so unlucky as to rob you of some of your popularity by
that unfortunate item, I claim . . . you neither increase nor diminish it
by so fruitless a proceeding as making speeches for the Fund.

Sam to Orion

Word of Sam's boisterous living in Virginia City reached Orion, and he
sent his younger brother a "fearful lecture," as Sam termed it, on the subject of dissipation and upholding the family name. When Sam didn't answer, the elder brother may have made a special trip to Virginia City to see
for himself, or to deliver the lecture in person. We know that he went there,
and that, whatever his reason, Sam was ruffled after he saw him at the
theater, for he complained to his mother and sister, "he will learn after a
while, perhaps, that I am not an infant, that I know the value of a good
name as well as he does, and stop writing such childish nonsense to me."[1]

Rather than infantile, Sam looked old to Jane Clemens in a photograph
he sent her, or so she told him. She admonished him that if he worked hard
and attended to business, someday he might aspire to a place on a big San
Francisco daily. The implication was that he wasn't growing any younger
and now that Orion had found his fulfillment, it was time Sam was working toward his.

Her son's response was alternately defensive and defeatist. "Ma," he wrote,
"you have given my vanity a deadly thrust. . . . Behold, I am prone to boast
of having the widest reputation as a local editor, of any man on the Pacific
coast. . . . But I don't suppose I shall ever be any account. I lead an easy life,
though, and I don't care a cent whether school keeps or not. Everybody
knows me, and I fare like a prince wherever I go, be it on this side of the
mountains or the other. And I am proud to say I am the most conceited ass

in the Territory."[2] If he hadn't the high office his brother held, he seemed to be saying, he made up for it with the brass Orion lacked.

Finally he mentioned Orion. A plebiscite on statehood had been scheduled, and Sam was sure the outcome would be affirmative. "We shall bud out into a State before many months," he wrote,

> which will relieve Orion of his office. If I have influence enough, I mean to get him nominated a candidate for some fat office under the State Government, so that you can come out and live with him. I am a pretty good hand at such things. I was a mighty heavy wire-puller at the last Legislature. I passed every bill I worked for, and on a bet, I killed a bill by three-fourths vote in the House after it had passed the Council unanimously. Oh, I tell you a reporter in the Legislature can swing more votes than any member of the body.[3]

Orion might still be on the hurricane deck, but Sam wanted it known he hadn't abandoned the pilothouse.

He was right about the outcome of the plebiscite. A convention to draw up a constitution for the new state was scheduled to open in Carson City on November 2. Sam went to the capital to report the First Annual Fair of the Washoe Agricultural, Mining and Mechanical Society for the *Enterprise*.[4] During the week or so he was there he no doubt stayed with his brother and family.

Toward the middle of October he returned to Virginia City, where, if we can credit the local reporter for the *Gold Hill Daily News,* he proposed marriage to an unidentified young woman. On the twenty-eighth, the local claimed that Twain had told him he couldn't "find nary a [girl] to keep house with. Mark says he 'popped it' to one the other day, but she couldn't see it."[5] If there was any substance to this report, it suggests Sam may have had occasion to contrast his own bachelorhood-by-default with the conspicuous domestic contentment of the Carson City Clemenses.

An indication of Sam's state of mind at this time is provided by a story he wrote that so outdid anything he had produced before for descriptions of bloody violence that it shocked readers for hundreds of miles around.[6] Published in the *Enterprise* on October 28, it told of "a man named P. Hopkins or Philip Hopkins" who lived with his wife and nine children not far from Carson City. Ordinarily mild and affable, when he discovered he had been swindled in a stock deal he slipped into homicidal insanity. In a mad rage he slaughtered his wife and seven of their children.

Twain described the murder scene in ghastly detail: Mrs. Hopkins lying across the threshold, her head split open and scalped, her right hand almost severed from the wrist; six children, their brains dashed out with a club, dead in one of the bedrooms. "The children must have struggled hard for their lives," the journalist elaborated, "as articles of clothing and broken furniture were strewn about the room in the utmost confusion." Two of the daughters were found bruised and insensible in the kitchen, and the eldest girl, Mary, was discovered dead in the garret, "frightfully mutilated, and the knife with which her wounds had been inflicted still sticking in her side."[7] As Twain told it, the murderer rode into Carson City on horseback, his throat slit from ear to ear, holding a reeking scalp from which warm, smoking blood was still dripping, and fell in front of the Magnolia saloon. There he died in five minutes without speaking. The long red hair of the scalp marked it as that of Mrs. Hopkins.[8]

Although it should have been apparent from internal clues and burlesque elements that the story was a "sell" (the target of Twain's lampoon was a stock investment scheme he deemed fraudulent), many readers took it at face value and were so appalled they couldn't finish their breakfasts.[9] The *Virginia Evening Bulletin* saw through the sham, labeled it "as baseless as the fabric of a dream," and reprimanded the author, but the nearby *Gold Hill Daily News* accepted it without question and even put out an extra edition.[10] Tough-minded editors in San Francisco seemed half inclined to believe the yarn, and small-town papers in distant parts of Nevada and California either reprinted it or published a summary of it as straight news.

When Twain admitted in print the report was a hoax, the *Virginia Evening Bulletin* editorialized: "The man who could pen such a story, with all its horrors depicted in such infernal detail, and which to our knowledge sent a pang of terror to the hearts of many persons, as a joke, in fun, can have but a very indefinite idea of the elements of a joke."[11] Dan De Quille later recalled that "there was a howl from Siskiyou to San Diego. Some papers demanded the immediate discharge of the author of the item by the *Enterprise* proprietors."[12]

Although Twain struck back in print, the critical barrage continued, and eventually the shots took effect. He was reported to be in "terrible agony," particularly over the damage he had done to the reputation of his paper.[13] According to Paine, Twain offered to resign, but Joe Goodman waved him off with the assurance that the storm would blow over.[14] Dan De Quille, who was at that time rooming with Sam, recalled that "one night when the persecution was hottest, he was so distressed that he could not sleep. He tossed, tumbled and groaned aloud."[15] One wonders whether it was the pestering that racked Mark Twain or remorse for the terrible violence he had visited on a blameless family—one whose name might or might not have been "Hopkins."

Sam went down to Carson City to cover the constitutional convention, which Orion, acting as territorial secretary, called to order on November 2, 1863.[16] While he was in Carson, again probably staying with Orion, Sam wrote a sardonic letter to the *San Francisco Daily Call,* with which he had contracted to be an occasional correspondent. "The murder of Abel, by his brother Cain," Twain wrote, apropos of nothing in particular, "would rank as an eminently justifiable homicide up there in Storey county [Virginia City's county]. When a man merely attempts to kill another, there, and fails in his object, our Police-Judge handles him with pitiless severity. He has him instantly arrested, gives him some good advice, and requests him to leave the country. This has been found to have a very salutary effect. The criminal goes home and thinks the matter over profoundly, and concludes to stay with us. But he feels very badly, for days and days together."[17] The Cain reference seems to have been the first time Mark Twain invoked in his writing the original biblical fratricide.

There were other reporters covering the convention, from California as well as Nevada, but none equaled Mark Twain in importance; he could outwrite them all, and he was reporting for the most influential paper in the territory (if no longer the most copied). It was not surprising, then, that when the hard work of constitution making was completed and a celebratory mock legislative body was formed, he was unanimously elected "Governor of the Third House."[18]

Sam did not spend Christmas with Orion and his family. Instead, he returned to Virginia City and enjoyed a riotous visit by Artemus Ward, the celebrated newspaper humorist and lecturer, who was on a speaking tour of the West. Ward made the *Enterprise* office his headquarters, and he reveled in the company he found there. In Mark Twain he discerned a special spark. He advised the reporter about his writing, urged him to make his name known in the East, and even offered to contact on his behalf the editor of the *New York Sunday Mercury.*[19] For his part, Twain wrote in the *Enterprise,* "The man who is capable of listening to the 'Babes in the Wood' [Ward's famous rambling speech] from beginning to end without laughing either inwardly or outwardly must have done murder, or at least meditated it, at some time during his life."[20]

When Ward left Virginia City, Sam returned to Carson to cover the convention of the Union Party to select candidates for Nevada's first state election.[21] The assembly chose a ticket that included Orion Clemens for secretary of state. According to a contemporary report, Orion was nominated "by acclamation," so it seems unlikely that Sam's machinations had anything to do with it, as he had told his mother and sister they would.[22] The day the meeting adjourned, Sam wrote to his mother that Artemus Ward had urged him to "leave sage-brush obscurity, and journey to New York with him. . . . But I preferred not to burst upon the New York public too suddenly and brilliantly, and so I concluded to remain here."[23]

Samuel remained in Carson City after the party convention to await the third territorial legislature.[24] As usual, Orion's home bustled with social activity, and according to Paine, "his brilliant brother [was] its chief ornament . . . no occasion was complete without him."[25] Effie Mona Mack observed, "There were now two governors in the same household."[26] And indeed, it did seem that for the second time in their lives the brothers were more or less on a par, both riding high, yet neither much more so than the other. Sam's recognition by the Third House, however much a spoof, was important to him, and, augmented by Artemus Ward's encouragement, gave his ego a much-needed boost. For the moment, at least, he seemed able to rein in his inveterate striving against his imposing brother. Things were looking so rosy, in fact, that Sam and Orion decided it was about time to bring their mother to live in the West. On January 9 the younger brother appropriated a sheet of the secretary's official stationery and scribbled: "Ma, we are going to send for you in the Spring. Make Aunt Betsy Smith come out with you—you two would enjoy yourselves in Carson and Virginia, you *bet* you! Then I could burlesque you occasionally, you know." He closed with "All are well. Good bye. Legislature meets day after to-morrow."[27]

On the second day of the session Secretary Clemens reported about the previous year's border difficulties with California. He informed the legislators that Mr. Kidder and Mr. Ives had established "the true location of the boundary line in the Honey Lake region, . . . thus preventing further difficulties, while in the south, upon the running of the line under this commission the State of California immediately yielded a jurisdiction long maintained over the rich Esmeralda mining region, and the position of the line and respective jurisdiction of California and Nevada, are now clearly known wherever there are settlements along our western border."[28]

Orion went on to confess that when he appointed Butler Ives survey commissioner for Nevada Territory he had exceeded his authority. He had been urged, he admitted, to call a special session of the lawmakers, but instead he had acted on his own recognizance, trusting that when he presented his case to them he would be vindicated.[29] The legislators duly appropriated the three thousand dollars Orion had promised Ives.[30] Throughout the report, Orion played down the dramatic circumstances of the conflict and his own key role in bringing it to a successful conclusion.

In the state election Orion was chosen secretary of state, but since the constitution was defeated, the election was voided.[31] All was not lost, however. Orion still had his job as secretary of the territory, and almost immediately machinery was set in motion to give statehood another chance.[32]

Orion had joined the First Presbyterian Church of Carson City soon after arriving in Nevada, and a year later he was elected to the board of trustees.[33] When Mollie and Jennie moved west, they too allied with the church.[34] The congregation was in the process of raising money to complete a brick house of worship they had begun building in 1862, and it must have occurred to Orion or Mollie, or both, to turn some of Mark Twain's popularity to that end.[35] He had never spoken to a paying audience before, but he now consented to deliver his "Third Annual Message [actually the first] to the Third House" as a benefit for the building fund, charging a dollar a head.[36] The event was held on January 27, and some two hundred dollars was raised.

Two days later disaster struck. Jane "Jennie" Clemens had been six years old when she came to Carson City, where she attended Miss Hannah K. Clapp's Sierra Seminary, a fashionable boarding school.[37] A bright student, she was a joy and comfort to her parents, and sometimes her Uncle Sam, after the labors of a legislative morning, would drop by the school and listen to her exercises and those of the other pupils.[38] Jennie was a religious little girl, fond of reading her Sunday school books. She had recently finished Bunyan's *Pilgrim's Progress,* and she was in the process of working her way through the large family Bible. She told her mother she prayed often through the day at school for aid in her difficulties.[39] When she learned there was no pulpit Bible for the new church, she began saving her pennies to buy one.[40]

On the morning of January 29, 1864, some five months after celebrating her eighth birthday, Jennie was suddenly stricken. She was seriously ill from the beginning, and in her delirious sleep that night she several times repeated portions of the Lord's Prayer as her parents and uncle sat anxiously at her bedside.[41] The affliction was diagnosed as "spotted fever" (presumably cerebrospinal meningitis), and there was nothing that could be done. For four days the helpless adults kept the death watch, until on February 1, at six o'clock in the evening, Jennie Clemens died.[42] (Curiously, Twain's official biographer makes no mention of this signal event.)

Throughout the ordeal Mark Twain continued to send his daily letters to the *Enterprise*. Two days after the funeral, he took to task the local mortician, who apparently had a monopoly and had, Sam felt, overcharged Orion. "Does not this undertaker take advantage of that unfortunate delicacy which prevents a man from disputing an unjust bill for services rendered in burying the dead, to extort ten-fold more than his labors are worth?"[43] When news of the death reached Jane Clemens she wrote to the bereaved parents: "Jennie was an uncommon smart child she was a very handsome child but I never thought you would raise her, she was a heaven born child, she was two [*sic*] good for this world."[44] A trace of these sentiments may have lain behind Mollie's statement years later that "I know it is best she were taken. I was not fit to bring her up."[45]

When the legislature adjourned on February 20, Sam returned to Virginia City.[46] From there, about a month later, he wrote to Pamela that "Molly & Orion are all right, I guess. They would write me if I would answer there [*sic*] letters—but I won't. It is torture to me to write a letter. And it is still *greater* torture to receive one—except yours and Ma's."[47] He said nothing further of the plan to bring Jane Clemens to Nevada. He told his sister he took "no sort of interest" in "politics or eastern news"—meaning the war, which was dragging on.[48]

This letter must have crossed in the mails one in which Pamela reminded her younger brother, "you talk of pursuing happiness, but never overtaking it" and implored him to "let the Spirit of God, which has been knocking at the door of your heart for years, now come in, and make you a new man in

Christ Jesus. All the family but you," she went on, "have given evidence of an interest in religion, and will you stand alone, and be separated from the rest, not only in this world, but in the world to come? No no it cannot be; I cannot bear to think it." She closed this impassioned appeal with "Sam I wish you would come to the fair, if you could do so without losing your situation."[49]

The festival referred to was the Mississippi Valley Sanitary Fair, to be held in St. Louis in May to raise funds for the western Sanitary Commission, and Pamela's endorsement of it was significant because the Sanitary Commission, forerunner of the American Red Cross, looked after federal soldiers' health and comfort.[50] Earlier in the war her sympathies had seemed not to be with the North, but this invitation clearly indicated she was now pro-Union.[51] That impression was confirmed when Sam and Orion soon received an appeal from their sister to "do something" for the fair.[52]

Orion and Mollie had long been supporters of the charity. Shortly after her arrival in Carson City, Mollie had helped organize a ball to raise funds for it, and Orion was now president of the Sanitary Committee of Ormsby County.[53] On April 25, Sam, who was on another visit to Carson, reported that "the ladies are making extraordinary preparations for a grand fancy-dress ball, to come off in the county building here on the 5th of May, for the benefit of the great St. Louis Sanitary Fair." Mollie served as secretary pro tem at the organizing meeting of the committee that planned the fundraiser. Twain went on: "The most pecuniary results are anticipated from it, and I imagine, from the interest that is being taken in the matter, the ladies of Gold Hill had better be looking to their laurels, lest the fame of their recent brilliant effort in the Sanitary line be dimmed somewhat by the financial achievements of this forthcoming ball."[54]

Not willing to "stand alone, and be separated from the rest" of the family, when he returned to Virginia City, Sam carried Pamela's request to Almarin B. Paul, head of the Sanitary Commission for all of Nevada. Paul then "went to work sending calls to the several counties to contribute, and I [Sam], being chief of our editorial corps . . . went to scribbling editorials."[55]

These efforts met with but meager success, however, and Sam and Almarin soon "began to think we were going to make a mighty poor show at the St. Louis Fair, when along came RUEL GRIDLEY."[56] In response to one of Paul's telegrams, Gridley had raised more than $5,000 in Austin, Nevada, by an unusual game of auctioning and re-auctioning the same ordinary sack of flour. When he took the bag to Virginia City, it was put on sale in the opera house, but it brought only $570.[57]

Disappointed, Paul decided to take it in style the next day to nearby Gold Hill. He got a brass band and two open carriages—one for the speakers of the day and the other for "Gov. Mark Twain and his staff of bibulous reporters," as the *Daily News* characterized them—and set off.[58] When Gridley told the story of the sack in Gold Hill, citizens and businesses gave nearly $7,000 in gold. Heartened, the fund-raisers moved on down the road to Silver City and Dayton, where respectable sums were also realized. At each stop free drinks flowed plentifully.[59]

The revelers had by that time covered about half the twenty-mile distance to Carson City, and apparently they considered taking the celebrated flour on to that larger community. For some reason, however, they instead turned back and retraced their path to Virginia City. On their way they learned that its citizens had been roused by reports of their success and were determined not to be outdone by their neighbors. When the cavalcade arrived in town the streets were jammed. In two and a half hours nearly $13,000 was subscribed.

Twain's report of that eventful day appeared in the *Enterprise* the following morning, May 17.[60] "Yesterday," he proudly proclaimed, "was the greatest day the Sanitary Fund ever saw in Nevada Territory."[61] The reporter also made an odd assertion. The flour sack was not taken to Carson City, he said, "because it was stated that the money raised at the Sanitary Fancy Dress Ball, recently held in Carson for the St. Louis Fair, had been diverted from its legitimate course, and was to be sent to aid a Miscegenation Society somewhere in the East; and it was feared the proceeds of the sack might be similarly disposed of." He softened the accusation by adding that "it was a hoax, but not all a hoax, for an effort is being made to divert those funds from their proper course."[62]

He was wrong in reporting the dance had been for the benefit of the St. Louis fair; it actually had been planned all along to raise funds for the eastern wing of the Sanitary Commission. Only afterward (perhaps at Orion's or Mollie's request) did the sponsors meet to discuss the possibility of redirecting the profits to the fair. When a member of the committee stated that "a portion of the proceeds of the St. Louis Fair, were to be applied to the aid of the Freedmen's Society," the meeting adjourned without reaching a final decision, except that the money "should go to the aid of the sick and wounded soldiers, who are fighting the battles of our country, *and for no other purpose.*"[63]

Naturally the sponsors of the Carson City ball were offended by the distortions in the unsigned *Enterprise* article. They wrote an angry letter to the paper calling it "a *tissue of falsehoods,* made for *malicious purposes,*" and demanded the name of the reporter.[64] After setting forth the facts of the case, they declared that they themselves would decide what to do with the money, "without the aid of outsiders, who are probably desirous of acquiring some *glory* by appropriating the efforts of the ladies to themselves."[65]

The fate of those funds, then, was still undecided at the time Twain wrote his report, and the sponsors correctly discerned that he was trying to influence where the money was to be sent. What they couldn't know was that they were not the real targets of his guile. It seems it was important to Samuel to demonstrate to Pamela, now that she was pro-Union, that he could outdo his brother in patriotic fund-raising. His reasons for writing the offensive item, then, were probably threefold: first, to prevent the ball proceeds from going from Orion's bailiwick to Pamela's pet project in St. Louis; second, to prevent the flour's ever being auctioned in Carson City; and third, to generally undermine his brother's efforts on behalf of the Sanitary Fund in Ormsby County. (There were probably other motives behind Sam's notorious article, including an ambivalent attitude toward the Union cause, but I believe his troubled relations with Orion were paramount.)

"I wished Pamela could have been there," he wrote to his mother and sister about the flour sack pilgrimage,

to see her own private project bringing forth its fruit and culminating in such a sweeping excitement away out here among barren mountains, while she herself, unconscious of what her hands had done, and unaware of the row she was kicking up, was probably sitting quietly at home and thinking it a dreary sort of world, full of disappointments, and labors unrequited, and hopes unblessed with fruition. I speak of the row as hers, for if she had not written us, the St. Louis Fair would probably have never heard from Washoe. She has certainly secured $30,000 or $40,000 worth of greenbacks from us by her own efforts.[66]

Though Sam used the collective "us," Orion was conspicuously absent from the letter. The closest the younger brother came to mentioning him was when he explained (somewhat differently than he had in the *Enterprise*) why the cavalcade hadn't gone on to his base of operations. "Carson is considerably larger than either of these three towns," he explained, "but it has a lousy, lazy, worthless, poverty-stricken population, and the universal opinion was that we couldn't raise $500 there."[67] There is an undated newspaper clipping in the Mark Twain Papers that reports "already" $31,820 in bricks (presumably silver) had gone from Nevada Territory to the Mississippi Valley Fair. Of that amount the largest portion, $6,548, came from Sam's county, Storey, while Orion's Ormsby contributed only $273, less than 1 percent of the total.[68]

Sam wrote in the *Enterprise* on May 18 that "we are told that the [Virginia City] UNION (or its employees, whichever it is,) has repudiated [its Sanitary Fund] bid. We would like to know about this matter, if we may make so free."[69] Once again the charge was groundless, as the *Union* proved by printing a receipt, but it took umbrage anyway, and in a long, bitter editorial, it denounced the *Enterprise*'s insinuations as "despicable" and without "parallel in unmanly public journalism."[70]

Unabashed, Twain replied that the *Union* had paid its contribution only because of his promptings, that it "had not intended to pay the bill, but on secondary consideration, and for the sake of saving an entirely imaginary reputation for virtue and honesty, concluded to do so."[71] When the *Union* responded with more inflammatory rhetoric, Clemens sent a note to James L. Laird, one of the three owners, demanding a printed retraction or "satisfaction."[72] More notes were exchanged, until Sam *"peremptorily"* demanded "the satisfaction due to a gentleman—without alternative."[73] Even then more messages were traded.

Finally, on May 24, Mark Twain published all the correspondence in the *Enterprise,* denouncing Laird as "an unmitigated liar," "an abject coward," and "a fool, because he cannot understand that a publisher is bound to stand responsible for any and all articles printed by him, whether he wants to do it or not."[74] (It will be recalled that the *Union* gave Orion a ringing endorsement when he needed it most—"Governor Clemens moves slow but very sure, and when he resolves to do a thing he does it.") Twain later alleged that a duel was averted only when, during early morning pistol practice, his friend Steve Gillis shot the head off a sparrow and convinced Laird's seconds that Clemens had done it.[75]

An agitated Mollie wrote to Sam that not only had Orion's standing taken a beating on account of his brother's item on the benefit ball, but nearly all the ladies of Carson City were disposed to withdraw their friendship from her as well. Already despondent over Jennie's death, Orion's wife must have suffered terribly from this blow, for it meant the end of her cherished position as de facto First Lady of Nevada. Only Mrs. Ellen G. Cutler, she wrote, president of the Sanitary Ball committee, "understood the circumstances under which" Sam's offense had been committed.[76]

Sam replied that he was "not sober" when he perpetrated the "joke," and it had been published by mistake. "Since it has made the ladies angry, I am sorry the thing occurred." He also wrote to Mrs. Cutler thanking her for showing a "disposition to be lenient with me" and for standing by Mollie. Then he published an expression of regret in the *Enterprise*—albeit a lame one. "We stated that the rumor was a hoax. And it was—we were perfectly right."[77]

The following day he sent Orion what amounted to a non-apology and coupled it with a demand that he not campaign further for the Sanitary Fund. "If I have been so unlucky as to rob you of some of your popularity by that unfortunate item, I claim at your hands that you neither increase nor diminish it by so fruitless a proceeding as making speeches for the Fund. I am mighty sick of that fund—it has caused me all my d——d troubles—and I shall leave the Territory when your first speech is announced, and leave it for good."[78] Before Orion had a chance to answer, Sam sent him another note, in which he announced that he and Steve Gillis were returning to the States. "Washoe has long since grown irksome to us, and we want to leave it anyhow."[79]

Apparently Mollie was wrong about Mrs. Cutler, for two days after Sam's latest letter to Orion, he received a challenge from her husband, William K. Cutler. Twain later claimed that a duel was averted, once again, through the agency of Steve Gillis.[80]

With at least two duels, or near-duels, behind him, Twain left Virginia City by stage bound for San Francisco on May 29, 1864. The *Gold Hill Evening News* editorialized the following day that

Mark Twain's beard is full of dirt, and his face is black before the people of Washoe. Giving way to the idiosyncratic eccentricities of an erratic mind, Mark has indulged in the game infernal—in short, "played hell." Shifting the locale of his tales of fiction from the Hopkins family to the fair Ladies of the Ladies' Fair; and the plot thereof from murder to miscegenation—he slopped. The indignation aroused by his enormities has been too crushing to be borne by living man, though sheathed with the brass and triple cheek of Mark Twain. He has vamosed, cut stick, absquatulated.[81]

The Hopkins family massacre had been bad enough, but the assaults on the ladies of Carson City and on the *Virginia City Daily Union* were worse: these were real attacks on real people. Following the apparent rapprochement during which the two "governors" agreed to bring their mother west in the spring, Sam saw in Pamela's plea an opportunity to go ahead of Orion once more and to recapture some of his lost stature in the family. But even as he gloried in Nevada's "greatest moment," the old gorge was rising anew, for once again he realized he was caught between the horns of a dilemma—he could neither decisively defeat his brother nor accept him on equal (much less superior) terms. This place wasn't Hannibal, and it wasn't Keokuk, but even in the vast Territory of Nevada there didn't seem to be enough room for both Sam Clemens and his brother Orion.

10
Sam's San Francisco Crisis

I put the pistol to my head but wasn't man enough to pull the trigger.

Samuel Clemens

On September 7, 1864, the voters of Nevada approved a new state constitution, and the following month the Union Party met in convention in Carson City to nominate candidates for state office.[1] Since Orion Clemens had been elected secretary of state in January it seemed likely he would again be nominated by his party for that office. The *Virginia City Daily Union* editorialized that "Orion Clemens, who has been Secretary of the Territory since its organization, will be a strong candidate. We believe he has given general satisfaction heretofore, and we shall not be surprised at his nomination."[2]

Many years later Mark Twain stated that "Orion was so sure to get the Secretaryship that no one but him [*sic*] was named for that office" but that on the day of the caucus he was "hit with one of his spasms of virtue . . . and refused to go near the Convention. He was urged, but all persuasions failed. He said his presence there would be an unfair and improper influence and that if he was to be nominated the compliment must come to him as a free and unspotted gift."[3]

As if that weren't enough, Twain went on to say, Orion "had another attack of virtue on the same day, that made [his failure of nomination] absolutely sure. . . . He suddenly changed from a friendly attitude toward whiskey—which was the popular attitude—to uncompromising teetotalism, and went absolutely dry. His friends besought and implored, but all in vain. He could not be persuaded to cross the threshold of a saloon. The paper next morning contained the list of chosen nominees. His name was not in it. He had not received a vote."[4]

Mark Twain had the broad outcome right, but the circumstances were considerably different. Despite his personal popularity, Orion was no shoo-in for the nomination—as the lukewarm endorsement by the *Daily Union* suggests. Depression had hit the Comstock, production had declined, and many stocks had collapsed. Nevada voters had soured on the political incumbents. This disenchantment spared no one, and the *Gold Hill Daily News* was probably expressing the consensus when, on the eve of the Union Party convention, it editorialized: "We trust in making their selections, the delegates will refuse to listen to any candidate who will presume to set up 'claims' for any nomination—for, as we have time and again remarked, it is an insolent presumption in any man, or any set of men, to set up 'claims' of office upon the grounds of having rendered party services."[5] Moreover, as we have seen, Sam's Sanitary Fund shenanigans seem to have "robbed" his brother, as Sam himself put it, "of some of [his] popularity." How much was lost is impossible to say, but Orion's public image was no longer untarnished.

Nor was Twain's recollection correct that Orion's was the only name considered for secretary of state. The article cited above also reported that Dr. A. S. Peck of Esmeralda County and R. M. Daggett of Storey were in the running, and the following day the *Gold Hill Evening News* reported that yet another hopeful, C. H. Noteware of Douglas County, "seems to be the favorite against Clemens, of Ormsby, and Daggett, of Storey, for Secretary of State."[6]

It was also erroneous to state that Orion "refused to go near the convention." On the contrary, not only did he go and allow his name to be placed in nomination, he (along with the other three candidates) gave his "hearty endorsement of the platform adopted by the Convention." Finally, Twain's memory that his brother "had not received a vote" was wrong. Of the total of sixty-one ballots cast, Orion received thirteen, second only to Noteware's forty-four. The other two candidates received just two votes apiece.[7]

If there is a nugget of truth in Mark Twain's story, it may lie in his assertion that Orion "could not be persuaded to cross the threshold of a saloon." But why should it be necessary to do that in order to secure his party's nomination? The answer lies in the practice of "button-holing," in which aspirants bought delegates drinks at local bars and pressed them for their votes. The *Gold Hill Evening News* reported on October 11 that "Carson, usually a quiet spot . . . last evening . . . was filled with delegates and button-holeing was indulged in at about the same extent as 'brandy and water.'"[8] It is possible that Orion found this practice repugnant and declined to participate.

Twain was at least accurate in one respect: This was a crucial juncture in Orion's life. Soon afterward his job expired (along with the territorial status that had provided it), and he, like his brother, fell on hard times. Unlike his brother's, Orion's career would never recover—nor would his spirit.

On October 12, C. N. Noteware was declared the nominee of the Union Party for secretary of state of Nevada.[9] Henry Goode Blasdel, the man nominated for governor, must have traveled directly from the convention to San Francisco, for a few days later he met there with Sam and told him there was talk of running Orion for the United States Senate. At that time each state's two senators were elected by the legislature; Nevada's first state lawmaking body was to meet several weeks hence, so there was time. "Do you think you stand any show?" Sam asked his brother. "If so, you had better make friends with your Carson enemies—that is, if you approve of the Scriptural doctrine which makes it a man's duty to love his enemies."[10]

Evidently Orion was still interested in a political life, for in a letter written three weeks later Sam warned him that "Dawson says Daggett and Fitch will be likely to euchre you out of the nomination. . . . Look out for them."[11] But Orion didn't look out—at least not to any good effect—for on December 8 his name did not appear on a list of nine aspirants for senatorial honors that ran in the *Gold Hill Daily News,* and a week later, when five names were placed in nomination before the Nevada Legislature, his was not among them.[12] When Orion turned over his office to C. N. Noteware in early December 1864, he found himself out of a job and without income.[13]

Little is known of Orion's activities in 1865. On March 14 he was admitted to the Nevada bar and, as his brother recalled in 1906, "put up his sign as attorney at law," but whether Twain was right in saying that "he got no clients" we don't know.[14] On October 10 the nominating convention of the Republican (Union) Party met in Carson City, and Orion seems to have been named a candidate for the Nevada State Assembly (the party met to select a nominee for member in the U.S. House of Representatives for the election of November 7, 1865; since Orion was elected to the state assembly in that election, I infer he was nominated at the October 10 meeting).[15] Oddly, he appears not to have mentioned that fact when he wrote Sam later that month, for his brother's reply makes no mention of it. On the other hand, Orion may have given Sam the impression he was torn between a career in the law and one in the ministry; in any case, Orion enclosed a sermon he had written.[16]

"Orion," began Sam's memorable reply, "there was **genius**—true, unmistakeable **genius**—in that sermon of yours. It is not the gilded base metal that passes for intellectual gold too generally in this world of ours. It is one of the few sermons that I have read with pleasure—I do not say profit, because I am beyond the reach of argument now[, but v]iewed as a **literary** production, that sermon was first-class."

Then he proceeded to preach a sermon of his own. He had had, he said, only two "**powerful** ambitions" in his life: to be a river pilot and to be a preacher of the gospel. "I accomplished the one and failed in the other, **because** I could not supply myself with the necessary stock in trade—*i.e.* religion."

But I *have* had a "call" to literature, of a low order—*i.e.* humorous. It is nothing to be proud of, but it is my strongest suit, and if I were to listen to that maxim of stern *duty* which says that to do right you **must** multiply the one or the two or the three talents which the Almighty entrusts to your keeping, I would long ago have ceased to meddle with things for which I was by nature unfitted and turned my attention to seriously scribbling to excite the **laughter** of God's creatures. Poor, pitiful business! Though the Almighty did His part by me—for the talent is a mighty engine when supplied with the steam of **education**—which I have not got, and so its pistons and cylinders and shafts move feebly and for a holiday show and are useless of any good purpose.[17]

Sam had been agonizing over his call for some time. The Civil War had ended, and the Mississippi was open to commercial traffic again—yet piloting was no longer Sam's measure of success. His new god was eastern publication. When Artemus Ward asked Sam for a sketch to include in a book about his western travels, Ward seems to have precipitated a crisis. Twain had never struggled over his writing before; everything he composed had flowed from his pen more or less effortlessly. But he labored over the story for Ward's book—a tale about a jumping frog he had heard during a sojourn in the Sierra foothills—making several abortive starts before he finally managed to write a version that satisfied him. Probably the day he received Orion's letter he had finally mailed it to Ward's publisher.[18] That symbolic act was clearly on his mind.

Having delivered himself of his threnody, he turned on his brother— and the gloves were off. "Now *you* aspire to be a **lawyer,** when the voice of God is thundering in your ears and you are wilfully deaf and will not hear. *You* were **intended** for a preacher, and lo! you would be a scheming, groveling, mud-cat of a **lawyer.**"

Like a tongue returning to a sore tooth, his mind ran back to the "poor, pitiful business" of his own call. "*You* see in me a talent for humorous writing, and urge me to cultivate it. But I always regarded it as brotherly partiality on your part, and attached no value to it." No doubt referring to a *New York Round Table* squib he had seen a day or two earlier, he admitted, "It is only now, when editors of standard literary papers in the distant east give me high praise, and who do not know me and cannot of course be blinded by the glamour of partiality, that I really begin to believe there must be something in it."

At last he came to the point. "But . . . I will toss up with you. I will drop all trifling, and sighing after vain impossibilities, and strive for a fame— unworthy and evanescent though it must of necessity be—if you will record your promise to go hence to the States and preach the gospel when circumstances shall enable you to do so." So that there could be no mistake, he added: "I am in earnest. Shall it be so?" And he went back to the first page of the four-leaf letter and wrote above the dateline and salutation: "P.S. You had better shove this in the stove—for if we strike a bargain I don't want any absurd 'literary remains' and 'unpublished letters of Mark Twain' published after I am planted."[19]

Apparently unaware that Orion had just committed himself to run for the Nevada Assembly, Sam appealed to him to join in a career change. In the pattern that was becoming a paradigm, he wanted his big brother to take the high road while he took the low. But now there was a difference, for he was asking him not merely to act as a figurehead but to dedicate himself to a special vocation—the ministry—while Sam strove for an "unworthy and evanescent" goal, that of exciting "the **laughter** of God's creatures." It was the clergy's bookish rather than its evangelical aspect Sam emphasized ("viewed as a **literary** production, that sermon was first-class"), and so it was a sort of partnership of letters he invited his brother to join him in.

As we have seen, Samuel and Orion shared an interest in literature and writing. When Orion showed Pamela his 1858 letter to Miss Wood concerning Henry's death, she was so impressed by the way he delineated his brothers' personalities that she judged he might become a good novelist. This support made him want to try his hand at a story.[20] Sam also encouraged Orion's writing. In March 1861 he commended him on the humor in one of his efforts and remarked, "That portion of it wherein the old sow figures is the very best thing I have seen lately. Its quiet style resembles Goldsmith's 'Citizen of the World,' and 'Don Quixote,'—which are my *beau ideals* of fine writing."[21]

But even more than uniting with him in a literary alliance, Sam now seemed almost to be asking Orion to become his ethical counterbalance, his better self—or, if you will, his conscience personified. Else why ask him to "strike a bargain" at all?

That letter was written on Thursday, October 19, 1865. Before mailing it Samuel received another message from its intended recipients. It must have contained bad news, for he added in pencil on the back of the fourth leaf, as folded: "You are in trouble, and in debt—so am I. I am utterly miserable—so are you. Perhaps your religion will sustain you, will feed you—I place no dependence in mine. Our religions are alike, though, in one respect—neither can make a man happy when he is out of luck. If I do not get out of debt in 3 months,—pistols or poison for one—exit *me*. [There's a text for a sermon on Self-Murder—Proceed]."[22]

How did Orion respond to this extraordinary appeal? Obviously he didn't obey Sam's directive to burn the letter, for it still exists, but more important, he didn't comply with its central plea. We don't have his answering letter (if there was one), but we know he didn't become a minister. Unlike Sam, Orion didn't seem to lack "the necessary stock in trade—*i.e.* religion." He had been an active member and an elder of the Presbyterian church in Carson City for years, and he even wrote sermons and prayers. But there is no reason to believe Orion shared Sam's exalted (not to say mystical) ideas about the brothers' joint destiny. He had his own life, and doubtless he gave priority to his personal responsibilities and proclivities.

Saintly though he appeared, Orion was human enough to harbor resentments. He must have been aware of Sam's mutinous machinations in the Ben Franklin Print Shop, and the ugly Sanitary Fund affair was still fresh in memory. It is not out of the question that he nursed a six-year grudge over Sam's taking the reins of the Clemens family from him in 1859. If what we have called the homicidal intent hypothesis is valid, there is a chance he suspected his brother of once contemplating his death (see page 41). Whatever the extent of Orion's knowledge, when Sam reached out his hand in October 1865, Orion seems to have turned his back.

Less than two weeks after Sam mailed his despondent appeal, Orion began campaigning, speaking in Clear Creek, Empire City, and Carson City.[23] On the eve of the election he gave a speech in the Theater in Carson that, according to the *Daily Appeal,* "gratified the audience and did credit to himself."[24] On November 7 he was overwhelmingly elected to the assembly, receiving nearly three times as many votes as his opponent.[25]

In December Orion received another urgent appeal from his brother— one of an entirely different nature. It was to "send me immediately all necessary memoranda to enable Camp to understand the condition, quantity and resources of the land, and how he must go about finding it." Herman Camp was an early Comstock mining claim locator and an aggressive speculator in Washoe stocks. He had been friendly with Sam in Virginia City and again in San Francisco. At the end of January 1865 Clemens recorded in his notebook, "Herman Camp has sold some Washoe Stock in New York for $270,000."[26] He must have kicked himself as he did so, for Camp had offered him half profits if he would go east and help him sell the claims— "and I, like a fool, refused."[27]

The letter told Orion that Camp was now back in San Francisco. When Sam learned of the bold trader's "large New York business associations and facilities" and that he was returning to that city soon, he told him about the Tennessee land with all its resources, including oil. Then he made a proposal: If Camp, when he arrived in New York, would send back five hundred dollars traveling money, provide an equal amount when Sam got there, and pay all his expenses while he assisted in selling the tract, Camp could have half the proceeds. "He is independent now," Sam explained, "and I had to make *him* a liberal offer."[28]

Even so, Camp was not willing to make a commitment on the spot, but he was sufficiently intrigued to agree to travel to St. Louis, meet with Jane

Clemens and Pamela Moffett, "and then go at once and see the land" before telegraphing his final decision to Sam. The speculator allowed that "the land is valuable now that there is peace and no slavery, even if it have no oil in it."

Time was of the essence. "He leaves for the east 5 days hence," wrote Sam, "on the 19th. . . . Write me these particulars at once," he implored, repeating, "as he leaves on the 19th." For good measure he added at the top of the letter, "Send the memoranda *at once.*" Sam, just turned thirty, told his brother he was feeling "tired [of] being a beggar—tired [of] being chained to this accursed homeless desert,—I want to go back to a Christian land once more."[29]

Orion mailed the documents, and evidently they arrived in time to accompany Camp when he sailed aboard the steamer *Sacramento,* which left on the scheduled date.[30] Among those papers was almost certainly a letter from one Nicholas Longworth, a successful Cincinnati winegrower who had propelled eastern wine into national preeminence during the mid-1800s and was famous for his Catawba wines, which were compared with the Hocks and Champagnes of Europe.[31] Sometime before his death in 1847 John Marshall Clemens had sent Longworth some samples of "a wild grape of a promising sort" that grew on the Tennessee land "to get his judgment upon them," and Longworth responded "that they would make as good wine as his Catawbas."[32]

The speculator's steamer arrived in New York on January 12.[33] Biographers of this period in Mark Twain's life have assumed (insofar as they have touched on the matter at all) that Camp then set off on the long trip to St. Louis and Tennessee as planned, but there is reason to doubt that he did. In Samuel's surviving letters to St. Louis there is no mention of the Tennessee land until June 21, 1866, at which time he told his mother and sister: "I *tried* to sell it once and he [Orion] broke up the trade."[34] If Camp had carried out his plan and visited Jane Clemens and Pamela Moffett, it seems unlikely Samuel would have had to impart that information to them.

An alternate possibility is that Herman Camp wired Sam an offer to buy the land himself as soon as he landed on the East Coast. As Twain related in his *Autobiography,* "He agreed to buy our Tennessee land for two hundred thousand dollars. . . . His scheme was to import foreigners from grape-growing and wine-making districts in Europe, settle them on the land, and turn it into a wine-growing country. He knew what Mr. Longworth thought of those Tennessee grapes, and was satisfied."[35] The last sentence suggests that Camp, having read Longworth's praise of "those Tennessee grapes" during his voyage, made up his mind to buy the real estate sight unseen. Such an act was in character for this person, whom Twain described as "a bold man who was always making big fortunes in ingenious speculations and losing them again in the course of six months by other speculative ingenuities."[36] No such telegram survives, but for the reasons mentioned, I suggest one was sent, probably on January 12, 1866.

The early telegram hypothesis can account for Samuel's unusual behavior of a few days later. Under this construal, as soon as Samuel received Camp's wire he had "the contracts and things" drawn up and mailed to Orion in Carson City. Mail took two or three days to cross the Sierra, so conjecturally Orion received them at mid-January. He may have been surprised at the alacrity of developments and pleased at the size of the offer—but after his initial reaction he must have paused. To allow the land to be turned to wine production went against everything he believed about temperance—and besides, how could he know that Mr. Camp was going to deal fairly and honestly with those people from Europe?

Whatever Orion's thoughts, as tempting as the offer must have been, he found he could not accept. He wrote to Sam that he would not be a party to debauching the country with wine or putting immigrants at risk. As Twain later recounted: "And so, without waiting to find out, he quashed the whole trade, and there it fell, never to be brought to life again. The land, from being suddenly worth two hundred thousand dollars, became as suddenly worth what it was before—nothing, and taxes to pay."[37]

If this schedule is accurate, for the second time in two months Orion had delivered Sam a fearsome blow—first by shunning his plea to balance Sam by becoming a preacher, then by acting like that preacher and canceling Sam's ticket home. Twain was writing a daily letter to the *Enterprise*. As we have seen, even in times of great personal stress he somehow managed to get off his dispatches. Because no file of the paper from this period has been found, it is impossible to determine exactly when specific pieces were written, but one strange item that was reprinted in the *Golden Era* on January 28, 1866, seems to have been composed shortly after Sam (conjecturally) received his brother's devastating refusal on or about January 18.

It was "Mark Twain's Kearny Street Ghost Story," and it told of disembodied spirits on a rampage in a San Francisco household. One of the tormentors approached the bedside of the young lady of the house one night:

> The ghost came and stood by the bed and groaned—a deep, agoniz-
> ing, heart-broken groan—and laid a bloody kitten on the pillow by
> the girl's head. And then it groaned again, and sighed, "Oh, God,
> and must it be?" and bet another bloody kitten. It groaned a third
> time in sorrow and tribulation, and went one kitten better. And thus
> the sorrowing spirit stood there, moaning in its anguish and unload-
> ing its mewing cargo, until it had stacked up a whole litter of nine
> little bloody kittens on the girl's pillow and then, still moaning, moved
> away and vanished. . . . What do you think of that? What would you
> think of a ghost that came to your bedside at dead of night and had
> kittens?[38]

"If a cat was to be drowned or shot," Orion wrote of the period when Sam worked for him in Hannibal, "Sam (though unwilling yet firm) was selected for the work."[39] The cat-loving fifteen-year-old dutifully carried out his brother's bidding, but the odious experience stuck fast in his mind, and when sixteen years later his big brother presented him with another hateful decree, the innocent victims reappeared in an eerie newspaper piece.

Debauch the country with wine? Sam must have thought, I'll show him debauch. Albert Evans was the San Francisco correspondent for the *Gold Hill Daily News*. For some time he and Twain had been trading insults in the pages of their respective journals. In a dispatch dated January 19, 1866, and signed "Amigo," Evans wrote of Twain's being "in the dock for being drunk over night."[40] In subsequent letters he elaborated, declaring that Twain was in the company of "Pacific street jayhawkers" when he was arrested. Pacific Street was the heart of the Barbary Coast, San Francisco's toughest and most vice-ridden neighborhood, a sector respectable people avoided entirely. In 1907 Twain identified "jayhawkers" as "pro-slavery Missouri-ans, guerrillas, modern free lances."[41] Evans went on to insinuate that Twain had lain on the ground and forced the police to drag him by the legs, and that after he had been searched and booked he stood "at the grating, curs-ing and indulging in obscene language." He wrote of Twain "losing $40 in the house of a lady, under peculiar circumstances" and of "how he lost his watch, and thought that the police had stolen it on the night previous, having been oblivious to the fact that his friend had taken it from him early in the evening, in order to save him from loss."[42]

Twain appeared before Justice of the Peace Alfred Barstow, who imposed the customary fine, but the prisoner pleaded poverty, saying he had "nothing in his pockets but a plug of tobacco and a broken jackknife." The fine was remitted.[43] Edgar M. Branch writes: "Clemens once admitted that he had spent a night in prison for drunkenness. Although this jailing happened in San Francisco, it came considerably later than autumn 1864 [as Paine placed it in the *Biography*]. After his night in the lockup he appeared before Alfred Barstow, justice of the peace for the Second Township, who released him. Barstow had first been elected to the bench on 18 October 1865. . . . A good possibility is that the jailing occurred in January."[44]

Possibly, Clemens then dragged himself back to his rented room in the house of Angus Gillis (Steve's father) at 44 Minna Street and wrote his next daily letter to the *Enterprise*.[45] "The air is full of lechery," it began, "and rumors of lechery." Then, giving full vent to his spleen, the correspondent went on to describe the state of moral corruption in San Francisco under the existing police government. It was the most vitriolic letter he had ever written, and after he had sealed and addressed it he wrote on the outside, "Be sure and let Joe see this before it goes in." As Joe Goodman told the story to Paine many years later, the foreman said to him when the piece arrived, "You can't afford to publish that." "Let it all go in, every word," he answered. "If Mark can stand it, I can."[46] The letter does not survive (although part of it may have been discovered by Gary Scharnhorst and reprinted in his "Mark Twain's Imbroglio with the San Francisco Police: Three Lost Texts"),[47] but on January 23, 1866, the *Gold Hill News* commented that "The principal topic of conversation this morning is the filthy letter of 'Mark Twain' published in this morning's Enterprise."

The crisis was not over. As Twain recalled in 1909, "I put the pistol to my head but wasn't man enough to pull the trigger."[48] If the schedule of events given above is correct, the date was probably January 19, 1866, which happened to be one day short of the deadline he set himself when he wrote, "If I do not get out of debt in 3 months,—pistols or poison for one—exit *me*." He was still in debt, and no relief in sight—thanks to Orion.

Recapitulating the early telegram hypothesis: (1) Herman Camp wired Sam his offer as soon as he arrived in New York on January 12, 1866; (2) Sam immediately had the necessary documents drawn up and mailed to

Orion in Carson City; and (3) Orion's negative reply arrived in San Francisco on or about January 18, at which time (4) Sam got drunk and landed in jail and (5) came near to committing suicide.[49]

11

The Brothers Head Home

Sandy Baldwin says I have made the most sweeping success of any man he knows of.

Sam to his mother and sister

In Carson City, Orion had begun his term in Nevada's second state assembly by winning seats on the important Ways and Means and Judiciary Committees, even being elected chairman of the former. After this auspicious beginning things went downhill. How much his brother's "filthy letter" hurt Orion we don't know, but more instrumental was probably his own determination, in an environment dominated by mining interests, to rein in those forces, or at least to abate their more glaring offenses. In the assembly's deliberations Orion often found himself in the minority, and on at least one occasion he cast the sole dissenting vote. Of the six bills he introduced during the two-month term, two seemed closest to his heart. One was designed to protect "every man, poor or rich, who might buy shares in any mining corporation" by securing and safeguarding that person's right to elect and remove officers and restricting the power of trustees to levy assessments on stockholders. The other was intended to change the state's revenue system by putting the appraisal of a mine's output on a more realistic basis than currently, by raising the rate of taxation from 50¢ per $100 of proceeds to $1.25, and by abolishing "the enormously expensive system of suits for [the collection of] taxes" and substituting seizure and sale of assets.[1]

Both bills were tabled without reading, and on February 26, 1866, an obviously disappointed and frustrated Orion tendered his resignation as chairman of Ways and Means, stating in a public letter that he had "failed to be as useful to the State as in my opinion I should have been."² It was little more than a gesture, for the legislature was about to adjourn anyway, but evidently Orion felt it important to apologize to the people of Nevada. If conscientious Orion had had the benefit of his shrewd brother's "wire-pulling" he might have been more effective, but the team that "could work miracles" was no longer intact.

Charles Henry Webb, cofounder of the *Californian* and San Francisco correspondent for the *Sacramento Daily Union,* was taking quiet steps to get Mark Twain a complete change of scene. Webb persuaded the proprietors of the Sacramento newspaper to engage his friend on a special assignment.³ "I contracted with the Sacramento Union," wrote Clemens later, "to go wherever they chose and correspond for a few months, and I had a sneaking notion that they would start me east—but behold how fallible is human judgment!—they sent me to the Sandwich [now Hawaiian] Islands."⁴ For his part, Twain would end his association with the *Enterprise,* stay a month, and write twenty or thirty letters.⁵

When the steamer *Ajax* left for the islands on March 7, 1866, Mark Twain, armed with letters of introduction from his associates ("my friends seem determined that I shall not lack acquaintces"), was aboard.⁶ He had brought missives from Carson City and St. Louis, but he did not open them until the ship was two days at sea. A notebook entry dated March 9 records, "Just read letters from home which should have been read before leaving San Francisco. Accounts of oil on the Tennessee land, and that worthless brother of mine, with his eternal cant about law and religion, getting ready, in his slow, stupid way, to go to Excelsior, instead of the States. He sends me some prayers, as usual."⁷

"On the 13 day of March 1866," Mollie noted in her journal, "we left Carson. Mr Clemens to go for the summer to Meadow Lake, and I to travel through California, or go home at my pleasure."⁸ They were writing an end to their western adventure. With Orion's career in public office finished, Jennie dead (the second anniversary of her death on February 1, 1864, had recently passed), and a depression gripping the economy, the dream of making a permanent home in Nevada was dashed. How much their lives had changed was evidenced by the fact that in 1862 Orion wouldn't hear of Mollie's coming west by stagecoach, but now he was willing to let her travel around California alone.

If Orion had won the nomination of his party for Nevada secretary of state and then the election, he might have been on his way to a distinguished career, for he had demonstrated an ability not only to lead but to grow in office. As a delegate to the state assembly, on the other hand, he had shown little aptitude for the give-and-take of legislative politics. Undoubtedly the death of Jennie had had a profound effect on him, and in retrospect it is clear that the loss of his only child was a turning point in his life. After Mollie brought her to Nevada he was buoyant and confident as he had never been before, but after she died he seemed to have lost his reckoning, and his heart was never again fully in anything he undertook.

Apparently there was money enough for Mollie's passage back to the Mississippi Valley and a little more, but Orion would have to try to raise cash for his own trip in the Excelsior District, high in the Sierra. He wrote to Jane and Pamela shortly after arriving at Summit City on Meadow Lake that he expected to spend the summer there "practicing law and acting as mining agent for persons at a distance, and I hope to make some money and go home in December."[9] He was no longer thinking in terms of pursuing a career, but simply of making a living. He hoped to be able to do that by writing for newspapers in the Midwest, and while he was in Meadow Lake he contributed to both the local semiweekly and the *San Francisco American Flag,* a two-year-old Radical Union paper.[10] These pieces were for the most part humdrum accounts of mining in the Excelsior.

Meanwhile, in the Sandwich Islands, Sam had realized he couldn't possibly visit the eight inhabited islands and write about them in the single month allotted, and he wrote the *Union* to that effect.[11] He then apparently received a letter from Mollie, for on May 22 he wrote to her, "It is no use to wait for me to go home. Go on yourselves." He told her the "old sore" was still so raw that he had begun "many letters" only to burn them when the subject of the Tennessee land crept into them. "It is Orion's duty," he lectured his sister-in-law,

> to attend to that land, and after shutting me out of my attempt to sell it (for which I shall never entirely forgive him,) if he lets it be sold for taxes, all his religion will not wipe out the sin. It is no use to quote Scripture to me, Mollie,—I am in poverty and exile now because of Orion's religious scruples. Religion and poverty cannot go together. I am satisfied Orion will eventually save himself, but in doing it he will

damn the balance of the family. I want no such religion. He has got a duty to perform by us—will he perform it?

It is no use disguising it—I always feel bitter and malignant when I think of Ma and Pamela grieving at our absence and the land going to the dogs when I could have sold it and been at home now, instead of drifting about the outskirts of the world, battling for bread.[12]

If this was the expurgated version, one wonders what the letters he burned sounded like. Paradoxically, in the same dispatch he told of visiting the United States minister resident, who was about to be replaced, on what was probably an attempt to secure that diplomatic post for Orion. But the position had already been filled—"so there is an end to *that* project."[13] Orion appears to have written Sam bidding him to go home and sell the Tennessee land. Not surprisingly, Sam told his brother to "go to thunder" and to take care of the land himself.[14]

By this time Mollie was missing her husband greatly, and Orion told her he would telegraph her to join him as soon as he had finished a prospecting expedition.[15] So anxious was she to be with him, however, that she wanted to proceed at once; she would "rather live in a snowbank" with him, she said, than elsewhere by herself. Orion told her to come immediately, and they were reunited in Meadow Lake on June 16, 1866, after which they took a rudimentary room at the Andrews Hotel.[16]

Orion wrote to the secretary of the Mount Blanc Mining Company asking for an advance on "what you expect to receive for one half of my remaining interest."[17] In the early 1860s Orion had invested in and become president and trustee of the company, which operated its diggings at American Flat, near Virginia City, but he had resigned his presidency in 1864, apparently because he was discouraged with the mine.[18] Now he must have received Sam's letter and realized that if anything was to be done about the Tennessee land he would have to do it himself, for he explained to the secretary that he intended to use the proceeds "to go to the States on the next Steamer, with my wife, to attend to our Tennessee land."[19]

On July 26 Orion and Mollie left Meadow Lake for San Francisco, presumably having raised money for Orion's passage back to the States either by disposing of the mining stock or their Carson City house, or both.[20] Twain wrote in his *Autobiography* that Orion "sold his twelve-thousand-dollar house and its furniture for thirty-five hundred in greenbacks at about 30 per cent discount."[21] However it was disposed of, the building that had been the symbol of Orion and Mollie's social stature in Nevada was gone, and with it all that had been inside—the piano, the furniture, everything. The only item they couldn't bear to part with was Jennie's little chair. That they took with them.[22]

Sam returned to San Francisco in August 1866. What had been planned as a one-month visit to the islands had stretched into four—but still it had not been long enough, as far as he was concerned. As he noted in his journal, "Aug 13—San Francisco—Home again. No—not home again—in prison again—and all the wild sense of freedom gone. The city seems so cramped, and so dreary with toil and care and business anxiety. God help me, I wish I were at sea again!"[23] His first task was to finish his letters to the *Union*, eight of which had yet to be published. That accomplished, he took them up the river and settled his account with the newspaper. "They paid me a great deal more than they promised me," he wrote home from San Francisco on the twentieth, adding, "Orion and Mollie are here."[24]

Sam's meeting with his brother was the first since Orion had thwarted Sam's efforts to form a literary alliance and to sell the Tennessee land—the first, in fact, since Sam departed Nevada under a cloud more than two years earlier. For that reason, and because of what happened subsequently, it was one of the most noteworthy encounters in the brothers' dealings. Evidently Orion told Sam of his intention to go to Tennessee to "attend to" the land—no doubt to try to sell it—and asked him to come along to assist him. When Sam declined, Molly suggested that her brothers might be willing to help, and Sam authorized Orion to reimburse them in acreage if they did so.[25] Conceivably Sam brought up the matter of Orion's becoming a clergyman—nothing, after all, was standing in the way of it now. There may have been a heated exchange, for two months later Sam would tell his cousin, niece, and nephew that "Orion would make a preacher. . . . but he won't touch it. I am utterly and completely disgusted with a member of the family who *could* carry out my old ambition and won't."[26]

The *Union* had paid Sam enough money to cover the fare home, but— "bitter and malignant" though he was at the thought "of Ma and Pamela grieving at our absence"—he was determined to remain a while longer in "this accursed homeless desert."[27] It seems there was something he had to do. He wasn't sure what it was—"I tortured my brain for a saving scheme of some kind," he wrote in *Roughing It*—but it had to be done.[28] Orion might be reconciled to going home a failure, but he was not.

Orion and Mollie sailed aboard the steamer *Golden City* on August 30, 1866, while Sam remained behind.[29] He worked for a while in September reporting the California Agricultural Society Fair for the *Sacramento Union,* and he did some other writing—but as busy as he was in these ways, inside he was casting about, urgently seeking that talismanic "saving scheme."[30] Among the options he was considering was a trip around the world, a book on the Sandwich Islands, and a paid public lecture on the islands. The last, according to Paine, "was a *fearsome* prospect—he trembled when he thought of it." His benefit lecture for Orion's church had been a success, but that had been thrust upon him. "To come forward now, *offering himself* in the same capacity, was a different matter."[31] What Paine didn't mention—but what no doubt Samuel was mindful of—was that becoming a professional speaker had been Orion Clemens's lifelong ambition.

At last overcoming his trepidation, on October 2, 1866, Mark Twain delivered an address to a packed house in San Francisco. The rousing success of the lecture resulted in a quickly arranged speaking tour of California and Nevada towns.[32] From the interplay of lecturer and listeners he bodied out more fully than before the unique persona he had created. That bold, impudent, roguish character had come into being largely in reaction to Orion; now that Sam's big brother was away he was free to make it more his own.[33]

And Sam was making money. From Virginia City he wrote home, "You know the flush times are past, and it has long been impossible to more than half fill the Theatre here, with any sort of attraction—but they filled it for me, night before last—full—dollar all over the house." He added proudly that "Sandy Baldwin [United States district judge for Nevada] says I have made the most sweeping success of any man he knows of."[34] At last he was ready to go home. "I'll leave toward 1st December," he wrote, "but I'll telegraph you."

In fact he did not depart until December 15, aboard the *America,* after having made a special arrangement with John McComb's *Alta California* to be that paper's roving correspondent. He hadn't made the fortune he had held as a precondition for his homecoming, but he had accomplished something in his mind perhaps even more important: Having seen Orion off packing, he had become a paid lecturer, something Orion had only dreamt of—and a successful one at that.

On September 19, 1866, Orion and Mollie arrived in New York, where they had a "wandering, sight-seeing stay of a few days" before returning to Keokuk for a reunion with Mollie's family. Orion then proceeded to St. Louis to see his own kindred, apparently leaving his wife with her parents.[35] Like his illustrious brother, Orion had made arrangements to contribute letters to a San Francisco newspaper, but unlike Sam he was paid very little for these, if anything at all.[36] On October 15, 1866, he dated what was apparently his first correspondence with the *San Francisco Times,* a staunch Union journal. Among other things, he told of how his watch had been stolen while he attended a political meeting in St. Louis addressed by Benjamin F. Butler, a Radical Republican ("These Secessionists here hate Ben Butler").[37] In another letter Orion wrote: "The civil war being dead, its ghost haunts some of the localities where its crimes were committed, indulging in such pranks as rail-tipping, by which a railroad train was yesterday thrown from the Louisville and Nashville Railroad, killing six, and wounding ten persons." He reported that General Ulysses S. Grant had visited St. Louis, but added wryly, "He did not call on me."[38]

By the end of December 1866 Orion was on his way to attend to the Tennessee land. From Nashville he wrote that "the people here talk over the war and public affairs with the same indifference they might exhibit in discussing the French revolution"—but this surface equanimity was belied by several acts of interracial violence he told of witnessing. He also reported that the captain of the steamboat on which he intended to continue his trip "prophesies and argues in favor of the re-establishment of slavery in six or seven years."[39]

The South, though vanquished, had not changed much. When Orion reached Gainesborough, the backwater hamlet of his birth, he took a room at the tavern. As he was "loitering about the streets" he was "accosted by a young physician, in brown jeans, who had been a rebel spy." When the doctor learned that Orion was from Missouri he asked what Missourians thought of the prospect of war with France, giving his own opinion that such a conflict would furnish an opportunity for "another split," and that "a man would be a fool to fight for a Government that wouldn't let him vote." Orion responded that the government would be a fool to let a man vote who had fought against the country.[40] He seems to have been equally outspoken with a woman (perhaps a family friend) who was a member of Gainesborough's "first class society" (she even had a rag carpet in her parlor) and seems to have invited Orion to dinner. Upon discovering how thoroughly "Union" her guest was, she treated him "with rude insolence." That evening Orion's landlady warned him he "must be fearful" how he talked. Later his roommate, "the only Union man in town," told him "they would not attack me in day time, but if they caught me out in the dark, might knock me on the head with a rock." The roommate added that during Orion's absence townspeople had gathered at the tavern "and 'lowed I [Orion] shouldn't hire a horse, as I desired, to go to Jamestown."

Gainesborough was on the way to the Tennessee land, some fifty miles farther east, but there may have been a special reason Orion stopped there—to remind himself how far he had come from his beginnings. "There generation after generation grows up and dies," he informed the *Times,* "with no more than neighborhood traveling, or an occasional visit to Nashville. . . . They hate Yankees with intense bitterness, and hope to see them obliged to 'bend the knee to a foreign yoke,' though they should have to do so themselves."[41] Not only had Orion traveled much farther than Nashville, he had bucked local custom by becoming a Union supporter. Hardly one to bend his knee, he was probably lucky to escape Gainesborough with his life.

When he got back to St. Louis he wrote about the trip, and as he warmed to the subject, his censure of the South came to focus on those who (not unlike Samuel Clemens) wavered in their loyalties. He spoke colorfully of "the wretched reptiles who slunk through the war, trailing their slimy tracks in crooked lines through the edges of both parties—at first giving hearty assistance to the rebel side, then deserting it to render lukewarm aid to the Government, and now cursing Yankees and praising rebel soldiers, and rebel Generals, and everything rebel, with hearts pouring out vitriol on all Union soldiers and Union Generals who were not Copperheads."[42]

12
Sam Tests the Link

As men, the Twins have not always lived in perfect accord; but, still,
there has always been a bond between them which made them
unwilling to go away from each other and dwell apart.

Mark Twain, "Personal Habits of the Siamese Twins"

While Orion was in Tennessee, Sam arrived in New York and checked
into the Metropolitan Hotel.[1] Before he went to St. Louis he planned to go
down to Washington and thought he would be there a month. One aim of
the visit (as he implied in a letter written later) was to "gouge" a government office for Orion out of Senator William M. Stewart of Nevada.[2] But
a week passed, and then another, and he did not go. On February 23 he
wrote in his dispatch to the *San Francisco Alta California* that he was suffering from "the blues" and that his "thoughts persistently ran on funerals and
suicide."[3] By March 2, Sam had decided to skip Washington and was preparing to go straight to St. Louis. As he packed his trunk he may have
thought of the other time he had made that journey, the first leg of his trip
to Muscatine thirteen years earlier.[4] On this eve of his departure, he ended
his *Alta* letter oddly with "I never felt so particularly unhappy in my life as
I do at this moment."[5]

Clemens left New York on the New Jersey Central on March 3, and
after a fifty-two-hour ride that involved sitting up all night, he arrived in
St. Louis at midnight on March 5. "I went straight home and sat up till
breakfast time, talking and telling other lies," he wrote later.[6] It had been
six years since he last saw his mother and sister, and there was much ground
to cover. They thought he looked old, Paine informs us, but in other ways
he seemed unchanged. "Jane Clemens had grown older, too. She was nearly
sixty-four, but as keen and vigorous as ever—proud (even if somewhat criti-

cal) of this handsome, brilliant man of new name and fame who had been her mischievous, wayward boy. She petted him, joked with him, scolded him, and inquired searchingly into his morals and habits. In turn he petted, comforted, and teased her."[7]

Orion was on hand too, back from Tennessee. His attempts to sell the land had failed, and he seemed generally down on his luck.[8] He had listed himself in the St. Louis city directory as a lawyer and was taking whatever work he could find, but that apparently wasn't much. Indeed, so straitened were his circumstances that he and Mollie couldn't afford to live together; she was still in Keokuk with her parents, while he boarded with his sister (now a widow) and his mother.[9] The sight of the former acting governor fallen so low must have disconcerted Sam. When he started to ask him if his law practice was going satisfactorily, he found he couldn't—the answer was all too obvious.[10]

While Sam was in St. Louis the *New York Weekly*, a large-circulation paper that paid its contributors liberally, began to reprint five of his letters from the Sandwich Islands. The journal had been courting him since early in the year, and on March 7 it proudly announced it had "made an engagement with the celebrated 'Mark Twain,' the California wit and humorist, who will furnish us with a series of his inimitable papers."[11] Sam may have suggested to Orion that he seek employment as a correspondent with the *Weekly*. In any case, Orion sent an article of his own to the paper.[12]

Before he left New York, Sam had made a down payment on a pleasure excursion to Europe and the Holy Land aboard the steamer *Quaker City*. In St. Louis he bought a scrapbook and asked Jane Clemens to paste into it the letters he intended to write to the *Alta* during that trip.[13] Twain arrived back in New York around April 14. There he learned that the *Alta* had agreed, as he had hoped, to pay his passage on the *Quaker City*.[14]

Meanwhile, Orion was preparing to return to Tennessee. Perhaps mindful of his close call in Gainesborough, he planned to take a firearm. "The Merchants' Union Express," he instructed his wife, "will probably be best for you to send the pistol by."[15]

In Tennessee he received word from Pamela that the article he had submitted to the *New York Weekly* had been published, and the paper invited him to "write as often as convenient." "Now I want to advise you," she went on (somewhat patronizingly), "to write several contributions, and wait until they are published, before you say anything about pay. I think this is important." Continuing in the same vein, she added: "Mrs. Green says she has always liked your writings. She thinks your style is particularly pleasing. I believe it is Mrs. Ludington who says, if any thing, she likes your style better than Sam's. I think your style will be popular if you once become known to the public."[16]

A search of the *New York Weekly* for this period turned up no articles bearing Orion's name, but a sketch titled "Saved by a Slave," in the issue of April 18, 1867, and attributed to "Leon Treulon," is very possibly Orion's work. It tells of how nineteen-year-old Frank Becker, a Union soldier, finds himself behind enemy lines and is pursued by a dozen rebels. Running for his life, Becker takes refuge in a plantation outhouse, where he comes across "an old negro." When Becker requests help in hiding, the black man asks if Becker is a Yankee. Becker allows that he is, and that the rebs are after him. "Jist git in dere," offers the negro, indicating a large iron-hooped cask near the doorway, "and I'll fix ye so ther' won't be no sich thing as yer bein' discovered." Thinking the fellow might betray him, Becker hesitates, but then decides to trust him. He climbs into the barrel, and the negro covers him with smoked ham.

When the rebels show up and ask about a "blasted Yank," the unnamed black man tells them he saw a man "runnin' like mad a little time since" and adds, "Hope you cotch de cussed Yankee." That night Becker makes his way back safely into the Union lines, "saved by a slave as were many others of our escaped prisoners." As we shall see (chapter 14), Orion would later pen a similar sketch about another estimable slave.

Pamela seems to have written Sam about this auspicious development and to have asked him to arrange to have the *Weekly* sent to St. Louis. In any case, he wrote back on June 1 that "I asked them to send the N.Y. Weekly to you—no charge." But then he added pointedly, "I am not going to write for it—like all other papers that pay one splendidly, it circulates among stupid people and the *canaille*."[17] Whether this knock reached Orion or, if so, affected him is not known, but he did not add his *New York Weekly* piece to his scrapbook (as he had some of the *Times* letters), and as far as can be determined, instead of the "several contributions" his sister recommended, he did not at that time write another article for the journal.[18]

On the eve of Samuel's departure aboard the *Quaker City*, he found himself in the clutches of "an accusing conscience." "I wish Orion were going on this voyage," he wrote to the family in St. Louis, "for I believe with so many months of freedom from business cares he could not help but be cheerful and jolly." Alluding to his missed opportunity to get a job for his brother, he continued,

> I wish I had gone to Washington in the winter instead of going west. . . .
> But I am so worthless that it seems to me I never do anything or accom-
> plish anything that lingers in my mind as a pleasant memory. My
> mind is stored full of unworthy conduct toward Orion and toward
> you all, and an accusing conscience gives me peace only in excite-
> ment and restless moving from place to place. If I could say I had
> done one thing for any of you that entitled me to your good opinions
> (I say nothing of your love, for I am sure of that, no matter how
> unworthy of it I may make myself,—from Orion down, you have
> always given me that, all the days of my life, when God Almighty
> knows I have seldom deserved it,) I believe I could go home and stay
> there—and I know I would care little for the world's praise or blame.

In other words, if he hadn't wronged his brother (not to mention the rest of them), he would gladly throw over his fame, go home, and settle down. But that was out of the question now, and "You observe that under a cheer-ful exterior I have got a spirit that is angry with me and gives me freely its contempt. I can get away from that at sea, and be tranquil and satisfied— and so, with my parting love and benediction for Orion and all of you, I say good bye and God bless you all—and welcome the wind that wafts a weary soul to the sunny lands of the Mediterranean!"[19]

As Sam sought escape at sea, Orion, once again unsuccessful in his ef-forts to sell the Tennessee land, returned to St. Louis. By this time he was growing desperate for any sort of employment.[20] A week or so after his famous brother and other passengers of the *Quaker City* were received by Tsar Aleksandr II of Russia and his family, Orion wrote to his wife of his many unsuccessful efforts to find newspaper work. "I am sorry you are not well and have been so unhappy," he commiserated. "It is my intention to have you with me as soon as I can." "I sent you a Democrat last Tuesday," he added, "with a telegraphic dispatch relating to the reception of the Quaker City excursionists by the Emperor and Empress of Russia."[21]

Just when Orion thought he was about to get a situation in a printing office and be able at last to bring Mollie to St. Louis, he was called back to

Tennessee to "fix up title papers."[22] Six weeks later he wrote from Jamestown, "I fear I am stuck here till February, there is so much surveying and investigating to do."[23] Jane and Pamela were worried about Orion's state of mind. "We feel truly sorry for you in your exile," wrote his sister, "and hope it will not be necessary for you to stay much longer, but I hope you will not think of leaving, so long as you can do any good by staying."[24] Orion answered dejectedly that it would "take many months yet, it may take years, to straighten up all these titles."[25]

In his seemingly endless "exile" Orion turned to a diversion; his next letter to Mollie suggested he had begun tinkering with an invention. "You want to know about the machine," he teased his wife. "You are my best friend, you stick closer to me than any other; and I like you better than any body else, but you will have to puzzle your head and guess till you cypher it out as the work progresses, if I ever get a chance to work at it again."[26]

When Samuel Clemens returned to New York from the *Quaker City* excursion on November 19, 1867, he must have found a letter from St. Louis (probably written by Jane Clemens) informing him that Orion was still in need of a job, for the following day he wrote home that "I will move Heaven and earth for Orion."[27] While he was away he had received an offer from Senator Stewart of Nevada to become his private secretary, and had accepted. "At least I can get an office for Orion," he wrote home, "if he or the President will modify their politics." Orion sided with the Radical Republicans in Congress against the pro-Southern Reconstruction policies of Democratic president Andrew Johnson.[28] Sam encountered obstacles, however, and by February 6, 1868, he figuratively threw up his hands in exasperation. "Some time in the course of the present century," he wrote, "I think they will create a Commissioner of Patents, and then I hope to get a berth for Orion."[29]

In February Orion returned from Tennessee to St. Louis—once again empty-handed—and proceeded to Keokuk to see Mollie. The visit evidently was not conjugal, for after he had returned to St. Louis he wrote to his wife: "Tell Mrs. Wempner we have carefully abstained from any attempt to make a baby till I should get into business. When that occurs we will again sleep together as do married folks."[30] Mollie seems to have offered to get a job, but Orion wouldn't hear of it. "I tell you again," he wrote sternly, "I don't want you to work for money."[31]

Back in St. Louis, Orion found employment setting type for the *Mis-*

souri Democrat, working as a "sub" but hoping for a "regular situation." He had been away from the printer's trade so long he was no longer good enough to hold a position in a job or book shop or on an evening newspaper. Since printing was the only work he knew other than the law, however (and since he didn't have enough capital to set up a legal practice), there was nothing left but to take what he could find on a morning paper—even though that entailed night work, irregular hours, and low wages.[32]

He was still pursuing the dream of inventing a machine, and he seems to have invested it with much airy expectation. As soon as it was perfected, he seemed sure, it would deliver him and Mollie from their destitute circumstances.[33] Perhaps it was this golden promise that prompted Orion to inform Sam he didn't want a patent office position after all. While Sam hadn't exactly moved "Heaven and earth for Orion," he had expended time and effort in his behalf—but instead of being annoyed by this announcement, he was pleased. Writing to "My dear Bro." he allowed that he was glad to learn "you do not want the clerkship, for the Patent Office is in such a muddle that there would be no security for the permanency of a place in it."[34]

If the younger brother felt disposed to point out that things might have been different had Orion chosen to become a man of the cloth, he restrained himself. "We chase phantoms," he philosophized instead, "half the days of our lives," adding: "It is well if we learn wisdom even then, and save the other half." Which of the two had attained to such an understanding? Clearly Sam felt he had—but for the present he was powerless to act on it. "I am in for it," he continued. "I must go on chasing [phantoms]— until I marry—*then* I am done with literature and all other bosh,—that is, literature wherewith to please the general public. I shall write to please myself, then."

He disdained his vocation as much as he had when he first struggled with his call, but unlike that time, when Orion seemed part of the equation, now his brother's choices had no bearing on his own; no longer were the respective careers two sides of a coin. Nonetheless, it still seemed important that Orion go on chasing this particular phantom. "I hope you *will* set type till you complete that invention, for surely government pap must be nauseating food for a *man*—a man whom God has enabled to saw wood and be independent."[35] Even if Orion's scheme was a chimera, it was at least worthy of his largeness of spirit.

Sam had left Senator Stewart and was at work on a book based on his *Quaker City* letters. At the invitation of Elisha Bliss, who managed the American Publishing Company, he had gone to the company's headquarters in Hartford, Connecticut, where he negotiated what he called a "splendid" contract.[36] "They pay me more than they have ever paid any author except Horace Greeley," he crowed to his mother and sister.[37]

Sam's plaint to Orion that "I must go on chasing [phantoms]—until I marry" was different from his usual wistful allusions to the wedded state, for this time he had a specific woman in mind. He had met twenty-two-year-old Olivia Langdon ("slender and beautiful and girlish"), sister of Charles Langdon, one of his shipmates aboard the *Quaker City.*[38] At Charles's invitation, Clemens became a guest at her parents' home in Elmira, New York, for two weeks in August and September 1868, and before he left he had proposed to Livy. She turned him down, but she did consent to correspond with him on a sisterly basis.[39]

Sam and Charles Langdon went from Elmira to Cleveland, Ohio, to visit Mary Mason Fairbanks, whom they had met on the voyage, and her husband, Abel, and afterward Clemens proceeded on alone to St. Louis. From there he wrote to Livy he was glad Charles hadn't come along. "He would have had no rest here—I have none."[40] Three days later he wrote to Mrs. Fairbanks that since arriving home "I have not once been in a happy humor. . . . There is something in my deep hatred of St. Louis that will hardly let me appear cheery even at my mother's own fireside. Nobody knows what a ghastly infliction it is on me to visit St. Louis. I am afraid I do not always disguise it, either."[41]

As he disclosed to Olivia in a letter written that Christmas, he sometimes felt "a stranger in my own home—(not that *I* ever seem a stranger to my mother and sister and my brother, for their love knows no change, no modification)—but then I see them taking delight in things that are new to me, and which I do not comprehend or take an interest in; I see them heart-and-heart with people I do not know, and who are nothing to me, and so I can only *look in* upon their world without entering."[42]

One of the new things to Sam was Orion's invention. This may have been a "modest little drilling machine," or it may have been a "wood-sawing machine" that Sam later recalled. "He . . . patched it together himself," he wrote in his *Autobiography,* "and he really sawed wood with it. It was ingenious; it was capable; and it would have made a comfortable little fortune for him; but just at the wrong time Providence interfered again. Orion applied for a patent and found that the same machine had already been patented and had gone into business and was thriving."[43] Orion and Mollie were at last reunited and were living with his mother and sister.[44] He was making $25 a week and paying Pamela board of $8.75 a week.[45]

Sam's St. Louis visit lasted less than a week, after which he returned to Hartford to work on the printer's copy for his book.[46] He finally managed to win Olivia's heart and to overcome her parents' objections, and on February 4, 1869, the couple became formally engaged.[47] If he ever entertained thoughts that joining a new family in New York would somehow free him from the old one in Missouri, he was wrong, for someone in St. Louis (again, probably his mother) suggested that Orion might get a job on whatever newspaper Sam bought into. Testily, Sam replied that "my head is so busted up with endeavors to get my own plans straight, that I am hardly in a condition to fix up anybody else's."[48]

Two months later Mark Twain wrote a curious article he called "Personal Habits of the Siamese Twins."[49] Because he knew "intimately" the renowned congenitally joined twins, Chang and Eng, he told the reader, he felt "peculiarly well qualified" to write about them. "As men, the Twins have not always lived in perfect accord; but, still, there has always been a bond between them which made them unwilling to go away from each other and dwell apart." During the Civil War, Twain's Chang and Eng took opposite sides; one of them was an inveterate smoker, the other not; one was a drinker, the other a temperance advocate.

Oddly, Twain had the brothers in the sketch fall in love with the same girl. Olivia and Orion had never met, although Sam evidently had told his fiancée enough about his brother to make her feel she knew him. On June 4, 1869, Sam, staying at Olivia's home in Elmira, wrote to St. Louis, "I want to write to Orion, but I keep putting it off—I keep putting *everything* off. . . . If Orion will bear with me and forgive me I will square up with him yet. I will even let him kiss Livy."[50] Three weeks later Sam wrote that "she is a staunch friend of Orion's, and I fancy she is about half in love with him."[51]

Sam was again in Elmira when he informed his mother and sister he had shipped a trunk and valise to them and intended to follow "in the course of a week or more," adding that "if I come to St Louis I want to shut myself up in the house and not see anybody. I must write my next winter's lecture."[52] After the luggage arrived, Jane and Pamela began watching expectantly as each carriage or omnibus approached their gate—but always they were disappointed. Meanwhile, Orion wrote to Sam that he and Mollie "can fix you a nice, quiet place to write your lecture" in a house they had "taken" for the summer while its owners were away.[53]

But the days passed—became weeks—and still the traveler did not arrive, nor any word from him. Finally, on July 25, 1869—one day short of a month after Sam's announcement—Jane Clemens took pen in hand and, in her inimitable fashion, gave him a piece of her mind. "My dear son," she wrote,

> I have been waiting, waiting, for you, your trunks have been here more than a month. Suppose I send you my trunks and a letter telling you I will be along in a week or so, and then I stay over four weeks what would you think of me especially if I had not been to see you for six or seven years but one time—would you conclude I was weaned from you and cared but little for you and how would you feel to think I had forgotten my own child. seven years ago all the people I know could not have made me believe that one of my children would not think worth while to come and see me. There is no excuse for a child not to go and see his old mother when it is in his power.[54]

If Sam answered, the letter does not survive. What does is a missive he directed to Pamela nearly a month later. "I am sorry I never got to St Louis," he apologized. "But I have been busy all the time and St Louis is clear out of the way, and remote from the world and all ordinary routes of travel."[55] He *had* been busy, but not so much that he hadn't found time to drop a note to Mary Mason Fairbanks, whom he apparently intended to visit on his way to St. Louis, explaining that he had "unexpectedly got aground" in Elmira.[56] Presumably a similar note to St. Louis would have been no more trouble. And he did find time to get to Cleveland, but instead of proceeding on to St. Louis as he had the previous September he turned around and went back to Elmira.[57]

One of several matters that had been occupying Clemens was preparation for the wedding. "Livy says we *must* have you all at our marriage," he wrote to Pamela, adding peremptorily: "and I say we can't." The long train trip in the middle of winter, he explained, would be "equivalent to murder and arson and everything else," and besides, the cost was prohibitive. Then, even though a date for the wedding had apparently already been set, he went on to write: "She says her father and mother will *invite* you just as soon as the wedding date is definitely fixed, *anyway*—and she thinks that's *bound* to settle it. But the ice and snow, and the long hard journey and the injudiciousness of laying out any money except what we are *obliged* to part with . . . settles the case differently." He enclosed the key to his trunk. "Mollie is welcome to all the shirts she can find in it or in the valise," he offered, perhaps thinking Orion could use them.[58]

It is difficult, in reading this letter and reviewing its writer's behavior, to escape the impression that Sam didn't want his family to come to the wedding and that, like the trunk and valise, the St. Louis Clemenses (not just Orion, but Jane and Pamela as well) had become excess baggage. In Elmira he had been welcomed into a household that was not only wealthy and socially prominent but embodied what must have seemed a high degree of culture and refinement. His own clan, by contrast, were really nothing more than provincials. Not that he had been "weaned from" them or "cared but little for" them, as Jane Clemens feared, but they *had* become something of a burden and an embarrassment. In "Personal Habits of the Siamese Twins," Twain had written that Chang and Eng "were ignorant and unlettered—barbarians themselves and the offspring of barbarians, who knew not the light of philosophy and science."

Least humiliating of Sam's relations was probably Orion. "The family all seem to know and like Orion particularly well," wrote Sam, "and want to see him"—adding as an afterthought, "They naturally want to see *all* of you."[59] Livy's parents probably found the story of Orion's early antislavery sentiments particularly intriguing, for they had been fervent abolitionists and had even been active in the Underground Railroad.[60] When Jervis Langdon died in August 1870, Sam wrote of him, "he was an Abolitionist from the cradle, and worked openly and valiantly in that cause all through the days when to do such a thing was to ensure a man disgrace, insult, hatred and bodily peril."[61]

The Langdons also probably respected Orion for his honesty. When Sam conveyed Mr. Langdon's offer to buy the Clemenses' land in Tennessee for thirty thousand dollars, Orion cautioned that Langdon "must not buy blindfold, or until he sends his Memphis agent there to examine." Then, in a rare display of pique, he added for Sam's benefit, "Neither you nor Ma nor Pamela know anything about the land. . . . I have laboriously investigated the titles, localities and qualities, and I would put its present value at about five thousand dollars."[62] Eleven years later he told Sam he had not sent a deed because "I feared you would unconsciously cheat your prospective father-in-law."[63]

As a counteroffer, Orion proposed that Mr. Langdon enter into an "equal copartnership" with the Clemenses, they to furnish the land and he the means to settle it with immigrants on seven- or eight-year leases, thereby perfecting the family's title and developing the property.[64] Nothing came of that proposal, however, and the sale did not go through. Thus did Orion quash another potential sale of the Tennessee land, and again for reasons of conscience.

13
Orion Shows Another Side

Look how it helps me. I should be an editor with something to edit.
This "Publisher" may as well be built up into something large as not.

Orion to Sam

The following month Orion received letters from R. W. Taylor, comptroller of the U.S. Treasury Department, demanding reimbursement of
$1,330 for disallowed payments Orion had made as Nevada territorial sec-
retary. Accordingly, Orion wrote to the Nevada printers in question and
asked them to return the money purportedly overpaid them, but, doubtful
that they would be able to do so, he respectfully protested to Taylor that it
was "rather severe to require me to refund to the United States out of my
own pocket all the profit those printers ever got." He explained that after
converting the government's greenbacks to coin, "which alone was used as
currency" in Nevada, at the rate of "40 cents on the dollar or less," and
after paying their compositors, the printers had received only "FIVE CENTS
per 1000 ems for profit, presswork, binding, paper, ink, delivery, &c! Even
if I paid them more, were they not justly entitled to a fair profit?"[1]

Taylor wrote back that allowance of $375 would be "considered" if Orion
paid the balance of $955. Orion had been bonded for $10,000 before assuming his post in 1861, but he was apparently too intimidated to remind
Taylor of that fact.[2] The only thing he owned that had any substantial
value was his share of the Tennessee land. When Pamela and Jane learned
of this new adversity, they were naturally upset. Not only might Orion lose
his part of the land, but the family name could be sullied as well. They
turned to Sam for help.

The restored head of the family wrote in reply that his first impulse was to send Orion a check for the money, "but a sober second thought suggested that if he has not defrauded the government out of money, why pay, simply because the government chooses to consider him in its debt?" Taking the high ground, Sam declared: "No. Right is right. The idea don't suit me." He suggested that Orion write to the Treasury and state his case once more, telling them he had no money. "*If* they make his sureties pay, *then* I will make the sureties whole, but I won't pay a cent of an unjust claim. You talk of disgrace. To my mind it would be just as disgraceful to allow one's self to be bullied into paying that which is unjust."

Then, as if to plant his flag, Sam made a grand gesture. Noting that Jane Clemens thought it "hard" that Orion's portion of the land "should be swept away," he wrote that "this letter is his ample authority to sell *my* share of the land *immediately* and appropriate the proceeds." The only condition was that when Orion was back on his feet, he should repay the sale price—not to Sam, but to their mother. "Tell Orion to keep a stiff upper lip," he added in closing, "when the worst comes to the worst I will come forward."[3]

When Sam told the Langdons what he had done, Jervis Langdon thought (as Olivia reported) "it was too bad for your brother to be such a drag to you." As for his fiancée herself, she wrote that

> I am very sorry that your brother is troubled, and very thankful that you are prospered, glad on your account and glad because you can help others—God gives diversities of gifts, he has not given to your brother money making wisdom, but, from what you say, he has given him a beautiful spirit nevertheless. . . . You are a good youth to say what you have to your brother about helping him to the money when he cannot get along longer without it because I know that while you are in debt you do not know very well how to spare money, but it is the gifts that really cost us something that are most valuable in Gods sight.[4]

Sam's gift actually cost him little, for, as Paine pointed out, he had "long since lost faith in [the land], and was not only willing, but eager to renounce his rights."[5] On the other hand, the gesture had moved his beloved Livy to call him "a good youth"—she even went on to add that she was "so proud of the true nobility of your nature." It was a small price to pay for such praise.

Samuel Langhorne Clemens and Olivia Louise Langdon were married in the Langdon home at Elmira on February 2, 1870.[6] Pamela Clemens Moffett and her seventeen-year-old daughter, Annie, were the only members of the groom's family to attend. Sam had, in the end, bowed to Olivia's wishes and sent travel money to both his sister and mother, but for some reason his mother opted out of the trip.[7] Paine stated simply that "Jane Clemens could not come, nor Orion and his wife."[8] The health of the sixty-seven-year-old woman may have been a factor, but then again, she may still have been nursing a grudge over her son's snub of six months earlier; if he "would not think worth while" to travel to St. Louis from Elmira to see her, why should she go in the opposite direction to be present at his wedding?

As for Orion, even if his brother had sent him the necessary funds, he couldn't have spared time away from his job. He was (as he informed R. W. Taylor) "penniless, and working for my daily bread on a daily morning newspaper (the Democrat) reading proof at $25 a week."[9] The Langdons would just have to wait a while longer to meet this man who seemed so admirable—and Orion would have to forbear that promised kiss.

If Orion was leading the life of a pauper, Sam had now attained a princely estate. His father-in-law had presented him with a beautiful house (complete with furnishings and domestic staff) in Buffalo, New York; he was buying on time (with Langdon's help) a third interest in the *Buffalo Express; The Innocents Abroad,* published in August 1869, was a commercial as well as critical triumph; and his recent lecture tour had been similarly successful.[10]

Samuel sporadically continued to try to help Orion. His old Virginia City acquaintance Thomas Fitch was now a congressman, and Sam contacted him in Washington about the treasury dispute. By January 1870 he was able to send Pamela "a note from Tom Fitch by which Orion will see that Tom is moving in the matter. Let Orion drop him simply a line, thanking him."[11] Three months later Sam sent his brother a letter of introduction to one of the proprietors of St. Louis's *Missouri Republican.* But the overture failed to get Orion a new job, and Sam considered doing what he had been too "busted up" to think about before—try to find Orion work on his own newspaper. As it turned out, however, The *Express* was not a growing enterprise but a shrinking one. "We shall not send for my brother," he informed his father-in-law in May, explaining that the evening edition was to be discontinued and the job printing shop farmed out—both "*leaks* from the start."[12]

In June a glimmer of hope appeared for Orion. He had approached a leading New York firm of patent solicitors with one of his inventions, and they reacted positively. When Sam received the news he exulted to Pamela, "I am *exceedingly* glad to hear that Orion's machine is so favorably thought of by Munn and Co." Then he launched into a long and impassioned paean to the inventor's art: "An inventor is a poet—a true poet—and nothing in any degree less than a high order of poet. . . . We would all rejoice to see Orion achieve a moneyed success with his inventions, of course—but if he can eventually do something great, something imperial, it were better to do that and starve than not to do it at all."[13]

Despite the reversal of Orion's fortunes Sam still seemed to perceive him as the better man. In the matter of Jervis Langdon, he had refused to bend his principles, while Sam had given in to pressure. Langdon, hard-headed businessman that he was, had probably considered his offer for the Tennessee land less an investment than an act of largesse to his prospective son-in-law and the other Clemenses. Orion, however—as much as he needed the money—probably recognized the bid for what it was and declined to sell (and would not allow Sam to do so) because he didn't think the deal would be fair to the purchaser.

Sam, on the other hand, had accepted Langdon's generosity even though he didn't need it and had implied he wouldn't take it. Shortly after he and Livy had become engaged, he had written to his family, "I am particularly anxious to place myself in a position where I can carry on my married life in good shape *on my own hook* [his emphasis], because I have paddled my own canoe so long that I could not be satisfied, now, to let anybody help me—my proposed father-in-law is naturally so liberal that it would be just like him to want to give us a start in life."[14] He was right about that. After the wedding, when he and Livy arrived in Buffalo and were driven to what he thought was to be their boardinghouse, Sam was surprised to find Mr. and Mrs. Langdon in the hall. What he didn't know was that the house, "a magnificent mansion," was, through Langdon's munificence, registered in Clemens's name.[15] In the end he accepted; it would, after all, have been embarrassing not to. But Orion would not have, and Sam knew it. He continued his letter about Orion's invention:

> To be Governor of Nevada is to be a poor little creeping thing that a man may create—a very pitiful little office-holding accident, with some better man's brass collar on—but to invent even this modest little drilling machine shows the presence of the patrician blood of intellect—that "round and top of sovereignty" which separates its possessor from the common multitude and marks him as one not beholden to the caprices of politics but endowed with greatness in his own right.[16]

Pamela was now living in Fredonia, New York, fifty miles southwest of Buffalo, with her two children and Jane Clemens (Sam had recommended that community because when he lectured there he was struck by the intelligence of the audience). Hoping Sam's words would "raise Orion's spirits, and Mary's [Mollie's] too," Pamela forwarded the letter to them in St. Louis.[17] Whether Orion was cheered to see the supreme achievement of his life disparaged as "a poor little creeping thing" and a "very pitiful . . . accident," however, is doubtful.

That summer Sam signed a contract with Elisha Bliss for a new book. "I propose to do up Nevada and Cal.," he wrote to Orion, "beginning with the trip across the country in the stage." He asked his brother if he had "a memorandum of the route we took—or the names of any of the Stations we stopped at? Do you remember any of the scenes, names, incidents or adventures of the coach trip?—for I remember next to *nothing* about the matter. . . . I wish I could have two days' talk with you."[18] By the end of the month Sam had received Orion's "note-book of the Plains trip."[19]

Orion ill-advisedly also sent a request for an advance of two or three hundred dollars to cover expenses of selling the Tennessee land. Sam was so upset that he was unable to pen a reply for twenty-four hours. When he had granted Orion authority "to sell *my* share of the land . . . and appropriate the proceeds," he had stipulated that the sale must be made "*immediately.*" During the nine months that had passed, no sale had been made, although a fifty-thousand-dollar offer was received in April and one for fifteen thousand dollars in May.[20] When he had cooled down a little, Sam agreed to provide the money Orion requested, but only with the proviso that he "either sell at some price or other, or give away" one full half of the land within four months—"but it must be honestly parted with, and *for-ever*. . . . this is the last time I will ever have anything to do with the care, protection, or sale of that doubly and trebly hated and accursed land."[21]

But Orion apparently ignored this warning, for Sam scrawled on the envelope of a letter he sent him a month later: "Leave it in Mellon's [the St. Louis agent's] hands but *give him 25 per cent*—can you never get that necessity before your face?" Despite this brass, the communication inside was civil, even gracious. "I find that your little memorandum book," it granted, "is going to be ever so much use to me, and will enable me to make quite a coherent narrative of the Plains journey instead of slurring it over and jumping 2,000 miles at a stride."[22]

Orion's journal was an indispensable tool to Mark Twain in writing the first twenty chapters of what eventually became the seventy-nine-chapter *Roughing It*. He used it to recall names, distances, times, landmarks, several particular incidents, and even the day-by-day happenings of the journey. He employed it as an outline from which he was able to diverge at will without losing the essential thread of actual events.[23] So grateful was the author that he wrote Orion, "I shall take the greatest pleasure in forwarding to you the third $1,000 which the publisher . . . sends me—or the *first* $1,000, I am not particular."[24]

Inspired by Sam's gratitude, Orion sent additional material having to do with "the difficulties of opening up the Territorial government in Nevada and getting the machinery to running."[25] Sam thanked him for "such full Nevada notes," but before he had a chance to do more than glance at them he misplaced them.[26] He asked his brother to "scribble something again, to aid my memory. . . . Don't tax yourself—I can make a little go a great way." Undoubtedly Orion complied, and Sam used the material in what became chapter 25 of *Roughing It*.[27] Later Sam would ask his brother to "torture your memory" and write down "in minute detail" every fact and exploit of "the desperado Slade" and also to describe his appearance and conversation when the brothers met him at Rocky Ridge station. Orion responded with an extended, circumstantial account of the notorious Slade, and Sam used most of this information to complete chapter 10 of *Roughing It*.[28]

Sam and Olivia's marriage idyll had taken a calamitous turn in June when they were called to Elmira for the beginning of the death watch at the bedside of Olivia's father, which ended when he died of stomach cancer on

August 6, 1870. After they returned to Buffalo and before Olivia, then five months pregnant, could recover from the loss, her visiting friend Emma Nye fell ill with typhoid fever and died on September 29 in the Clemenses' bedroom. Exhausted, the bereaved couple left for a week's visit with Sam's mother and sister in Fredonia.

Sam was probably in no mood to sympathize when Pamela informed him that Orion's night work in St. Louis was "putting his eyes out."[29] What was needed, she said, was "*easy work* at $100 a month, no night work, [and] liberty after supper to rest and work at [his] machine."[30] Once again the question of a job on the *Buffalo Express* seems to have come up, but Sam said only night work was available there.[31]

He took the matter under advisement, though, and when he got back to Buffalo he wrote to his publisher in Hartford. Elisha Bliss was starting a monthly publication to advertise his books; he envisioned a circulation of one hundred thousand and hoped eventually to charge for it and make it a lucrative literary periodical. He had offered Mark Twain "in effect $4,000 a year" to edit it.[32] Twain turned the offer down, but he did promise to furnish an article. It now occurred to him that the editorship might be just the thing for Orion.[33]

"Say, for instance," he wrote to Bliss offhandedly, "I have a brother about 45—an old and able writer and editor." He explained Orion's circumstances and casually touted his accomplishments in Nevada, informing his publisher that he "came out with the name of an able, honest and every way competent officer. He is well read in law, and I think understands book-keeping. He is a very valuable man for any sort of *office* work, but not worth a cent *outside* as a business man." Although he knew Bliss had only one assistant, Twain ingenuously inquired: "Have *you* got a place for him at $100 or $150 a month, in your office?" Only in closing did he mention the periodical. "When is your paper coming out? Did you ever receive the article I sent you for it from Fredonia?"[34]

The publisher rose to the bait. "How would your brother do for an editor of it? Would he be satisfied with $100. per month for present, until we could do better by him?" Intrigued that Mark Twain had a sibling who was also a writer ("Say! Is he anything like his younger brother?"), Bliss was nevertheless wary of overcommitting himself. He further hedged by pointing out that he had no "real place" for the brother just then, "but would like for *your sake* to *create a position* for him, if possible."[35]

Though Sam used indirection in coaxing the half-offer out of Bliss, he conveyed it to Orion with a bluntness that bordered on effrontery. "I desire," he wrote, sounding like the imperious Mississippi pilot of old, "that you throw up that cursed night work and take this editorship and conduct it so well that editorships will *assail* you at the end of a year." He suggested that the businessman wanted Orion mainly to prevent his eminent brother from leaving the fold and to get an occasional article out of him. "But all right," he deigned, "I am willing." Orion should enter into the job, he lectured, without showing "any shadow of timidity or unsoldierly diffidence, for that sort of thing is fatal to advancement. I warn you thus because you are naturally given to knocking your pot over in this way when a little judicious conduct would make it boil."[36]

Then he wrote to Bliss. "It is a splendid idea!" he enthused. "He will make a tip-top editor—a better than I, because he is full of talent and besides is perfectly faithful, honest, straightforward and reliable. There isn't money enough in America to get him to do a dishonest act—whereas I am different." He went on to instruct Bliss on the care and handling of Orion Clemens. "You just take him in hand and laugh with him and talk with him and keep him jolly, and I will answer for his editorial ability. I don't fancy that you will have much trouble keeping him jolly, either, though he is not quite so sprightly and idiotic as I am." Utterly sure of Orion's competence, Sam predicted that within a year Bliss would find him "really worth a deal of money to you." He would even be willing to bet on it, he said.[37]

When Orion pointed out to Sam that he was making more money in St. Louis than Bliss offered (he had received an increase from twenty-five to twenty-seven dollars per week) and had the boldness to ask about a future raise in Hartford, Sam's reply was curt.[38] "You have got the same curious ideas that all novices have—you must stipulate *before*hand what shall be done *in case* you prove a literary treasure." With caustic sarcasm he continued: "If you would rather slave all night in St Louis for $8 more a month than do easy and gentlemanly work in Hartford in daylight, I applaud your wisdom and say nothing against it. I will only remark that Bliss offers you exactly three times as much as the work is worth." Implausibly, he added that "I would take the job myself at less money if I were living in Hartford and my name did not appear as editor." He also noted that he had offered Bliss to make up the difference in salaries if Bliss couldn't.[39]

Still Orion demurred, and apparently Mollie was opposed to the move.

Sam wrote ten days later, "Be hasty. Be quick. Sell out *clean,* in St. Louis." And on the back of the note, as folded: "I hope you will pack up and leave for Hartford *instantly* and finally."[40] It was not until several weeks had passed, however, that Orion, probably accompanied by Mollie, stopped in Buffalo on his way to Hartford.[41] We don't know what advice Sam may have had for his brother and sister-in-law at that time, but he seemed concerned they get off to a good start. "Both of you *go slow,*" he would write a month later, "don't *hurry* in the matter of making friends, and don't get impatient. Making friends in Yankee land is a slow, slow business, but they are friends worth having when they *are* made."[42]

On December 20 Bliss wrote to Twain, "Your Brother is here and we are getting at work in earnest."[43] Sam had asked his new friends the Reverend and Mrs. Joseph H. Twichell to make Orion and Mollie's acquaintance, and he urged Bliss to get them season passes to the playhouse. "It will keep them in good spirits to go often to the theatre," he explained, "and besides I want him to get drawn away from thought, and have a bracing and revivifying relaxation from his long siege of hard night work."[44]

Bliss wasted no time in using his new leverage. On January 25, 1871, Orion wrote to Sam conveying his employer's request that he give up writing for the *Galaxy* and instead contribute to the *American Publisher.* Bliss offered to pay him five thousand dollars a year (three thousand dollars more than the *Galaxy*) if he would write "exclusively for this paper, if you will give him all your books, which he thinks you ought to do."[45] A few weeks later Sam received another letter from Orion appealing for a contribution. His employer, he said, "is decidedly worked up about it. He says, put yourself in our place. A new enterprise, in which 'Twain' was to be a feature, and so widely advertised." Orion got in a thrust of his own. Throwing back at his younger brother an image he had used earlier ("you are naturally given to knocking your pot over"), Orion asked, "Are you going to kick the pail over?" From that point on, the letter was not so much Orion speaking for Bliss as pleading on his own behalf:

Think of yourself as writing for no periodical except the Publisher. "Have you seen Twain's last?" says one. "It's in the Publisher." He goes and buys it because there is no other chance to get it. It gives us prestige. Look how it helps me. I should be an editor with something to edit. This "Publisher" may as well be built up into something large as not. With a great circulation, giving only once a month a taste of "Twain," to whet people's appetites for books, it acts as an advertisement. . . . Under these circumstances, with your pen withdrawn from the Galaxy, and held aloof from small books, and confined to the larger and more elevated description worthy of your mettle, and writing only for us, who publish a paper as a branch of your publisher's enterprise, you would not be writing too much nor too little, but just exactly enough. Squarely, we must have something from you or we run the risk of going to the dickens. Bliss says he will pay you, but we must have something every number.[46]

Olivia Clemens had fallen gravely ill with typhoid fever, and Sam had been busy nursing her. This hardship was compounded by the recurrent illness of three-month-old Langdon Clemens, who had been born prematurely on November 7, 1870.[47] Orion pointed out that he was not unmindful of "the shadow of a gigantic and irreparable sorrow" that hung over his brother. "I could not have found it in my heart to insist now on the imposition of the least labor upon you if it had not been for the very serious moment the matter is to us."[48]

This is an Orion Clemens we have not seen before, and probably Sam hadn't either. It was no disgrace to fall from a position of worldly power so long as one preserved one's "beautiful spirit," as Olivia called it, but to wheedle, to implore—that was not worthy of Orion. "Look how it helps me" sounded a little like: "You got me into this, now it is your duty to help me make the most of it."

Though Sam had pledged to "try to give him a chapter from the *new* book every month or nearly every month," he balked. "Now why do you and Bliss go on urging me to make promises? I will not keep them. I have suffered damnation itself in the trammels of periodical writing and I will *not* appear once a month nor once in *three* months, in the Publisher nor any other periodical. . . . You talk as if I am *responsible* for your newspaper venture. If I am I want it to stop right here—for I am not going to have another year of harassment about periodical writing."[49]

Meanwhile, in Hartford, Orion and Bliss had gotten off to a bad start. Orion found it difficult to write when his employer was in the office, "where he can holler at me to go after a proof or do something about the paper." But when the new editor "spent time walking to think in the fresh air" or worked at home after meals polishing rough drafts he had written while Bliss was away, the publisher became upset, "for he thinks I aint doing any thing, and instead of hiring a girl to write on wrappers [address mailers] has put me at it." Orion hesitated to complain to Bliss about these "girlish duties," however, for fear that if the publisher granted him "time to think" and he failed to produce something valuable, "he would consider that I had merely made a shirking excuse and was humbugging him."[50]

Obviously this was not the "easy and gentlemanly work" Sam had promised, and Orion was tempted to throw in the towel. "I'll work along here the best I can till I get my machine out," he penned, "and then I shall hope for better things." After he had written that he crossed it out—but not so heavily that Sam couldn't read it.[51]

The main thing Orion was trying to write was a children's story embodying a character he had introduced in the first issue of the *American Publisher*.[52] In a long introductory sketch (pronounced by Sam to be "tip-top"), he spoke of a genie who promised to "girdle the earth in thirty minutes; traverse either pole; dive to the centre of the globe; walk under the ocean; fly above the clouds; or make excursions into genii land or fairy land" to gather materials for "the children's department of this paper."[53] It was this omnipotent genie (along with other fantastic creatures, such as a grotesque fisherman, Mother Goose and her gander, the man in the moon, and an armed giant) that Orion was trying to work into a long, multichapter tale to run in sequential issues. But when he showed a draft to his employer, his fears were realized, for Bliss dismissed it, said he could get plenty of people to write better for children, and insisted that Orion confine himself to clerical tasks.[54]

Wounded, his confidence shaken, Orion sent the story to Sam, telling him Mollie thought it good and suitable for children. "If you think with Mollie please send it right back for the children's department of the Publisher. . . . If you think that with the alterations noted it will do for some paper or magazine please send it—and if you don't like it at all throw it in the fire."[55]

Replying that his opinion of a children's article was valueless ("for I never saw one that I thought was worth the ink it was written with"), Sam proceeded to give it nevertheless:

You mount a high horse and a dismally artificial one, and go frothing in a way that nobody can understand or sympathize with. Your heart and soul are not in this article. Then you certainly can't get anybody else's into it. . . .

Now that is only my opinion—Mollie's is on the other side and is really worth more than mine, since I have no love for children's literature. . . .

But lay this away (never destroy MS.) for 3 months and then read it and see if you can't better it.

He also allowed that Orion's experiences in Bliss's office would, at any other time, distress him greatly, "but I am and have been for weeks so buried under beetling Alps of trouble that yours look like little passing discomforts to me—molehills."[56]

Despite all his grousing, Twain finally sent an offering to the *American Publisher,* an excerpt from the western book, but when he transmitted another selection, Orion wrote back to point out it resembled a published story by another of Bliss's authors. "Do not put it in the paper, *at all,*" Twain responded. "I cannot alter it—too much trouble."[57]

But Bliss had yet to be heard from. "Your brother says he wrote you Knox[58] had written up something similar to the Bull story—I never saw it and do not know anything about it. Yours struck me *as a good thing, every way.*"[59] Clearly he felt Orion had spoken out of turn, and he made a veiled threat to close down the *Publisher* "rather than to have any dissatisfaction on its account arise."[60]

Twain was stymied by these letters. "Yours stopped my pen for two days," he wrote to Orion, "Bliss's stopped it for three. Hereafter my wife will read my Hartford letters and if they are of the same nature, keep them out of my hands. The idea of a newspaper editor and a publisher plying with dismal letters a man who is under contract to write *humorous* books for them!"[61]

14
Orion and *The Gilded Age*

~

Their happiness was complete. This cosy little house, built entirely of glass and commanding a marvelous prospect in every direction, was a magician's throne to them and their enjoyment of the place was simply boundless.

Mark Twain, *The Gilded Age*

In June 1871 Mark Twain paid a visit to Hartford, where he delivered a section of manuscript to Bliss, continued to work on the western book, and spent time with Orion and Mollie, who were living at 149 Asylum Street.[1] Orion, as his job allowed, continued to work on his inventions. One of them was a paddle boat, apparently employing a wheel and a chain mechanism, that was intended to cross the Atlantic in twenty-four hours.[2] Sam told his brother he found this contrivance "marvelously ingenious," but it was Orion's "Anti-Sun-Stroke hat" that particularly impressed him. "It is possible, useful, and worth a thousand wheels," he wrote. "It would have an enormous sale. Go at it at once. Mind, the hat must not *weigh* perceptibly more than it does now."[3]

After he returned to Elmira (where he had moved Livy and Langdon in March, putting the Buffalo house and his interest in the *Express* on the market), he promised Jane Clemens he would "help Orion with any machine he wants help on."[4] Later he informed Orion and Mollie that he was sending Bliss three original articles for the *American Publisher,* charging him $125. That amount, he said, was to be paid not to him but to Orion, in weekly installments of one-tenth each until it was exhausted, although "Orion can also draw small amounts from time to time as requirements demand."[5]

When Orion tried to do that, however, he and Bliss found themselves at an embarrassing impasse, for Sam had privately instructed Bliss not to go over the limit of one-tenth at a time, "otherwise he will do no sort of good with it."[6] Bliss could see, when Orion showed him Sam's letter, that the author had issued conflicting charges, and he wrote to Sam for clarification. Using some fancy footwork, Twain told his publisher he had authorized Orion to borrow small amounts from his account "outside the pay for those 3 articles. So it is all right."[7]

Although Sam praised Orion's brainchildren to him, to his sister and mother he expressed reservations about the marine invention, saying he wanted to see "the machine working in the water" before he formed a definite opinion. When he learned Jane Clemens had passed these doubts on to her elder son, he was, not surprisingly, upset. "Ma has been making mischief, I fear," he wrote Orion, "and without good grounds." He would not presume to offer an opinion, he said, on a matter another man had "put all his mind and heart on for four years and I had only looked into for 2 hours. . . . I may have conjectured considerable to Pamela [who had been visiting him and Livy in Elmira]—I don't remember, now—but my main idea was that I was not competent or worthy to express an *opinion,* at all."[8] Orion replied that Jane Clemens's letter, although it had caused him "a day's sky-colored absent-mindedness," had done no permanent harm. "I considered that your opportunities for judging of the concern were not so good as mine, and went ahead."[9]

It was probably about this time that Mark Twain began writing about his Sandwich Islands trip in the western book. Although he originally intended to include "4 or 5 chapters about the Islands," in the end he put in no fewer then fifteen.[10] By contrast, the year that led up to that four-month sojourn, the one commencing with his return to San Francisco from the mining camps, was dispensed with in a single paragraph. "The vagabond instinct was strong upon me," it read in part. "Fortune favored and I got a new berth and a delightful one. It was to go down to the Sandwich Islands and write some letters for the Sacramento *Union.*"[11] His struggle with his call to literature, his futile appeal to his brother, Orion's vetoing the sale of the Tennessee land, Sam's near suicide—in other words, all the events that made that year one of the most critical of his life—received not a word of mention.

Most Mark Twain scholars would probably agree that the Sandwich Islands chapters are "padding" added to *Roughing It* to stretch it to the six hundred pages called for in the contract, but really having little to do with a book devoted mainly to Nevada and California. Had the author wanted to, he no doubt could have instead filled those pages with more truly relevant material from that missing year in San Francisco. It is understandable, of course, that he had no stomach for reliving such trials. What is harder to accept is Mark Twain's failure to acknowledge Orion's resounding impact on him, particularly as evidenced by the events of late 1865 and early 1866.

The July 1871 issue of the *American Publisher* contained Orion's announcement of "A NEW BOOK BY MARK TWAIN." "It is a lively account of travel and a stirring recital of adventures in the Far west," it read. "He was miner and reporter, and had some experiences, which, though sober reality, will tax credulity."[12] On the same page, in the Children's Department, appeared a one-column piece headed by an engraving of a barefoot black boy seated in the driver's seat of a wagon and holding the reins. It was titled "JIM": "'You's done been sole, honey, an' I's gwine to tuk you to yer new mas'r. Yer needn't ter cry, coz he's a good mas'r, an' taint fur away, an' I'se comin' to see you ev'ry Sunday.'"

The story continued:

> It was in the days of slavery, in Missouri, and little colored Jim, six years old, was being taken by his mother to his new home. Jim did not want to leave his mother and felt very homesick when she put him down from his seat behind her on the old raw-boned horse, but that could not be helped, and had to be endured.
>
> "Say, mas'r Ben, won't you larn me to read?" Jim one day asked his master's son, who was about eight years old.

By dint of pluck, determination, and native intelligence, Jim masters the skill, and his owner lets him read as much as he pleases. When Jim is driving a carriage some "bad boys, white and black," cause the horse to rear, and Jim is thrown out and breaks a leg so badly it has to be amputated. "When he got well, he did not go about grieving and moping because he had met with such a loss, but he made himself happy with the chances he had."

When the war comes, a Union officer who has escaped from prison takes shelter in the stable. Jim feeds and befriends him and eventually leads him back through the lines to the Union army. "He did it because he loved freedom." Jim obtains an education, and, the writer observes, "who knows but some day he may run for Congress, although he is now studying for the ministry." The story concludes with a moral: "Jim's example, though not perfect in all respects, should shame into better conduct many boys with abundant advantages of school. It shows what even a poor, despised negro can do with energy and perseverance."[13]

It was Orion's sketch, and it may have owed something to the *New York Weekly* piece. He proudly wrote to tell Sam about it.[14] His brother, in turn, must have read it with special interest, for somewhere in that fertile imagination a seed was apparently planted, a germ that over the next few years would take root and grow. Its first budding would be in *Tom Sawyer,* wherein a slave child named Jim makes a walk-on appearance, but its full fruition would come in another tale about an adult slave named Jim, a story that also had a Missouri setting and used local dialect. Like Orion's little piece, it would relate Jim's separation from his family, his love of freedom, his intelligence, and his heroism. In its final form that story was to be published under the title *Adventures of Huckleberry Finn,* but it seems that in its humble beginnings it was called simply "JIM." No one but Mark Twain could have created that great American classic, yet its antecedent appears to have been a negligible but poignant sketch by the author's unsuccessful brother.

When Sam made another trip to Hartford in August to put his book to press, he spent a good deal of time at Orion and Mollie's new boarding-house at 54 College Street; he may even have temporarily lodged there with his mother and niece, who were visiting.[15] Sam was surprised to see "how hale and hearty" Jane Clemens "is getting."[16] He wrote to Livy that she had bought a new silk dress "to swell around in" and that Annie Moffett was "a very attractive and interesting girl."[17]

Turning to his brother, whom Livy had no doubt met in Buffalo when he was en route to Hartford, Sam wrote, "Orion is as queer and heedless a bird as ever." He told of how his brother, mistaking a young lady he met in the hall for the landlady's daughter ("the resemblance being equal to that between a cameleopard and a kangaroo"), had startled her by shouting heartily, "Hello, you're back early!" and how he had made "an ass of himself again" by insisting on escorting another lady home from the boarding-house, realizing only when she led him to an unfamiliar residence that she was not who he thought she was.[18]

If Sam ridiculed Orion to Olivia, to his face he treated him with respect. As we have seen, he encouraged him in his inventions and took them seriously, even if he did have reservations. In September he suggested to him: "The biggest thing in the world is to invent a *steam* railroad break [brake] that the *engineer* can apply throughout his train without needing breakmen. . . . Can you contrive it?"[19] It may have been in unconscious emulation of his brother that Sam brought to fruition an invention of his own—"an improved vest strap"—that he had been thinking about for "four or five years." As he lay in bed in Hartford, "an *elastic* strap suggested itself and I got up satisfied." After breakfast, he took the scheme to Orion, and as the brothers discussed it a new application occurred to Sam.[20] Later he asked Orion's advice about refinements, and his brother obliged and even set his "model maker" to work on a hinge for the device.[21]

In the fall of 1871, Sam, Olivia, and little Langdon moved to Hartford. They had decided to make a new start, and the Connecticut city seemed a natural location. It was headquarters for Twain's publisher; it was the home of Joseph Twichell, who was rapidly becoming Sam's closest friend; Olivia knew and liked several of the residents; it offered a "congenial literary and social atmosphere," as Paine put it—and Orion Clemens and his wife lived there.[22]

Sam and Olivia moved into the large, many-gabled Victorian Gothic house, surrounded by spacious, wooded grounds, that they had rented from John Hooker.[23] Within two weeks Mark Twain set out on a lecture tour that took him through the East, New England, and the Midwest.[24] At Christmas he was in the last-named region, and Olivia, at his direction, sent to Orion and Mollie "our fraternal love, and our loving wishes for your Christmas and future happiness"—and some money with which to buy themselves gifts. She added that she and Sam hoped "we may spend many happy years in Hartford together" and stated that "if Mr Clemens was here we would spend this Christmas together."[25]

In working on illustrations for *Roughing It,* Orion noticed that Bliss had borrowed some engravings from other books rather than have originals made, and also that he seemed to overstate their costs. Later he became suspicious of his employer's accounting in regard to the quantity and quality of paper used in the book's manufacture and the number of copies bound. He was also concerned about the "country newspaper style of printing the cuts" and the quality of binding.[26] When he came to the conclusion that

Bliss was committing types of fraud, he was faced with a difficult choice. Should he confront his employer and risk losing his job, or should he take the easy course and keep quiet? A brief piece he wrote for the October 1871 *American Publisher* may have reflected his dilemma. Titled "MORAL COURAGE," it asserted (apropos of nothing in particular): "Moral courage is a child of thought. Many a man is a moral coward, not because the natural courage is not in him, but because he does not take the trouble to think. Your mental vision must forecast the place you should put your mental foot, or you will be afraid. . . . You may lean on other people and ask their advice, but they can only aid you a few steps."[27]

As soon as publication of *Roughing It* was formally declared, Orion accused Bliss of dishonesty in its manufacture. The unsurprising result was that he and the American Publishing Company parted ways.[28] Whether Orion was fired or resigned is not on record, but the important point is that he precipitated a crisis knowing full well what the consequences were likely to be. If he asked anyone's advice before bringing the situation to a head it was not his brother, for when he conveyed his charges to Sam, the latter wrote back condemning "your assault upon Bliss" as an "indefensible" act, even while acknowledging "the brotherly goodness and kindness of your motive."[29]

No doubt Sam was exasperated. He had put his reputation on the line when he told Bliss, "I guess that after you have had [Orion] a year you will find that he is really worth a deal of money to you"—and even offered to bet on it. More than a year had passed, and now, rather than fulfilling that prophecy, Orion was causing Bliss trouble. On the other hand, this was the Orion of old, the heroic big brother putting principle before self-interest. At some level Sam must have been heartened by that, especially after watching Orion become something of a cat's-paw for Bliss and even stoop to badgering Sam on his own behalf.

Perhaps Sam's denunciation was a test; maybe he wanted to see if Orion's restoration was complete. Surely he realized it was his own position—that a properly loyal employee winks at the boss's infractions—that was morally "indefensible," not Orion's. Sam's getting Orion a job with Bliss had been a generous, brotherly act, comparable to Orion's efforts to secure *him* a position on the *Territorial Enterprise*—but at the same time it was something like throwing him into the lion's den. It was one thing to refuse to cheat the honorable Jervis Langdon on a land deal from a remove of many miles; it was an entirely different matter to comport oneself with honor and dignity in the offices of the freewheeling and forceful Yankee businessman Elisha Bliss.

Sam counseled his brother simply to "forget it. There is no profit in remembering unpleasant things. Remember only that it has wrought one good: It has set you free from a humiliating servitude; a thing to be devoutly thankful for, God knows." In closing, he seemed to wash his hands of the whole affair: "Being now free of all annoyance or regret in this matter, I hasten to say so."[30]

One of the reasons Sam was able to remain calm in the face of Bliss's skullduggery was that it couldn't affect his income from *Roughing It*, for that had been indexed to the retail, or subscription, price of the book, not the profit or loss of the publisher. On the other hand, he had agreed to a 7.5 percent royalty instead of a higher one (a competing publisher had offered 10) because Bliss had convinced him the figure represented "half the profits."[31] The more Sam thought about it, the more agitated he became. If Bliss was juggling figures about small matters, what was to have prevented him from doing so about larger ones?

Less than a week after advising Orion to forget the matter, Sam himself went to Bliss's house and confronted him. The publisher denied any wrongdoing, and he took pains to show his author "by facts and figures and arguments" that the contracted royalty gave him that talismanic half of the profits.[32] Sam later claimed he left that meeting convinced, but if so, he didn't remain so for long, for he soon consulted a lawyer. Charles E. Perkins, "an old personal friend and the best lawyer in Hartford," advised him that, because Bliss's assertion was oral and not part of a written understanding, his case was weak. As Clemens recalled the conference in 1875, "he advised me to leave the law alone—and charged me $250 for it."[33]

Putting Orion and Mollie in charge of the Hooker house, Sam took Livy to her mother's home in Elmira, where on March 19, 1872, his wife gave birth to daughter Olivia Susan (called Susy).[34] But even the birth of a healthy child couldn't take his mind off the *Roughing It* contract, and the following day he wrote to his publisher asking him to alter it "in such a way that it shall express that I am to receive half the profits."[35] Bliss evidently declined to do that. Despite his lawyer's initial advice, Clemens then decided to sue.[36] In May he wrote to Orion from Elmira: "Ask Chas. Perkins if he wants you to give him points in my lawsuit. But give none otherwise."[37]

Sam's letter surprised Orion. "I don't know how to approach Perkins," he replied. "I didn't know you had commenced a law suit. My plan did not contemplate a law suit by you. I suppose it is a suit for damages. I did not think there was any chance for enough to be made that way to justify such a proceeding." Assuming that Sam wanted to be released from his contracts, Orion went on to detail his scheme. If Bliss sought an injunction to stop Sam from publishing with another house, Sam should use "the fraud you can prove concer[n]ing the printing of Roughing It" to scare him off. As a subscription publisher (that is, one who sold directly to customers rather than through bookstores, which the more respectable trade publishers did), Bliss was particularly vulnerable to this stratagem.

> Bliss can see then that there is only needed to be added the testimony of some prominent engravers, book binders, and book publishers in the trade, at Boston and New York, to overwhelm with devastating ruin the subscription business and the American Publishing Company in particular—besides inevitably beating them if they should sue[,] your case would be one of the "causes celebre." . . . This indirect quiet threat would be so terrible that he would never bring a suit against you if you simply went quietly along and wrote your next book which you have contracted with him to publish, and put it into the hands of somebody else.[38]

Nor did Orion stop there. On a separate scrap of paper he wrote: "If you will let me open a law office here, and put me on a salary of ($100 a month same as Bliss's) $1200 a year for two or three years, I will study all the points of your case with such zeal, and watch your witnesses so closely, and so take advantages when opportunity occurs, that I would insure you the full enjoyment of your rightful profits of the next book."[39]

Sam didn't follow Orion's scheme. While it wasn't exactly the "dishonest act" that he had told Bliss there wasn't enough money in America to make Orion commit, it wasn't what he expected from his brother either. In fact, it must have smelled suspiciously like something cooked up by that "scheming, groveling, mud-cat of a **lawyer**" Sam had once accused Orion of want-ing to become. He wasn't particularly interested in parting ways with Bliss anyway. *Innocents Abroad* had been a great financial success in the publisher's hands, and *Roughing It* promised to be the same. In Bliss Sam had found a kindred spirit, one whom he could understand, even if he couldn't entirely trust. Sam's main concern was making sure he got from Bliss what he thought he deserved. To that end, Perkins and an unidentified "expert" called on the publisher and went through his books with him. They satisfied them-selves that 7.5 percent did indeed represent half of his profit, and Perkins persuaded Sam to drop his suit.[40]

Orion's trouble, then, had been for nothing. Instead of separating Sam from Bliss, it had driven him further into the publisher's arms (Sam soon bought five thousand dollars' worth of stock in the American Publishing Company).[41] Meanwhile, Orion had lost not only his job but the moral high ground as well.

In June, Livy and Sam were ready to take baby Susy and eighteen-month-old Langdon home to Hartford. Even though Langdon was very ill, they decided to make the trip, thinking it might do him good, but within days of their arrival he died of what was diagnosed as diphtheria. Apparently Orion and Mollie were still living in the Hooker mansion, and so it seems the brothers were united by yet another family death, the latest in a long string. According to Susy's later account, "After that, mamma became very very ill, so ill that there seemed great danger of death, but with a great deal of good care she recovered."[42]

Sea air was prescribed for Livy and the baby, and in July the grieving parents took Susy to a resort hotel named Fenwick Hall at New Saybrook, Connecticut, on Long Island Sound, about two hours by rail from Hart-ford. As before, the couple left Orion and Mollie in charge of their rented house. Sam and Livy spent a quiet summer at the coast, Sam writing little but planning a trip to England to lecture and to seek protection for *Rough-ing It* from the ravenous English literary pirates.[43]

Meanwhile, Orion made a trip to Vermont, where he investigated a number of newspapers with a view to investing in one and working for it. The money evidently was to come from Sam, for Orion wrote Mollie that "I look upon a purchase of an interest in [the *Rutland Herald*] by Sam in his own name as an investment as sure as bank stock, and as certain as investment can be to bring him his 7 per cent. . . . If I could get a third interest, and a salary of a hundred dollars a month, I could pay Sam his interest, and still have a nice income left."[44]

When he returned to Hartford, Orion kept Sam informed of his ongoing investigations and told him that until something was settled he was going to seek work at a local printer.[45] But Sam had other plans for his brother. He wrote him about a new invention of his, "a *self-pasting scrapbook*," and said, "I'll put it into Dan Slote's hands and tell him he must send you all over America to urge its use upon stationers and booksellers—so don't buy into a newspaper."[46]

In 1906 Twain recalled that he once helped Orion secure a job on a Hartford newspaper. "I made him go to the Hartford *Evening Post*," he wrote, "without any letter of introduction, and propose to scrub and sweep and do all sorts of things for nothing, on the plea that he didn't need money, but only needed work, and that was what he was pining for. Within six weeks he was on the editorial staff of that paper at twenty dollars a week."[47] As apocryphal as that sounds, there is evidence it actually happened, apparently before Sam sailed for England on August 21. On September 25 he wrote to Livy from London, "Let Orion . . . publish the enclosed," suggesting that his brother was in an editorial position of some sort, and on October 3 he told Livy that "it is indeed pleasant to learn that Orion is happy and progressing. Now if he can only *keep* the place and continue to give satisfaction, all the better. It is no trouble for a man to get any situation he wants—by working at first for nothing—but of course to hold it firmly against all comers—after wages begin—is the trick."[48]

If Twain's recollection was correct, it raises questions. Why did he "make" Orion apply for a job in such a humbling manner? Why didn't he write him a letter of introduction as he had to the *St. Louis Missouri Republican*? With his extensive newspaper connections he must have known people at the *Evening Post*, at least by name, and they surely would have recognized his. Perhaps he wanted to punish his brother for failing what might be called "the Bliss test."

In any case, the stratagem seems to have worked, and Orion was now gainfully employed. He and Mollie probably moved out of the Hooker mansion when Livy and Susy returned to Hartford in September. They may then have gone to live at 55 Sigourney Street, and they were evidently well enough off to furnish their quarters rather sumptuously, for Sam would later speak of the "high-toned" furniture his brother and sister-in-law owned in Hartford.[49]

Sam, homesick for Olivia and Susy, returned from England in November, and on December 20 Olivia reported to Jane and Pamela that "we took dinner last night with Orion and Mollie and had an exceedingly pleasant time. They are very cozily situated—Yesterday was the anniversary of their wedding." To which Sam added, "Orion is as happy as a martyr when the fire won't burn."[50] Perhaps it was at this get-together that Orion told Sam he had been offered another job, possibly by one of the New England papers he had been looking into. In 1906 Twain recalled that "he was presently called for by some other paper at better wages, but I made him go to the *Post* people and tell them about it. They stood the raise and kept him. It was the pleasantest berth he had ever had in his life. It was an easy berth. He was in every way comfortable."[51]

At another dinner party, probably the same month, Sam and his friend Charles Dudley Warner decided to write a novel together. According to Paine, "Clemens, in fact, had the beginning of a story in his mind, but had been unwilling to undertake an extended work of fiction alone. He welcomed only too eagerly, therefore, the proposition of joint authorship. . . . Clemens immediately set to work and completed 399 pages of the manuscript, the first eleven chapters of the book, before the early flush of enthusiasm waned."[52] Livy told her mother that "Mr Clemens . . . is perfectly brim full of work, says he never worked with such perfect ease and happiness in his life. . . . It is splendid to see him so heartily love his work, he begrudges every moment[']s interruption."[53]

The Gilded Age is remembered today for giving its name to the post–Civil War era it satirizes and for introducing the colorful character Colonel Sellers, but its beginning chapters are what interest us here. These draw on the early history of the Clemens family. When Jane Clemens visited Orion in Hartford in 1871 Sam may have asked his mother and brother about their life in Tennessee and the family's trek to Missouri. In any case, it was this story he had in mind when he agreed to a collaboration with Warner and that he wrote while he was still in "the early flush of enthusiasm."

To ensure the future prosperity of his family, Squire Hawkins buys seventy-five thousand acres of undeveloped land and promises his children, including his son Washington, that one day it will make them rich beyond their dreams. Although Samuel Clemens was not born until after his parents arrived in Missouri, his counterpart in the story, Clay, shows up while the Hawkinses are still en route to that state; he is adopted by them when he is orphaned. This device allowed the author to make Clay and Washington the same age, ten (Orion's age at the time of the Clemenses' move).

The augmented Hawkins family, along with their two slaves, board a steamboat to continue their journey, and as the vessel wends its way up the Mississippi, the children and the slaves fall under the spell of the passage, which "became a glorious adventure, a royal progress through the very heart and home of romance, a realization of their rosiest wonder-dreams."[54] When the sun goes down and the moon comes up, Washington and Clay wander off together to the hurricane deck "to revel again in their new realm of enchantment." There they run races, climb about the bell, and make the acquaintance of passenger dogs chained under the lifeboat. Rendered brothers by accident, they have discovered they can also be friends. When the pilot notices them and invites them into his aerie, "their happiness was complete. This cosy little house, built entirely of glass and commanding a marvelous prospect in every direction, was a magician's throne to them and their enjoyment of the place was simply boundless."[55]

If this begins to sound vaguely familiar, it is because it evokes a journey two other brothers once made. The trip described in *Roughing It* (which, it will be recalled, began on a river), even though presented more as a burlesque than a romance, was also an adventure, one that likewise led to an important discovery. In the "great swinging and swaying stage" that conveyed the Clemens brothers—that "imposing cradle on wheels"—all differences of age or status seemed to vanish, and they too found companionship ("smoked the pipe of peace") and boundless enjoyment (the "one complete and satisfying happiness in the world").[56]

In the pilothouse, Washington and Clay "sat them down on a high bench and looked miles ahead and saw the wooded capes fold back and reveal the bends beyond; and they looked miles to the rear and saw the silvery highway diminish its breadth by degrees and close itself together in the distance." Compare that passage with one in *Roughing It:* "We stretched our cramped legs full length on the mail sacks [and] gazed out through the windows across the wide wastes of greensward clad in cool, powdery mist, to where there was an expectant look in the eastern horizon."[57] The image of two innocents thrown together by fate and borne by a cozy transport into unknown territory, and in the process discovering their fellowship, seems already to have become a motif for Mark Twain. He would give it its fullest and most famous embodiment four years later.

In *The Gilded Age,* this fraternal idyll is followed immediately and without transition by a deadly race between the boys' steamboat, the *Boreas,* and the *Amaranth,* a larger vessel that approaches from behind: "The Amaranth drew steadily up till her jack-staff breasted the Boreas's wheel-house—climbed along inch by inch till her chimneys breasted it—crept along, further and further till the boats were wheel to wheel—and then they closed up with a heavy jolt and locked together tight and fast in the middle of the big river under the flooding moonlight!"

Their vessels thus joined, the opposing captains fire pistols at each other. They miss, but suddenly the *Amaranth*'s boilers explode, causing fearsome damage and loss of life. Mortally wounded, the *Amaranth*'s head engineer drags himself to his brother, the second engineer, who is unhurt, and declares: "You were on watch. You were boss. You would not listen to me when I begged you to reduce your steam. Take that!—take it to my wife and tell her it comes from me by the hand of my murderer! Take it—and take my curse with it to blister your heart a hundred years—and may you live so long!" Tearing off his wedding ring, he throws it down and falls dead.[58]

So too had the brothers Clemens had a potentially violent contention in the years following the discovery of their camaraderie while traveling to Nevada Territory. To mix Twain's images somewhat, pilot Sam had been on watch, had been boss, when Orion, with his new papers from Washington, began to draw steadily up, to advance inch by inch till the brothers "locked together tight and fast." ("By the Lord God! you must clear the track, you know!") And when lecturer Sam decisively bested Orion, if the loser didn't ever accuse or curse his brother, Sam's never-failing conscience surely did.[59]

Having minimized the role of "my brother, the Secretary," in *Roughing It,* Mark Twain in *The Gilded Age* gave the fictional Washington Hawkins a central part. Perhaps it had not occurred to him in writing the "nonfiction" book that Orion had comedic possibilities, but in this first novel he explored those "queer and heedless" qualities of his brother's personality he had held up to Livy. After Washington has grown up we discover that he is a flighty, gullible, shiftless dreamer. When, in chapter 6, his father asks him if he has finished his invention for making window glass opaque, he answers: "No, sir, I have given that up. I almost knew I could do it, but it was so tedious and troublesome I quit it." In the same chapter, Squire Hawkins urges his successful and responsible son to "keep yourself informed of poor Washington's condition and movements, and help him along all you can, Clay." In chapter 8, Washington is dominated and bedazzled by the silver-tongued Colonel Sellers, with his references to "we old veterans of commerce" and "a man who has been all his life accustomed to large operations."

15
Sam "Banishes" Orion

I hope the change is going to be a change to prosperity and contentment—for you *are* aging and it is high time to give over dreaming and
buckle down to the simplicities *and* the realities of life.

Sam to Orion

When Orion assumed his editorial responsibilities at the *Post* he took
them seriously, and others viewed his efforts in the same vein. He began
preserving his articles in a scrapbook, the first time he seems to have done
so in five years.[1] When he sent a copy of the newspaper to Schuyler Colfax,
vice-president under Ulysses S. Grant, Colfax called his pieces "very striking in their illustrations and cogent and unanswerable in their arguments."[2]

From Vermont the previous summer Orion had reported to Mollie that
"the Rutland Independent man wants to start a daily, and wants an editor;
but I am afraid the Daily would die at the end of the presidential campaign."[3] Now two Vermonters, John Baxter ("a big, rough fellow") and
Henry Clark ("a high, thin nose, wore a white necktie, and looked like a
preacher"), came down to Hartford and met with Orion at the Allyn House,
Hartford's best hotel. It seems that "a stock company of well-to-do politi-
cians"—dissident Republicans who were unhappy with President Grant—
planned to absorb the *Independent* and Rutland's Democratic paper, the
Courier, into a new daily to be called the *Globe.* They wanted Orion for
editor, and they recommended Clark for his associate.[4]

By Twain's recollection Orion was offered three thousand dollars a year,
and "he was eager to accept. His wife was equally eager—no, twice as eager,
three times as eager." But Sam opposed the move. "I said: 'You are as weak
as water. Those people will find it out right away. They will easily see that
you have no backbone; that they can deal with you as they would deal with

a slave. You may last six months, but no longer. Then they will not dismiss you as they would dismiss a gentleman: they will fling you out as they would fling out an intruding tramp.'"[5]

It is doubtful Sam used such insulting language to his brother's face, but the vehemence with which he recalled the incident more than thirty years after the fact testifies to the bitterness of his disappointment. In 1874 Orion recalled that "you were willing to buy for us a place near Hartford to cost . . . four thousand dollars," saying that "I gave weight to that when I left to go to Rutland; but not enough."[6] Whether Sam made the offer before or after the Vermont Republicans approached his brother is not known, but clearly he wanted Orion to remain in Hartford. (Twain was wrong about Mollie, incidentally; she *didn't* want to go to Rutland. Orion would remind her in November that "I left both St. Louis and Hartford against your protests.")[7]

Despite his wife's and his brother's opposition, Orion was determined to accept the bid. For one thing, the salary must have seemed astronomical, since a few months earlier he had spoken of getting by comfortably on less than half that amount. The prestige and independence of being in charge must have been another powerful incentive. The fact that he had secured the offer by his own devices must have also appealed to him. And finally, he may not have been quite as "cosily situated" in Hartford as Sam and Livy thought, for seven years later he would recall that "I lost interest in Hartford" and speak of his "indigo hued emotions fatally poisonous to my usefulness [there]."[8] The last clipping Orion added to the scrapbook was dated March 21, 1873, and on the eighteenth of the following month the *Hartford Courant* informed its readers that "Mr. Clemens, brother of 'Mark Twain,' who has been editorially connected with the *Evening Post* of this city for some time past, is about to take the editorial direction of a new daily to be established in Rutland, Vt."[9]

Around the latter part of April 1873, Orion moved to Rutland and took lodging at the Bardwell House (Mollie seems to have joined him later).[10] The first issue of the *Rutland Daily Globe* appeared on May 1. During its initial week of publication the journal set forth its editorial position in no uncertain terms:

Of course a paper ought to be independent. . . . Party hacks, slaves of avarice, fawning sycophants, may crawl where men should walk, but let us be spared any attempts to exalt abasement into a virtue. . . .

When the Globe hears the evidence and gets ready to express an opinion it will not be afraid to speak if that opinion should be adverse to the management of the Vermont Central [Railroad].[11]

Like all pieces in the *Globe,* this one was unsigned, but Orion almost surely wrote it. Evidently, the railroad interests were powers to be reckoned with in Vermont politics (as they were elsewhere), and Orion was fully prepared to take them on. "I like Orion's editorials," responded Sam when his brother sent him some samples. "I like their gentlemanly dignity and refinement as much as their other virtues."[12] Whatever pieces he may have seen, the one quoted above doesn't seem to have been among them, for "gentlemanly dignity and refinement" hardly describes it. Orion had come out swinging.

A week later "Treatment of Indians" ran in the paper, and it must have been written by the former acting superintendent of Indian Affairs in Nevada Territory. "We may yet learn to treat all men as brethren," the piece read, "and seek sincerely to elevate the lowest. We made a very good commencement with the negroes, after pocketing their earnings for two centuries. . . . It is time now to treat the Indians more as we would like to be treated by them."[13]

By July the Globe's competitor in Rutland, the (loyal) Republican *Daily Herald,* was taking on the upstart. "We are sorry to speak disparagingly of our cotemporary," it asserted, "whose inception—heralded with much shouting and high-sounding words—promised so much toward the enlightenment of our people and the welfare of the community." The editorial went on to attack the *Globe's* founders as "soreheads and Greeley candidates, who in a time of emergency had deserted their party and principles." It spoke of the paper's inclination "to frequently lose its temper and reason, and to break out with phrases and sentences replete with naughty words and petty spite" and asserted cuttingly that "something [is] the matter with its brains—probably owing to the immense fall it had from the pedestal it stood on, according to its own assertions, at its beginning, to its present position."[14]

The *Globe* lost little time in responding. "The editor of the Herald . . . knows he is not fooling anybody," it declared, "but if he can get a dollar and a half worth of printing and a free ride occasionally, he would sell out every principle he had in the world, and throw in his shirt." It went on to belittle the Vermont press and to single out orthodox Republican papers as "the most unmanly, the most sneaking, the most cowardly, the most pusillanimous, the weakest and poorest of the lot. . . . If the people of Vermont do not declare independence from the slavery under which they now groan, they will have occasion to reflect."[15]

Gone was the "gentlemanly dignity and refinement" of the editorials Sam had seen; a red-hot newspaper war was in progress. "We would here say we are afraid the 'Globule' has attacked too many persons," returned the *Herald*.[16] A week later it spoke of "a bitter, personal, mean, malicious, silly piece of composition as originated from 'The Globule' office Saturday" as deserving a special rebuke. That piece has not been found, but it must have been incendiary, for the *Herald* went on, "We would kindly caution 'The Globule' against the use of any such language in the future."[17]

That piece ran on July 14, some ten weeks after the *Globe* began publishing. One week later the *Herald* announced, "The New York *Herald* says: 'Mark Twain's brother, Orion Clemens, has retired from the Rutland *Globe*.'"[18] Orion had indeed left the *Globe,* and on the day the *Rutland Herald*'s piece ran he wrote a letter from Oil City, Pennsylvania, to Mollie, in Fredonia, New York, telling her of his efforts to find newspaper work there.[19] Oil City is about one hundred miles south-southwest of Fredonia; Orion seems to have taken his wife to stay with Jane and Pamela before proceeding on there. He and Mollie must have departed Rutland in something of a hurry, for they left some of their "traps" (clothing, personal belongings, etc.) behind.[20] Later Mollie told her husband, "I am going to be mum hereafter and not tell folks how we have roamed, it dont look well and it dont feel good."[21]

What had happened? Had the owners of the *Globe* discovered their editor in chief "had no backbone" as Sam had predicted they would, and ejected him "as they would fling out an intruding tramp"? Despite his assertion in the *Autobiography* that "it happened just so," it seems unlikely. The bare-knuckles tone of the *Globe*'s attacks on the *Herald* hardly reflects cowardice. Indeed, the heat of the exchange between the rival papers hints that Orion may have gotten into the same sort of trouble that caused Sam to leave Nevada with similar alacrity in 1864. In October Orion would confess to Mollie (in a different context) that "my impatience of rebuke manifested against my father's reprimands and ever since against any who found fault, has doubtless been a great source of trouble to me."[22] Later he would write Sam of "the cloudy obscurity" that "was beginning to draw over my mind" and that "drove me from Rutland."[23]

Having gone to Vermont against the advice of both his brother and his wife, Orion must have been determined to make a success of his new job, but his truculent attitude and intemperate words seem not to have gone down well with the locals. Whether he narrowly escaped a duel or offended his employers is unknown, but he seems to have gotten into hot water on account of "my impatience of rebuke"—and that, interestingly, he traced to John Marshall Clemens. Orion seemed to be acting under a need to strike out at authority. In this case it was the Republican establishment, but probably any convenient symbol of influence and control would have done as well.

To further complicate matters, in 1882 Orion wrote Sam, "I should have given [heeded?] more fully your advice to me about editing a newspaper, such as never to sell a line of editorial for a railroad pass, or to an advertiser, or for any purpose."[24] During his editorship the *Globe* ran a puff for "Dixon's Pencils" ("equal to any, if not superior, to any [of] foreign manufacture") that truly sounded as if it had been "sold."[25] How such a breach of editorial integrity might have contributed to Orion's departure is, however, unclear. (The *Rutland Daily Globe,* incidentally, continued to publish for several years after Orion's departure.)

When Orion moved to Rutland, Samuel and Olivia were preparing to depart for Europe. Before they left they arranged for a fabulous mansion to be built.[26] A year after its publication, *Roughing It* was a splendid success, having sold more than ninety-three thousand copies and earned Sam royalties of more than twenty-three thousand dollars.[27] In March he wrote to "Friend Bliss" that he not only wanted to buy more stock in the American Publishing Company, he wanted to become a member of its board of directors.[28] He, Livy, and Susy sailed for England on May 17, 1873.[29]

Orion had no success in Oil City, and he seems to have returned to Fredonia. From a subsequent reference he made to that community ("a pretty place to stay a day or two in; but as a residence . . . dreary and exasperatingly dull") he seems to have spent some time there, and if so, it is likely he at least tried to find work at the local newspaper.[30] By October 15,

1873, we find him in New York City, responding to a letter from Mollie.

> My Poor dear, unhappy, suffering wife, I do deeply feel for you and
> sincerely and heartily sympathise with you. But do not be distressed.
> Have confidence in me. I will find something to do. I took a commu-
> nication to the Tribune to-night. I have paid my bills up to to-night,
> including washing, and have twenty dollars, two cents, 4 postage
> stamps and four envelops left. So you need not think of sending me
> money. I have plenty to last me two weeks, feel in tip-top condition,
> and fully expect to get into business before the end of that time. At
> the earliest possible moment I will have you come.[31]

"My Darling Sweetheart," Mollie replied, "I am just ready to cry for joy
at receiving *a letter*. No matter if you have not got work—only do write. . . .
Just feel my arms about your neck and my lips to yours in a good loving
embrace." She assured him that "really and truly and way down in my
heart" she did have confidence in him. She was tired of boarding, she said,
but she wanted to be sure they had a permanent place to live before coming
to join him. She had run across his Bible the day before, and she wondered
if he had purposely left it behind. "I sincerely hope and do try to pray with
my whole heart and soul that you are settled in the true religious faith."[32]

Orion picked up the pace of his letter writing, getting one off nearly
every day. Unfortunately, printing work seems to have been as rare in New
York in 1873 as it had been when Sam was looking nineteen years earlier.
Orion waxed alternately pessimistic and optimistic; he told Mollie if he
could not find an editorial job he would settle for reading proof or setting
type, even subbing.[33] As to the abandoned Scriptures: "I thought you put a
bible in my trunk till I came to look for it. I bought one at the bible house
for 70 cents."[34] Molly was not propitiated. Their better days, she complained, were "just as far off as the day is, in which you will take Our
Heavenly Father at his word."[35] According to Paine, Orion was doing other
things in the big city besides looking for a job. "He was inventing a flying-
machine, for one thing, writing a Jules Verne story," and even "contemplating the lecture field."[36]

On November 2, Sam, Livy, and Susy arrived back in New York, and
Orion met them. Sitting in their hotel room, he was greatly impressed by
his brother's "towering importance" when the president of the Mercantile

Library Association sent up his card *"four times"* in an effort to secure Mark Twain's services as a lecturer. "This great blaze of international appreciation," Paine observed, "which had come to the little boy who used to set type for him in Hannibal, and wash up the forms and cry over the dirty proof, made him gasp."[37]

When Sam heard Orion's plight he gave him a check for $100. Rather than an outright gift, this seems to have been an installment on the $1,000 from *Roughing It,* which had a remaining balance of $385.[38] Even so, Sam decided there would be no more payments, and Orion wrote to Mollie two days later: "I am sorry Sam has announced his determination to let me have no more money. I do not think I would do so towards him. However, I might, under similar circumstances."[39]

Sam may have been annoyed because Orion declined his recommendation to return to the town where his wife was. "Sam advised me to go to Fredonia to stay," he told Mollie, "but I would not do that. I want to stay here and keep in view my one chance of employment, at a time when opportunities are so scarce."[40] Four days after meeting the returning travelers, Orion informed his wife that he had found temporary work reading proof for the *New York Evening Post.* Sam later wrote that his brother told him the foreman there "swore at him and ordered him around 'like a steamboat mate.'"[41] He also characterized Orion's situation as "slaving night and day in [a] New York newspaper sty."[42]

Intending to return to England shortly, Sam took Olivia and Susy up to Hartford, from where he wrote to his mother that he had meant to make a proposition to Orion in New York but was too rushed to do so. He would therefore make it to her, and "you can tell him." It was this: If Orion would go to live in Fredonia, where "he would be a comfort to your old age," Sam would pay him a pension of fifteen dollars a week, which was as much as Sam thought he could get in New York.

The only copy of this letter that survives is in Mollie Clemens's careful hand and is labeled, "Extract of a letter from S. L. C. to Ma." Sam included a note to the effect that Orion might read it ("It has no harsh thought in it, but is kindly meant, as from brother to brother"), and evidently Jane Clemens let her daughter-in-law copy the relevant parts and send them to Orion.[43]

Six days after he arrived in New York, Sam departed again for England to continue his lecture series and to protect his copyright, this time leaving his family behind in Hartford.[44] Whether he had an opportunity before sailing to discuss his proposal with Orion is not known, but if so, Orion must have reiterated his determination to remain in New York. He was resolved to make a go of his invention, and, if Paine is right, he also seemed to be nursing hopes of finding a career as a writer and lecturer, even though he must have realized he would never equal, or even approach, his brother in those fields.

Living in a tiny garret at 97 Varick Street, Orion continued to work irregular hours at the *Post*, hoping to send for Mollie in January. He informed her that he had "got some new light on my flying machine" and said he was subsisting on one meal a day, "a quart of milk and ten cents worth of graham bread." At first this regimen had made him feel weak going up stairs, he allowed, but now his body seemed to have adjusted.[45] The picture he painted caused alarm in Fredonia. Jane Clemens wrote to him in her neat, steady hand:

My dear son You remember days gone by that Sam took an oath before his mother, that oath saved him. Now my dear son I wish with my whole heart you will take a solemn oath and write it on paper and send it to your mother . . .

This oath is that you will not let a single word come from your mouth nor even one thought come in your mind about an invention of any kind. . . . My dear son when you have made a good liveing a regular income make that over to your wife and you have nothing to do with it. then work on your invention. . . . Now my dear son you and Sam are my own children one is just as near to me as the other. One is just as well fitted for making a living as the other but not alike. Sam gives his whole attion to his book writing and managemen. But the secret with you is Orion you work with your pen but your mind is not on it.[46]

A few days before this was written Orion had told his wife that Jane Clemens "has been a dear, good mother—much better, all my life, than I deserved to have, and it grieves me to think of the unnecessary trouble I have given her."[47] Nevertheless, he now wrote defiantly to Mollie that "I am not going to let you and Ma and Annie bully me out of my flying machine. You seem to have made up your minds that a thing can't be done, and then go at me with the serene confidence of people who have received a revelation from the Almighty."[48]

Livy invited Mollie to spend the holidays in Hartford, and she may also have said something about her sister-in-law staying on there indefinitely, rent-free. While Mollie accepted the short-term invitation, she seems to have taken offense at the other. "I presume you are right," Orion told her, "and that Livy writes you from a sentiment of charity and pity. If you can feel any less beholden at Pamela's stay there. As you pay your board it is at least not charity."[49]

Orion's resolve about his flying device wavered, and on December 30, 1873, he wrote to his mother: "Ma, I have stopped the machine, though it was not the real trouble, as you supposed. I will take your advice, though, as to putting off its further prosecution till I get comfortably provided against pecuniary embarrassment."[50] In addition to proofreading, Orion had found work as a night reporter, and the couple agreed that Mollie would join him in New York.

When Sam returned from England on January 26 he must have been dismayed at meeting his brother and sister-in-law, who were then living at 40 West 9th Street. "God knows yours is hard luck," he wrote to "My Dear Bro" a few days later from Hartford, "and one is bound to respect and honor the way in which you bear up under it and refuse to surrender. I thought you were heedless and listless; that you were content to drift with the tide and never *try* to do anything. I am glad indeed, and greatly relieved to know that this is not so. I grieve over the laying aside of the flying machine," he continued, "as if it were my own broken idol. But still it must be done."[51]

The same day Sam wrote this to Orion, Jane Clemens, in Fredonia, wrote to him: "Sam my dear son you are going to write to Orion. If you are going to give him advice that is good, all right. Kind words will always do good. Orion troubles me very much but I cannot speak a short word to him, at any time. I love to see brothers live and love each other and look over faults." She added: "I am *sorry* for Mollie."[52]

Orion was working on the *Evening Post* mornings and into the early afternoon. He had evidently lost his night job, but he had found a new enthusiasm: writing a book about an unidentified "vast subject." His plan was to stay at the *Post* for "three or six months or a year, if the exploration of the vast subject should necessitate so long a time . . . searching through geology, books of travel, and any other books I could find with facts bearing on my theories."[53]

But Mollie had other ideas. Unhappy in New York, she wanted to move back to Keokuk. Sam, as he apparently had in Hartford, agreed to help his brother and sister-in-law buy some real estate, and Mollie had her eye on a riverfront tract her father owned a mile north of town, "a beautiful place" with six houses on it.[54] "Some can be rented," she wrote to Jane Clemens, "and others exactly do for chickens. The whole property is exactly what we want."[55]

Orion tried to resign himself to returning to Mollie's hometown, and he manfully came up with a plan to work "on the garden and chicken business during the day and refresh my memory in law at night," so that in two or three years he could open a law office in town. "I could not become at this late time of life a distinguished lawyer," he wrote his brother, "but I might made a comfortable living with it."[56]

But in his heart he sensed that such a move would mean crossing a threshold of no return. He was nearly fifty years old. If ever he was to salvage the tattered remnants of his career, it would have to be now, here in New York. Keokuk, he confided to Sam, "would be a sort of gloomy exile for me," while remaining in the city and continuing to work on his book would be "my idea of elysium."[57] Before he threw in the towel he wanted to give his dreams one last chance. In a touching gesture that brings to mind Sam's appeal for help in accepting his call to literature, Orion sent his manuscript to his brother. "Now *you* can judge whether a book continued in the strain I sent you is likely to be a waste of time," he wrote the following day.[58] The wheel of fortune had come full circle, and now it was Orion's turn to look to his brother for help in a career choice. But unlike Sam, who had temporarily resisted a vocation for which he was eminently suited, Orion was grasping at straws.

Did Jane Clemens sense that a move to Keokuk might break her eldest son's heart? To be sure, she had warned him off his machine, but at the same time she had expressed confidence in his ability to make a living—and she didn't counsel him to leave New York. In any case, she seems to have written Sam asking him not to finance the move. We know this only from Mollie's reaction: Exasperated, she scolded her mother-in-law, "I don't know what to write. I am indeed sorry you wrote to Sam not to help us get a place."[59]

It seems that Orion and Sam met and discussed the situation, probably in New York, for on April 27 Orion apologetically wrote his brother that "I talked to you as I did I suppose from sheer habit of gloomy foreboding." He said he had been "ready to decline going" to Keokuk because he feared that once there he would "have to go to St. Louis and go into a printing office," leaving Mollie to run the farm by herself. Obviously what he wanted to hear from Sam was: "Look here, this project of yours shows promise. Ask Mollie to wait. Don't pass up this golden opportunity, but stay in New York and avail yourself of its fine libraries and other facilities to continue your intellectual work." He did not hear those words, or anything like them. Sam may not have received the manuscript (let alone found time to peruse it) by the time the brothers met, but whether he did or not he seems not to have encouraged Orion to continue his project but rather, for the sake of his mental health, to return to the Mississippi Valley. Orion wrote: "It begins to creep into my mind that your desire to rid me of some of my discontents weighs more with you than the consideration of the money needed." Still the elder brother seems to have resisted, and when he left the meeting, "the cloudy obscurity was beginning to draw over my mind that drove me from Rutland, that has neutralized my forces so often, [and] that seems so independent of circumstances."

Under this dark cloud, and unfortified with any encouragement from Sam, he had gone back and talked with his wife. Now he informed Sam that "Mollie has inspired me with her faith and hope" and that he was resolved that "I shall go intending to work faithfully, and believing I shall be more cheerful with out-door employment." It was a pathetic surrender, and it ended: "So, if it please you, we will go to Keokuk." Of the "vast subject" that had so beguiled him he wrote not a word.[60]

Mollie also sent Sam a letter telling him she and Orion wanted to go to Keokuk. In writing to his mother Sam described it and Orion's communications disingenuously: "The spirit of them is . . . we are anxious to go, we are in a frenzy to go, we can't, we don't *want* to live anywhere but on that farm!" Consequently, he told her, he had sent them seven hundred dollars "to get out there and start business with" and another two hundred dollars "to meet the first payment on the purchase with." He confessed that he had also done "a very disagreeable thing . . . but it seemed the wise course." He had advised his brother and sister-in-law to "*be* chicken farmers and not hifalutin fine folks; put on no airs till they earned the wherewithal to do it with; eschew fine clothes; sell their Hartford furniture as being too high-toned for their circumstances; in a word, to banish the American sham of 'keeping up appearances.' . . . In fact I gave them a lot of advice which none but children ought to need, but which THEY richly need."[61]

If he gave that counsel, it is not in the letter written on that date that survives in the Mark Twain Papers. What *is* there is a friendly wish and a mild chastisement: "I hope the change is going to be a change to prosperity and contentment—for you *are* aging and it is high time to give over dreaming and buckle down to the simplicities *and* the realities of life."[62]

That day he drafted yet a third letter, this one to his Boston friend William Dean Howells, editor of the *Atlantic Monthly:*

I am so strongly tempted to afford you and Mrs. Howells a glimpse of my brother's last, (just received), that I can't resist.

You observe that he is afraid the interest might fall in arrears, so he pays it some weeks ahead of time.

You perceive that he is still in some way connected with the infamous Tennessee land which has been our destruction for 40 years (see opening chapters of Gilded Age—my brother is "Lafayette [*sic*] Hawkins.") . . .

P.S. Do not fail to note the hopeful-glad-hearted, school-boy cheeriness which bubbles out of every pore of this man who has been ALWAYS a failure.[63]

There is about this note the conspiratorial air of a man who had previously enlisted his correspondents in the ridicule of his victim. One can only guess at the shock and embarrassment those polite gentlefolk felt the first time Sam mocked his own brother in their presence. Now he seemed compelled ("so strongly tempted . . . I can't resist") to go beyond that breach and foist off on them Orion's private communication—and to rewrite history in the bargain. In 1881 Jane Clemens reminded Sam of an occasion "when you banished your brother [and] I consented."[64] She seemed to be referring to the move to Keokuk. Even taking her opposition to that change into account, "banished" may seem a strong word—until we consider Sam's letters. They show that despite his generosity, his feelings toward Orion were, at the very best, decidedly mixed.

16
Orion's Excommunication

Whereas, Orion Clemens hath been, by sufficient proof, convicted of heresy, and after much admonition and prayer, obstinately refuseth to hear the church, and hath manifested no evidence of repentance; therefore . . . I pronounce him to be excluded from the communion of the church.

> The Reverend Dr. Willis Green Craig, from the pulpit

Orion did not make a success of his chicken farm, and within a year of his arrival in Keokuk he was showing signs of restlessness. He seems to have peppered his brother with legal and literary projects; he made yet another trip to Tennessee; and he looked into several positions, including attorney for a railroad and editorial posts with newspapers in Indianapolis, Louisville, and St. Louis.[1] He asked Sam for help in setting up a law practice in Keokuk—but what he really wanted, he went on without pause to tell his brother, was to return to the *Hartford Post:* "I have waked up enough to work mentally, and take bodily exercise sufficient to keep me from paralysis with the blues. . . . I desire no longer to be judged by what I said and did when I was asleep. I desire to cease to scatter. I want to concentrate. . . . If I were back in Hartford I should keep cheerful, make friends, seek companionship, and concentrate my ambition."[2]

Sam did not encourage his brother to return to the East, but he did continue to send him money. In January 1876 Orion asked for a loan of "five hundred dollars a year for two years, while I try to get into the practice of law."[3] Sam obliged, but by June Orion's practice had brought him only fifteen or twenty dollars.

Preparations were being made to disinter the remains of John Marshall and Henry Clemens from the Baptist cemetery on the north side of Hannibal and to rebury them in the newer Mount Olivet Cemetery south of town.[4] Samuel would pay for the transfer, and John L. Robards would carry it out that summer.[5] The planning, with its inevitable reminders, may have affected Orion. On June 28 he wrote to Sam: "I went yesterday and frankly told our pastor, of whom I think a great deal, my views on religious matters, and asked his advice, telling him I had been bothered about it thirty years."[6]

Although the ostensible reason for this pastoral visit was Orion's religious questioning, his reference to thirty years suggests that recollections of the 1847 autopsy may have lain behind it. In any case, the counseling seems to have done some good. "Thank God!" Orion wrote. "I feel this much better—that I am over the craziness of saddling my misfortunes on my loving, well meaning, innocent and only humanly defective relations, living and dead." Was this a cryptic reference to John Clemens, code for "I've finally forgiven my father his misstep and ended the lunacy of blaming him for my adversities"? "I want," Orion went on, "the balance of my life to be kept too busy for miserable, idle, whimsical, wicked foolishness. I am sure a busy life will bring out my best emotions."[7]

When Orion came home and told Mollie about his meeting, she burst into tears, and when word of his religious doubts reached Jane Clemens, she too became upset.[8] Orion sought to calm her: "It grieves me to see you and Mollie so distressed. . . . Do not suppose that I allude to anything occurring to myself in childhood. The books I had and the influences around me were towards belief in all that is in both the old and new testament. But I am thankful that I have always felt free, whatever I might openly say, to think and read on both sides of any question."[9]

By midsummer 1877, when Jane Clemens came to visit them, Orion and Mollie had left the farm, moved into a rented house in Keokuk, and taken in boarders. Orion's religious struggle raged on. On October 20 he wrote to his minister informing him that after thirteen years as a member of the Presbyterian Church he wanted to resign. He did not share the church's beliefs, he explained, that Christ was the Son of God, that the miraculous events told of in the Bible actually occurred, or that "The First Person in the Trinity satisfied His sense of justice by sacrificing the Second Person in the Trinity for faults he did not commit." His decision, he informed Dr. Willis Craig, was "the conclusion of thirty years internal conflict."[10]

As I have suggested, Orion's crisis may have had less to do with theology than with his rankling loss of faith in his father. When he told Sam he was over his "craziness" of blaming his bad luck on his "only humanly defective relations" he seems to have been overly sanguine, and now it was perhaps not so much the Presbyterian Church he was seeking to detach himself from as that other symbol of authority in his life. Nor would it do simply to turn his back and walk away; Orion Clemens needed to go through the full formality of resigning. But it was not to be. He was called before the Presbyterian session, and Dr. Craig informed him that although that body would excuse him from communion while he was in his present state of doubt, it could not accept his resignation, nor could it expel him when there was no suspicion of "unmorality."[11]

Years later Jane Clemens informed Samuel and Olivia that while she was visiting Orion and Mollie "friends told me they never felt so sorry for a man as they did for him" and that Mollie confided to her she feared Orion would lose his mind.[12] Jane left Keokuk nine days after Orion's letter to Dr. Craig.[13] Three days later Mollie lamented to Sam and Livy, "ALL I want is to see Orion come out right." She did not, however, tell them of her husband's religious plight; she spoke only of his legal practice: "I want him to stick to the law—but I dont know whether I can have influence enough to [word illegible] get him to try or not. . . . I feel sure Orion attends to other peoples business better than he attends to his own, therefore he should attend to other peoples business; and he is very careful with his law business. But he does not push as he ought—and others do push and get the practice."[14]

Orion rented an office for his legal affairs, but, as he informed Sam, it "was so private—rarely anybody disturbed me— that I could not resist the temptation to write—by the ream."[15] One of his compositions was an article on immigration, and this he submitted to none other than William Dean Howells of the *Atlantic Monthly.* Blithely unaware that Howells knew only too well who he was, he introduced himself thus: "I happened once to cypher out for my brother Sam, 'Mark Twain,' some hidden information I think was very useful to him [probably for *Roughing It*], and I imagine if you choose to write to him he will indorse me as a painstaking, conscientious, correct plodder, sticking like an absorbed and abstracted burr to a thing once commenced till it is completed."[16]

Painstaking perhaps, conscientious maybe, correct probably not, and persevering definitely not—Sam had already made his reading of his brother amply clear to Howells. How the editor handled this embarrassing predicament we do not know, but no article by Orion Clemens appeared in the *Atlantic.*

Orion bombarded Sam with weekly letters. He sent part of his manuscript for "The Kingdom of Sir John Franklin," inspired by the British explorer who perished when he tried to find the Northwest Passage in 1845. And Orion decried his "dreary dependence on a brother and sick wife," confessing that if it continued, "I shall want to go to hell awhile for rest and comfort. . . . I am like a man in a cave, hunting a ray of light in *any* direction."[17]

On a sudden inspiration he suggested that Sam use his Sir John Franklin story "as a skeleton or as memoranda" to expand into a book and "send it out in your name and mine (with some nom de plume, if that is best) (or all in your own name, if you prefer that) give me such part of the profits as you please, and enable me to pay you and the government and my other creditors, and leave me something over." (Presumably Orion still owed the federal government for alleged overcharges in the 1860s.) The story had to do with some travelers who "get into the centre of the earth," where they find "prehistoric vegetation and animals" and strange-shaped people. "Couldn't you imagine lots of queer adventures and romances under such circumstances?" he asked.[18]

Sam replied that if he wrote all the books he himself had in mind "I shall see the middle of the next century," but he encouraged Orion to "go ahead and write it yourself." Obviously the law practice was no hindrance, he observed, but Orion would have to give up "temperance, amateur theatricals, religion, and other dissipations, and [give] your entire mind to the one thing."[19]

For two years Sam had been sending Orion checks for forty-two dollars a month in quarterly installments so that he could "get into the practice of law." Now the term Orion had asked for was up, but he was no closer to his goal (or to being able to repay the "loan") than he had been at the beginning. He wrote to Sam: "I am satisfied that I am an idiot. I was an idiot to leave Hartford." He had heard that his brother was editor in chief of the *Hartford Courant.* "Can't you try me again?" he pleaded. "Put me at *anything* you think I can do, if it is setting type, collecting, or sweeping out and running errands at any wages you please, and if I ever [leave?] the track again, cut my throat and bury me four thousand feet down so I cannot hear the last call to rise again and make trouble in heaven."[20]

He enclosed more excerpts from his story. These pages tell of some whalers, under the command of Sir John Franklin, who have been stranded by

mutineers in arctic wastes, their two ships "incased in ice seven feet thick."
It is a fairly interesting story and in spots vividly written, but mainly it
concerns us for what it may reveal about Orion's general state of mind, his
experiences as a maverick Southerner, and his feelings toward Sam.

When the men discover open water some twenty miles from the ships,
they decide to transport the whaleboats to it on sledges and attempt an
escape. The problem is that the water is open only to the west and north.
"Mr. Gorin" argues that without dogs or provisions it would be madness to
strike out south—"Our way," he declares, "is *north!*"

"North!" exclaim the others in shocked disbelief.

"Aye, gentlemen," he responds assuredly, "to the north. It would be going somewhere, with a chance. To stay here is certain death."

But the others will have none of it and decide to proceed as planned, by
water as far as possible and then on the surface. After much difficulty they
manage to get the boats into the open sea and set sail. "We proceeded,"
wrote Orion, sounding somewhat like his brother, "with lighter hearts than
ever school boys felt at leaving school."

That night, however, they run into a terrible storm. Sir John is knocked
unconscious, and when he revives he seems surprised at where he is. The
reader discovers that for nearly six months he has been "dreaming" that he
was, as Mr. Curts informs him, "King of Lady Jane Land, and this is your
majesty's royal navy! But I am heartily rejoiced," Curts continues, "that
you are now only the plain commander, Sir John Franklin, to whom I yield
my authority."

In copying his story for Sam, Orion indicated an ellipsis here, and then
he resumed at page 45, where it seems that owing to a faulty compass the
voyagers have lost their way and sailed back to where they started. "If you
please, sir," suggests "the colored American" Herbert Spencer, "it's my opinion it's the power of Satan. That compass p'inted all right when we sailed,
and without anybody knowin' where it was done, it's turned round and is
p'intin' right the other way."

Orion's narrative continues: "Then, lowering his voice, he said, 'Some
of us has got sins that ought to be done like unto Jonah,' with a gesture of
his head and eyes toward Brown, x x x 'What we ought to done was to
throw the sinful man overboard in the storm, and then we wouldn't 'a'
been sent back.'"[21]

The checks continued to arrive in Keokuk. "The remittances I got from you today," wrote Orion on February 5, 1878, "will enable me to go on and finish my story, and get it in good shape before sending it to you." Three days later he sent several more sample pages and wrote, "I feel more encouraged to go on with my story since you like the second extract."[22]

"I have a badgered, harassed feeling, a good part of the time," wrote Sam to his mother in Fredonia a week or so later. "Well, the consequence is, I cannot write a book at home. . . . Therefore, I have about made up my mind to take my tribe and fly to some little corner of Europe."[23] There were many reasons for Sam's urge to get away (including a controversy about his remarks at the Whittier birthday dinner)—and not least among these was his importunate brother Orion.

Not a hint about the European flight did Sam drop when he wrote to Orion four days later. Instead, he concerned himself with his brother's story. It appeared, he said, to be "poaching upon Verne's peculiar preserve," referring to Jules Verne's 1864 science fiction novel *Journey to the Center of the Earth*. "If you *burlesque* Verne, of course you can use his ideas as much as you choose—but not otherwise."[24]

Jane Clemens had gotten wind of her eldest son's writing efforts and of Sam's involvement, and she contacted Sam. He replied in a defensive tone: "I wrote him that this story seemed to promise quite fairly. So it did—but from a lot of extracts which I have since received I begin to fear it is going to be only a wandering, objectless, motiveless imitation of the rampaging French lunatic, Jules Verne. . . . Well, Orion is absolutely destitute of originality, wherefore he *must* imitate; there is no help for it; so, let him go ahead and imitate Verne."[25]

On the evening of March 16 Orion took up a Keokuk newspaper and read that Mark Twain and his family were sailing for Germany in less than a month to be gone for two years. He was so shocked and upset he couldn't sleep that night. At two o'clock he got up and finished writing his story. He didn't take time to read it but wrote Sam a letter that was desperate altogether and inchoate in part. "I feel lonesome and disappointed," he keened. "I have had a longing to get back to Hartford, and be with you. . . . I feel that I have suffered the hell I have for forty or more years, in consequence of the infernal doctrine of government by fear. I have been trained a coward, and I mean to put out the fire of hell, and this is the gist of the Kingdom of Sir John Franklin. Do with any part of the manuscript, however, or the whole of it, as you think best." He added: "I send the manuscript by express," but before he did so he apparently asked Mollie to read it. She did so as far as "the hanging scene," at which point she laid it down, "shocked and despondent at its horrors and heresies. . . . But why," Orion asked rhetorically, "should not people be brought to face and realize what they profess to believe? It is radical, but it is the honest expression of my thoughts."[26]

"This work of yours is exceedingly crude," replied Sam within a week, "but I am free to say it is less crude than I expected it to be, and considerably better work than I believed you could do." Fortunately, he said, there was a market for "apprentice work" such as this, and "so I shall speak to the N.Y. Weekly people." He had read the manuscript through, and in four pages of notes he suggested how Orion might modify it, cutting about a third.[27] He then delivered a long lecture on the difficult art of writing, using one of his own stories as an example.[28]

After a quick trip to Fredonia to say good-bye to his mother and sister, Sam took his family to New York City, and on April 11 they sailed for Europe—but not before Sam made Howells promise to put Orion into a book or play.[29]

In Keokuk, Orion had conceived a new project. He was writing a course of lectures "to rescue," as Sam later characterized it, "our 'noble and beautiful religion' from the sacrilegious talons of Bob Ingersoll." Robert Green Ingersoll (1833–99) was a popular writer and spellbinding orator who, as the spread of Darwinism provoked wide and violent controversy, advocated scientific and humanistic rationalism and propounded the view called by T. H. Huxley "agnosticism."[30] Sam's account suggests that Ingersoll's skepticism was too strong for Orion. He evidently planned to inaugurate his course in Keokuk and then, if it was successful, take it around the country. He wrote to Sam asking for money.

Apparently believing his brother had changed his views from the time he tried to resign his church membership, Sam wrote a sarcastic reply.

I enclose a draft on Hartford for $25. You will have abandoned the project you wanted it for, by the time it arrives,—but no matter, apply it to your newer and present project, whatever it is. You see I have an ineradicable faith in your unsteadfastness,—but mind you, I didn't invent that faith, you conferred it on me yourself. . . . I don't feel like girding at you any more about fickleness of purpose, because

I recognize and realize at last that it is incurable; but before I learned to accept this truth, each new weekly project of yours possessed the power of throwing me into the most exhausting and helpless convulsions of profanity.[31]

He had not, of course, "learned to accept this truth," and he proceeded to demonstrate it by going on for nine pages before Livy saw the letter and "shut down on it." It was cruel, she said. Send the money, she advised, raise Orion's monthly pension, and wish his lectures success.

Obligingly, Sam wrote a new letter. "I shall be sincerely glad to hear that you[r] success meets your highest expectations," he avowed, and he enclosed the draft and told his brother his new monthly check would be for fifty dollars. But he also admonished Orion to leave his own (Mark Twain's) name out of his dealings with the press.[32]

Still, the first letter was too good to waste. Livy suggested he send it to Howells, and he did. "Take care of it," he charged his friend, "for it is worth preserving." "You *must* put him in a book or a play right away. You are the only man capable of doing it. You might die at any moment, and your very greatest work would be lost to the world. *I* could write Orion's simple biography, and make it effective, too, by merely stating the bald facts—and this I will do if he dies before I do; but *you* must put him into romance. This was the understanding you and I had the day I sailed."[33]

He then launched into a long, ten-point recapitulation of Orion's career ("that is, a *little* of it") that to some extent drew upon the "bald facts" but that went beyond them as well. There seems to be no evidence, for instance, that Orion belonged to "as many as five different religious denominations," that he voted both Democrat and Republican in the same election, that he proposed to lecture around the country as "Mark Twain's Brother" on the topic of "the Formation of Character," or that he "ran a bold tilt against total Abstinence and the Red Ribbon fanatics." Admittedly, Orion was not the steadfast and self-assured paragon Sam seemed to want him to be, but neither was he the bumbling idiot painted here.

"Now come!" Sam exhorted Howells. "Don't fool away this treasure which Providence has laid at your feet, but take it up and use it.—One can let his imagination run riot in portraying Orion, for there is nothing so extravagant as to be out of character with him."[34]

The remarkable letter rose in pitch as its author turned his fire on Orion's wife. Mollie harried poor Orion into the Presbyterian Church several times, he charged, then drove him back out again with "her prayings and Bible readings and her other and eternal pious clack-clack." She wouldn't allow her husband to pursue his trade as a printer because "she can't abide the thought of being a mechanic's wife." She "gobbles all the money and buys clothes and new wigs for herself" to the extent that Orion didn't have any decent garments for himself. "She won't let him work at a trade, but in the privacy of the boarding-house she makes him get up in the cold gray dawns of winter and go from one lodger's room to another (young fellows not half his age,—and they pity him and protest, too,) and build the fires, and go down on his knees and bow his gray head and blow them, to save the parlor bellows from wear and tear."[35]

Since Samuel Clemens had never set foot inside Orion and Mollie's boardinghouse, this affecting picture with its telling details must have come from the only other member of the family who had. Sam had probably received it from his mother in Fredonia, and the helpless pity it produced in him had grown during many months until Orion's letter announcing his new lecture scheme arrived and triggered the long, ardent outpouring that climaxed in the passage just quoted. "Orion is in his 54th year," Sam went on. "He and she are two curses which are dovetailed together with marvelous exactness. She is such a vain, proud fool; he is so utterly devoid of pride."[36]

Inasmuch as Orion's letter does not survive we have no way of verifying Sam's characterization of the theme of his lecture course as "to rescue our 'noble and beautiful religion' from the sacrilegious talons of Bob Ingersoll." What we know is that on March 6, 1879, Orion rented Red Ribbon Hall in Keokuk and delivered a lecture on "Man the Architect of Our Religion."[37] From the title—and from what happened afterward—he appeared to be more on Ingersoll's side than the angels'.

As we have seen, Orion had been called before the Presbyterian session two years earlier when he tried to resign his church membership. That body had counseled him "*not* to give utterance" to his views. Evidently members of the session had been keeping an eye on him since, and, according to Fred Lorch, four of them were in the audience that night "with pencil and pad to record the heresies of their church brother."[38] The next day Orion received a citation to appear before the session again, this time to answer charges that he had (1) publicly delivered a lecture in which he "disavowed the divinity of the Christian religion and attributed it wholly to man," and (2) "avowed sentiments contrary to the fundamental doctrines of this church."[39] Orion acknowledged receipt at once, stating that "I desire that the matter of said charge and specifications, be immediately heard and decided," and he even provided the committee with a handwritten synopsis of his lecture.

On the evening of Wednesday, March 8, 1879, he presented himself at Dr. Craig's study. There he found, in addition to the pastor, six other persons—the clerk of the session, the prosecutor, and the four members who had attended the lecture. These men were important members of the community. The Reverend Dr. Willis Green Craig was an eminent divine who would later be associated with the McCormick Theological Seminary of Chicago and in 1893 would act as moderator of the Presbyterian general assembly in Washington, D.C. One of the witnesses was Justice of the Peace J. Henry Westcott, a legal colleague of Orion's, and the clerk of the session was P. T. Lomax, a dignified and gentlemanly Virginian, who was also a lawyer.[40]

The charges were read and elaborated, and Orion stipulated that the summary he had furnished might be used as evidence. To the first charge Westcott testified he had heard Orion deny the inspiration of the Scriptures in the sense that he believed the fundamental principles of the Bible originated with man, and also that he believed Abraham, first patriarch of the Jews, was an idolater.

Orion cross-examined Westcott, asking: "Was not the idea of Abraham in planting the tree, and at the same time calling upon the name of the Lord, the Everlasting God, intended as an act of dedication of the tree to the purpose of afterward being converted into an idol by cutting symbols upon the stem?"

"I understood that the tree was ultimately to be an idol," allowed the witness.

On the second charge Orion waived the production of witnesses, stipulating that he could not recognize Christ as co-equal with God, but on the contrary, while he regarded his mission on earth as a great beneficence, he considered him to be human in origin. His death on the cross was an "outgrowth and modification" of the human sacrifices practiced by the ancient Jews and others, and as to the resurrection, that belief had resulted from the traditions of Christ's life not having been written down until perhaps a century after his death. Orion remained unconvinced of its historical truth.

The moderator asked Orion: "Did you feel impelled by a sense of duty and privilege to give public utterance to these views?"

"Yes," he replied. "I consider it the duty of every man to think soberly upon these subjects, to make up his views satisfactorily to himself and then express them to others, in order that if he be in error he may be corrected and the truth reached through free, full and open discussion."

"Were you earnestly counseled and repeatedly besought by the session *not* to give utterance to these views?"

"I was."

"Do you understand the views enunciated in your lecture and freely expressed here to be directly contrary to the fundamental teaching of the Presbyterian church?"

"I do."

"Have we, the session, according to our best ability, sought to resolve your doubts?"

"You have sought to resolve my doubts. You will have to judge as to the best of your ability."

"That is a correct answer."

Two days later Orion received through the mail the following message:

Dear Sir—I have to inform you that the session on Wednesday evening last, unanimously found you guilty under the charges tabled against you, and their sentence was that you should therefore be excommunicated from the church, and said excommunication be pronounced at morning service on Sabbath next.

Very respectfully,
P. T. Lomax, clerk of session.

The following Sunday Dr. Craig preached a sermon adapted to the occasion, after which he gave a short narration of the steps that had been taken with the accused, cited the biblical authority of the church to cast out unworthy members, and explained the nature, use, and consequences of the censure. He warned his congregation to avoid all unnecessary intercourse with the person about to be cast out, as they might be contaminated with his opinions. Then he announced: "Whereas, Orion Clemens hath been, by sufficient proof, convicted of heresy, and after much admonition and prayer, obstinately refuseth to hear the church, and hath manifested no evidence of repentance; therefore, in the name, and by the authority of the Lord Jesus Christ, I pronounce him to be excluded from the communion of the church."

The *Keokuk Daily Constitution,* pointing out "the prominence of the characters participating, and the fact that the matter originated from a lecture delivered in a public hall," printed the full text of the proceedings, the conclusion of the court, and the final sentence of excommunication.[41] The whole bizarre episode, far from being laughed off, became an event in the religious history not only of Keokuk but of the nation, being mentioned and discussed as a notable incident in both secular and religious publications.[42] The *Chicago Tribune* published a story, for instance, that was rerun by the *New York Times.*[43]

In the same issue the *Constitution* ran this announcement: "Orion Clemens will repeat his lecture on 'Man the Architect of Our Religion,' at Red Ribbon Hall, on Monday evening, May 19. Admission 25 cents." Orion's second lecture was not well attended. Those who were on hand heard the speaker refer briefly at the close of his remarks to his expulsion from the church. He stated that no attempt had been made to refute his statements, but that the session had concluded he had formed his views owing to "weakness of mind." As a parting shot, Orion told his audience he did not advise people not to associate with Dr. Craig, but trusted that everyone would fraternize with him as usual.[44]

Having failed in his attempt to resign from the church, Orion had at last forced the issue and been expelled. It is probably safe to say that other members of Dr. Craig's congregation would have been hard pressed to affirm all the church's doctrines, but Orion alone found it necessary willfully and openly to defy and deny the denomination. His excommunication was probably the outcome of a mental process he himself didn't fully understand.

When Sam learned of the affair he wrote to his mother and sister from Paris: "He'd better look out how he prances around with that lecture—some of the godly will hang him. However, I wish him better luck than that."[45] To Orion he wrote: "Never mind the Excommunication. If you made a square deal and told your honest thought in the lecture, I wouldn't care what people say. . . . I judge you wrote a good lecture. I am bound to say you showed a deal of moral courage to deliver it."[46]

One cannot help but wonder whether as he penned these words Samuel was reminded of a notebook entry he had made two weeks earlier (the day before Orion's second lecture), one that almost certainly referred to his brother: "The Autobiography of a Coward. Make him hideously but unconsciously base and pitiful and contemptible."[47] It will be recalled that two months earlier Orion had written him, "I have suffered the hell I have for forty or more years, in consequence of the infernal doctrine of government by fear. I have been trained a coward." Sam's entry became the germ of a project that would come to term nine months later.

17
Orion's Autobiography

~

I have read the autobiography with close and painful interest. It wrung
my heart, and I felt haggard after I had finished it. . . . But the writer's
soul is laid too bare; it is shocking.

William Dean Howells to Mark Twain

Sam and his family returned to the United States on September 3, 1879,
and promptly paid a brief visit to his mother and sister in Fredonia.[1] Naturally, the subject of Orion came up, and afterward Jane Clemens wrote to
her firstborn that she wanted him to "stride forth in search of work." Orion
replied to Sam that he would be glad to do that "if my writing fails" and
enclosed a preface for a proposed book, in which he asserted that he wanted
"to come to the rescue of morality" and "show that morality and religion
are developed independently of each other, and without divine interference."[2]

Nevertheless, he had given up on his book, closed his office, and was
preparing to leave for St. Louis in search of work when he received a letter
from Sam that changed his mind.[3] Even though the younger brother had
seen only the brief, poorly written preface, for some reason he encouraged
Orion to proceed with the work—told him, in fact, it was "probably a
duty" for him to do so.

Orion wrote Sam thanking him for his "kind letter" and telling him he
planned to work at home, using the money saved by closing his office to
buy some books he needed. "If I find I cannot write well at home, I think
I can get a private room for a dollar a month. I am going to write with all
my might," he averred, "and put *work* into it."[4]

Sam was called to Chicago to address the thirteenth reunion banquet of
the Army of the Tennessee, at which Ulysses S. Grant, former commander

of the Union armies (and past president of the United States), was honored. Mark Twain's speech was a rousing success, and he himself was deeply moved by several addresses he heard, especially one by the eloquent Robert Ingersoll. At five in the morning, having been up all night "talking with people and listening to speeches," he wrote a letter to Livy from his hotel room. "I guess this was the memorable night of my life," gushed the former rebel and Marion Ranger. "By George, I never was so stirred since I was born." Ingersoll's speech was "just the supremest combination of English words that was ever put together since the world began." He told his wife how "out of compliment" his own after-dinner toast had been scheduled last so as to "hold the crowd" and how afterward General William Tecumseh Sherman came up to shake his hand. "Lord bless you, my boy," Sherman exclaimed, "I don't know how you do it—it's a secret that's beyond me—but it was great—give me your hand again." Even the usually stone-faced Grant "told me he laughed till the tears came and every bone in his body ached."[5]

It was a quarter past six when Samuel finished his long epistle to Olivia, but he was still too thrilled to sleep. At seven he wrote to Orion: "Well, it was a memorable night. I never shall see its like again. I never shall hear such speeches any more in this life." Oddly, considering his brother's interest in Ingersoll, he didn't mention that particular speech, nor the fact that he had become acquainted with its author. "I'm mighty sorry I can't go to Keokuk," Sam wrote in closing, "but I must rush home right away."[6]

The topic of Twain's speech was "The Babies: As They Comfort Us in Our Sorrows, Let Us Not Forget Them in Our Festivities." When Orion read a copy he wrote to his brother: "Another Ten Strike for the family! Let me shake hands with you across the continent. . . . Your speech was the diamond of the 15 diamonds of speeches. And what an audience you had! No other man in the world could have so magnificently improved so grand an occasion as you did."[7]

Sam offered to pay for a month-long trip for his brother and sister-in-law.[8] The couple jumped at the chance, traveling to Fredonia to see Pamela and the ailing Jane Clemens and then continuing on to Hartford. When the two brothers got together in Sam's stately mansion, Sam apparently let Orion read the unfinished manuscript of *The Prince and the Pauper*. Orion liked it very much and found that his sympathies were with "the true prince" and "the interesting character who saved him from the mob," but whether he saw the parallels between this story of two boys who exchanged estates and himself and Sam we shall never know.[9] The brothers also probably discussed Orion's book, but unfortunately there is no record of what they said.

The day Orion and Mollie arrived back in Keokuk, Sam wrote what was perhaps the strangest letter he had addressed to his brother since October 1865, when he had offered to "toss up" and "strike a bargain" with him. After describing a patent he had bought a share in, he went on to say he was "grinding away now, with all my might, and with an interest which amounts to intemperance" at *The Prince and the Pauper.*

> Well, I must get one more exciting thing out of my head, and then I shall be ready to slide back into Edward VI's time wholly untrameled. It is this—to suggest to you to write two books which it has long been my purpose to write, but I judge they are so far down on my docket that I shan't get to them in this life. I think the subjects are perfectly new. One is "The Autobiography of a Coward," and the other "Confessions of a Life that was a Failure."[10]

He went on to describe his incredible plan of attack: To take the "absolute facts" of one's life and tell them "simply and without ornament or flourish"—with the one exception that "I would turn every courageous action (if I ever performed one) into a cowardly one, and every success into a failure. You can do this," he assured Orion, but only if he banished all idea of an audience and addressed his words exclusively to himself, "for few men can straitly and squarely confess shameful things to others."

An even better approach would be, he went on, "to tell the story of an abject coward who is *unconscious* that he is a coward" and of a failed man who "is blissfully unaware that he was unsuccessful and does not imagine the reader sees he was unsuccessful." If this approach were followed, the suggested titles could not be used, for they would of course give away the secret. "This latter plan," wrote Sam, "is the one I should use. I should *confine* myself to *my own* actual experiences (to invent would be to fail) and I would name everybody's actual name and locality and describe his character and actions unsparingly." Persons and places could be disguised later.

Holding up Casanova's *Memoirs* as a model, he told Orion, "Your coward should also be, unconsciously, the meanest and lousiest of the human race. . . . Rousseau confesses to masturbation, theft, lying, shameful treachery, and attempts made upon his person by Sodomites. But he tells it as a man who is *perfectly aware* of the shameful nature of these things, whereas your coward and your failure should be happy and sweet and unconscious. . . . Tackle one of these books," he continued, "and simply tell your story to *yourself,* laying all hideousnesses utterly bare, reserving nothing." If the book was well done, he assured Orion, there would be a market for it. "There is no market yet, for the one you are writing—it should wait. Love to Molly and all."[11]

Thus the book Orion had invested so much time and energy in, the book Sam a few weeks before had termed "probably a duty" for Orion to write—that book was suddenly declared marketless, and "should wait." In its place loomed the specter of a grotesque parody of an autobiography, an exercise in literary self-abuse. This was the project Sam had referred to in his notebook entry nine months earlier. At that time it seemed to be little more than the seed of an idea. What had brought it to fruition and caused him to offer it to his brother?

Two things, it seems. The first was the Grant banquet, where Sam had been accepted as an equal by the greatest heroes of the Republic—an overwhelmingly validating experience. The former Southern sympathizer had been welcomed into the ranks of the national elect. The second was Orion's congratulatory letter. In Chicago Sam had thrilled when he heard Robert Ingersoll tell the assembled throng: "The Southern people. . . . were wrong, and the time will come when they will say that they are victors who have been vanquished by the right. . . . Freedom . . . will . . . educate their children . . . execute their laws, and fill their land with happy homes."[12] Orion was one Southerner who had seen early on that his people were wrong and had thrown his allegiance to the North, while the younger sibling adhered to the old ways and even bore arms for the rebels. Now the older brother had at last declared Sam's exoneration. When Orion referred to Sam's speech as "a grand sermon," it may have evoked a time when Orion had written a religious discourse of his own. "Orion there was **genius**—true, unmistakeable **genius**—in that sermon of yours," Sam had written in 1865. And that, in turn, may have reminded Sam of the entreaty contained in his letter—and of the cold reception it met.

If so, it must have been with a supreme sense of irony that he now made his astonishing proposal, for it was an utter reversal of the earlier plea. If in that letter he formerly appealed to Orion to soar with eagles ("Now I don't know how you regard the ministry," he had written, "but *I* would rather be a shining light in that department than the greatest lawyer that ever trod the earth"), in this one he was telling him to feed with buzzards. At that time he had pledged to "strive for a fame—unworthy and evanescent though it must of necessity be—if you will . . . preach the gospel"; now he allowed that he would continue writing his novel while Orion might take up a couple of projects Sam had no time for.

On one level Sam no doubt wanted to know what Orion had to say, what "hideousnesses" he would "lay utterly bare." Having tried to put himself inside his brother's head by writing what he called "Orion's autobiography" (Paine's "Autobiography of a Damned Fool"), he had gained some insight but had ultimately been stymied when Livy forbade him to continue.[13] Now Sam was turning to the one man who could hardly fail to shed light on the subject that so gripped him—Orion himself.

But on another, deeper level, the proposal was something else. Sam wouldn't settle for just the "absolute facts"; he wanted Orion to turn his every valorous act into an ignominious one, his every victory into defeat. The courage Orion had shown in Missouri and Nevada, for instance, was to be turned on its head. Not satisfied with his big brother's acquittal of him, Sam seems to have felt that only a reversal of roles would suffice, that his own glorification had to be met by Orion's total humiliation. Sam had abashed himself when he asked his brother to toss up with him; now it was Orion's turn to go to his knees. It is probably no exaggeration to say that Sam saw Orion's autobiography as his punishment for preceding him into the winners' circle and as a surety that he would never make public his role as Sam's ethical guide. (Significantly, Samuel was asking his brother to drop a book about morality in order to take up this new project.) Moreover, Sam knew his brother was in a battle, of which his recent excommunication was but one manifestation. Now he was proposing a mental exercise that might tip the scale. "You can do this," he assured his brother, but only if you "*banish* all idea of an audience"—that is, only if you internalize the process. And he didn't stop there. When Mark Twain engaged in self-ridicule he figuratively winked at the reader or listener. This gesture was to be denied Orion. He must present himself as *unconscious* he was being a milksop, "blissfully unaware that he is unsuccessful and does not imagine the reader sees he was unsuccessful."

As difficult as it is to believe that Samuel still considered Orion a rival, this incredible proposal strongly suggests just that. In worldly matters, in affairs pertaining to letters and lectures and honors, he had so far outstripped his brother that there remained no basis for comparison, let alone competition. In only one theater did Sam still fear and envy Orion. Even though the elder brother had ultimately failed the Bliss test, Sam still saw him as his moral better. But now that Sam had attained standing with the nation's certified heroes he was at last prepared to challenge Orion on his home ground. If Sam could induce him to undertake this degrading project, he would have turned the tables and given him a taste of the desolation he felt at being abandoned to "scribbling to excite the **laughter** of God's creatures."

Amazingly, Orion didn't even need to think the matter over. "Yours of 26th just received," he answered on the spot, "11.35 A.M. in post office. 'The Autobiography of a Coward' will be commenced within an hour, and the first chapter sent to you within a week. The writing will be according to your suggestions." He even congratulated Sam on his "invention."[14]

Orion was better than his word, for two days later he sent "samples of modes of treating one of the subjects you suggested"—although he disparaged his efforts. "Don't let any of the family see either of the MSS," he cautioned. "Mollie read your letter, and she knows I am writing accordingly, but I told her she should not see a line of the MSS."[15] But this compliance with Sam's stipulations didn't last long. Two weeks later Orion remarked that "my autobiography looks now as if it might take in the whole family," and the following day he reported that he would have to make some changes "in consequence of conversation this morning with Squire Stotts [Mollie's father] and Mollie's Sister Ann" and that more alterations might be required "if I can get further information from ma and Cousins Jo and Allen Casey."[16]

Sam's reply does not survive, but a message he sent to Howells does. He thanked his friend for his laudatory *Atlantic* review of *A Tramp Abroad* and told him it had arrived at exactly the right moment, "for I had just laid down a long letter from Orion and was feeling haggard." Concealing his directing hand, he wrote: "Having reached 20th chapter of his work whose purpose is to destroy Christianity. . . . he abandoned the work, and—on the same day—began 'The Autobiography of an Ass,' and encloses chapter 1 to me for revision, opinion, and suggestion. . . . If I could have a new book and a new review every time Orion assaults me, I could defy him and tell him to do his worst."[17]

Even though the project seems to have been transmuted, a few days later Sam informed Orion that, having "stolen part of my Sunday holiday and . . . read your chapters," he had found that "I like them very much."[18] He even sent a couple of reminiscences from the Hannibal days for inclusion.[19] His only request was that future installments be sent in larger batches so they couldn't be mislaid.[20]

Orion was even more grateful for his brother's approval than usual. "The original of your letter I shall preserve as a Bible," he gushed, "to be often read, and to be observed as an article of faith." He intended to send a copy to Jane Clemens, he said, so she would stop hounding him to get a job.[21]

Samuel also wrote to their mother, feigning ignorance of her involvement in the autobiography and telling her that her eldest son was writing "an exceedingly readable book—a sort of narrative which I suggested to him—but he began to flood me with *daily* chapters of it, and I wrote and protested against this thoughtless invasion of my time, and told him to send his MS monthly—which of course knocked him and his book in the head at once; for he is like any other baby, and must have his pattings on the back and his encouragements every few hours, else his purpose peters out."[22] Orion's drive didn't peter out. He continued to send weekly (not monthly) installments and asked Sam to read them and return them with comments, which he did.

By this time Jane Clemens and Pamela Moffett were caught up in the project. Jane wrote Orion a long memorandum about the early days of the Clemens family and told of how at the age of sixteen or seventeen she had been thrown from horseback into a creek.[23] Pamela added her two cents' worth, saying she was "glad to help you in your work and will do the best I can," although she added, "If you were writing a romance a great many interesting incidents might be woven in that would hardly do to use in writing a veritable history, because it would hardly do to drag other people before the public in all cases." Evidently Orion had been less than transparent in conveying to his mother and sister what Sam had commissioned him to do; he may even have presented the project as his own idea.[24]

When the undertaking was two months old Samuel told Orion he was writing "a model autobiography. Continue to develop your own character in the same gradual, inconspicuous and apparently unconscious way."[25]

Going against an earlier warning that "you must expect to have to tear up and rewrite," he cautioned against revising, apparently preferring the spontaneity of the first draft.[26] Albert Bigelow Paine, who saw at least part of the manuscript, said that Orion "wrote . . . of his childhood with a startling minutiae of detail and frankness."[27]

In Fredonia, Jane and Pamela were trying to dredge up memories, but they were not having much success, and in any case neither of them felt well enough to write extensively. Jane Clemens's solution was to suggest to her eldest son that he use money she had sent to visit them. "If you were here only a short time Mela you and myself might call to mind a great many incidents that we cant think of now. And you could write them. . . . I will pay your board here and you can have my room to write in."[28]

When Sam got wind of this cozy prospect he put his foot down; he was, in fact, prepared to scuttle the endeavor rather than allow such a meeting. "My Dear Bro—" he wrote, "Drop the book and give your entire mind to the newspaper. [Orion had finally landed a job as a reporter at the *Keokuk Gate City*.] The bane of Americans is overwork—and the ruin of *any* work is a divided interest. Concencrate [*sic*]—*concentrate*. One thing at a time. Yrs in haste Sam."[29]

Jane Clemens was, of course, glad to learn of Orion's employment, but she didn't on that account give up the idea of a family writing session. Rather, she wanted to postpone it until July or August, when she and Pamela would be at Pamela's cottage on Lake Erie. By that time, she reasoned, Orion would have secured his position and could take a few weeks' leave of absence to join them. Pamela wrote to Samuel seeking his approval, explaining, "In that way many things will come to us that we have forgotten." In closing, she declared, "We are all very much gratified with the high opinion you express of Orion's book."[30]

Sam would not hear of it. "My advice to Orion (strenuously expressed) was to drop his book utterly, and give his undivided attention to his newspaper work." Professing concern for his brother's job security as well as health, he wrote: "No reporter will long remain useful who fritters away his resting time in writing on a book. . . . Now the minute he has at last gone to earning a living, do you want him to go to planning a holiday? Let the holiday alone."[31] A skeptic might wonder whether Sam was as concerned about Orion's soundness and livelihood as he was about what forgotten incidents his mother and two siblings might recollect. If his original scheme involved learning what Orion knew, it certainly didn't entail encouraging the family to "call to mind a great many incidents that we cant think of now."

Blithely ignoring Sam's directive, Orion began getting up at four or five in the morning to write before going to the *Gate City* at eight. "I will send some more autobiography to-morrow," he told his brother on May 15. "I wrote two pages Monday, and got in seven yesterday."[32] But Sam seems to have been right, for three days later Orion informed him that "I have just lost my situation, after receiving $2.20."[33] Once again Orion was free to devote all his time to his memoirs. "I will try to crowd it through," he told Sam, "and then go somewhere to hunt some kind of a situation, unless you think I had better quit fooling with the autobiography and go now."[34]

Orion's firing whetted Mollie's desire to leave Keokuk, the town she had grown up in and in which she and he had lately been subjected to humiliation. As for the life story, she thought there was little chance of getting it published, that Sam was merely "amusing" Orion with it, and that her husband was in danger of throwing away a year or two at an age when he didn't have any to spare. She wanted him to ask his brother point-blank: "Will the manuscript I am writing be published in book, magazine, pamphlet or any other form?" If yes, she could wait patiently until it was finished; otherwise Orion should hunt for work immediately. Her husband complied, telling his brother that "I would like to continue the autobiography, and will do so till I hear from you," for "without a suggestion from her I am obliged to face the fact that if I should die she would be without anything except the thousand dollars of Insurance money. I thought I might enjoy or might leave her a copyright of a book 28 years. But if no book is to be published, or will lie stillborn in the accouchement chamber of the publisher, I should at least avoid the stigma and discomfort of living on borrowed money."[35]

Sam's reply has not survived, but evidently it had a monetary component, for Orion wrote back: "I am deeply touched by the generosity of yourself and Livy toward myself and Mollie. She is grateful and happy." Then he revealed his motive in accepting his brother's charge in the first place.

Let me clearly explain myself. If there were no point to be gained I could not endure the pain and disgust of writing and publishing my own autobiography. If you have looked at the ms. I sent last Saturday you have noticed a skip of 28 years, and the introduction of the excommunication. If I can get my religious ideas widely read, I am willing to let the public think of me personally as they please. . . . With this idea I propose to paint myself as a dark background for your bright biography. I will only have to tell the simple truth.

He went on to say that he intended to end the excommunication episode with "a weakening on my part, a mistrust of my own powers, and attempts to prevail upon the preacher and session to let me back." That wasn't what had happened, "but it will be agreeable to my character, and will leave the reader mad." Then, instead of reproducing "the stupid lecture I delivered," he would present "the best I can write now, lightened up by explanations answering interruptions by the session, whether they occurred or not."[36]

If Orion had in mind a sounding board for his religious views, Sam— no doubt prodded by Mollie's pointed question—was now interested in publication for pay. "Some time ago," he wrote to Howells, finally owning up to the facts (to a degree), "I told Orion to sit down and write his autobiography—and do it in a plain, simple, truthful way, suppressing none of the disagreeables." He went on to explain that the names, dates, and localities in his brother's history were real but would be changed. "I think the result is killingly entertaining," Sam continued, "in parts absolutely delicious." He said he was going to mail a hundred pages or so to Howells. "Read it; keep his secret; and tell me, if . . . you'll buy the stuff for the Atlantic."[37] When he forwarded the manuscript, he added that after it had been culled and reduced by half "it will be worth printing, Howells—and that is a pretty fair result for a lunatic like the author of it, poor fellow. Lord what a hard time of it he has had."[38]

It took Howells only a few days to reply. "I have read the autobiography," he wrote,

with close and painful interest. It wrung my heart, and I felt haggard after I had finished it. . . . But the writer's soul is laid too bare; it is shocking. I can't risk the paper in the Atlantic; and if you print it anywhere, I hope you wont let your love of the naked truth prevent you from striking out some of the most intimate pages. *Don't* let any one else even see those passages about the autopsy.

The light on your father's character is most pathetic.[39]

Sam seems not to have shared Howells's rejection with Orion; in any case, his brother continued writing, but rather than distract Sam with weekly installments, he promised not to send any more manuscript until the work was completed.[40] In July, Jane and Pamela prepared to go to the cottage on Lake Erie, but there was no further talk of Orion joining them, even though the ostensible reason for Sam's objection—Orion's job—no longer existed. Jane wrote from Fredonia: "Orion if you had some out doors work it would strengthen your mind very much."[41]

In Elmira, on July 26, 1880, Olivia gave birth to her third daughter (Clara, her second, was born in 1874). Just as Orion and Mollie had done twenty-five years earlier, the parents named their little girl after Jane Clemens (though she was always known as "Jean"). From Keokuk the delighted brother and sister-in-law sent their congratulations. "You are right to stick to that sex," wrote Orion. "I think a good deal more of it than of my own." He also reported that he was on page 348 of the autobiography, "and not yet out of St. Louis—well satisfied, so far."[42]

When Sam wrote to Orion in the spring of 1880 that Elisha Bliss "has heart disease badly, and . . . his life hangs upon a thread," Orion replied magnanimously that "I am sorry for Bliss, and would like to have him know that I feel for him now both sympathy and friendship."[43] Orion's former employer clung to life until fall, finally succumbing in September. The following month Sam wrote to his brother that he estimated he had lost sixty thousand dollars over the course of his association with the publisher because Bliss, by misrepresenting his costs, had duped him into accepting a royalty that was less than his fair share—that is, half the company's net above the price of paper, printing, and binding.

If Bliss were alive, Sam warranted, he would stay with the American Publishing Company and "get it all back; for on each new book I would require a portion of that back pay." Then, enjoining Orion to secrecy, he told him he would probably go to a new publisher in six or eight months. "Out of the suspicions which you bred in me years ago," he continued, "has grown this result—to-wit, that I shall within the twelve-month get

$40,000 out of this 'Tramp' instead of $20,000." He had, he explained, caused his reimbursement for *A Tramp Abroad* to be stipulated as "1/2 profits" rather than a percentage of the retail price of the book.

> Twenty thousand dollars, after taxes and other expenses are stripped away, is worth to the investor about $75 a month—so I shall tell Mr. Perkins to make your check that amount per month, hereafter, while our income is able to afford it. This ends the loan business; and hereafter you can reflect that you are living not on borrowed money but on money which you have squarely earned, and which has no taint nor savor of charity about it—and you can also reflect that the money you have been receiving of me all these years, is interest charged against the heavy bill which the next publisher will have to stand who gets a book of mine.[44]

It was a specious rationale—Orion hadn't blown the whistle on Bliss in 1872 to "breed suspicions" in Sam but to get him out of the clutches of someone he considered an unscrupulous businessman—but it was good enough for Sam. For some time he had been looking for just such a fig leaf. "If I ever become able," he had told his mother and sister five years earlier, "I mean to put Orion on a regular pension without revealing the fact that it *is* a pension."[45] So here it was: Not only was Orion's monthly check increased a hefty 50 percent, he was also relieved of "the stigma and discomfort," as he had called it, "of living on borrowed money."[46] Let us give Samuel his due: Flawed as his reasoning was, his act was generous, and he gave Orion to believe it was no more than he deserved.

18
Orion Unravels

O my dear Sam I fear you have more to answer for than you think. . . .
Now his mind is not right.

Jane Clemens to Sam

"If you could have seen and heard us," exulted Mollie to Sam after she
and Orion received his letter, "I dont know but you would have thought us
both demented." Comparing her husband to a slave who, no matter how
well cared for "and even love shown," was always painfully aware of his
bondage, she declared: "That Slave has had his free papers given him."[1]

Perhaps emboldened by these fictive credentials, Orion admonished Sam,
when the latter wrote expansively about a new process he had thought of
for producing bookbinders' stamps, not to let "the fascinations of invention" deflect him from his humorous writing. "I had rather see my brother
remain in the lead in the exhibition of an intellectual power which alone
man possesses exclusively of beasts and birds," he wrote, "than to see him
fall to a secondary position as an inventor."[2] He may have had in mind his
brother's paean to invention ("an inventor is a poet—a true poet") when
his own drilling machine seemed about to succeed. Even though Sam had
used that occasion to belittle Orion's achievement in Nevada and contrast
it to the nobility of invention, there was probably no irony in Orion's high-
flown pronouncement. As it turned out, however, that declaration had the
perverse effect of stopping Sam from sharing literary confidences with him
and instead emphasizing his mechanical projects in future letters.

Orion continued to toil at his autobiography, and Sam sent incidents
for inclusion as they occurred to him.[3] Despite his promise to hold the
manuscript until it was completed, however, Orion once again began send-

ing installments to his brother, requesting, "If there is anything wrong please let me know."[4]

Jane Clemens was worried about her elder son. It had been more than four years since she had visited him and Mollie in Keokuk, but she couldn't forget what she had seen and heard there. In Fredonia, she lay awake many a night. Among other ghosts that haunted her was the memory of Sam's "banishing" his brother from New York. She remembered how she had finally consented, but when she saw what the exile had done to her firstborn her heart sank, and she had grieved ever since. The excommunication had made matters worse, and now he was out of work again. When she learned that Orion was writing his autobiography she had been heartened, especially when she heard Sam had a high opinion of it—but when Samuel wrote her that he had told his brother to stop bothering him with "*daily* chapters" and compared Orion to a baby, she couldn't understand. She didn't treat her sister that way; she was never so happy as when she could write something to please her.

What caused her ruminations to erupt in a letter to Sam and Livy we don't know, but spew out they did in meandering, strung-together sentences. "I have grieved until I am sick," she wrote, "and all the medecin will not help me. my trouble is my only two sons are not like brothers. I know I used my best to raise my children right many nights I lie awake most of the night and how I feel next day. O my dear Sam I fear you have more to answer for than you think." She reminded him of his sending Orion away and told him how she had felt when she saw him. "It is no better now," she despaired. Although she didn't say so, she seems to have received a report from Mollie. After telling Sam what she had experienced on her last visit to Keokuk, she declared: "Now his mind is not right."

Her head began to ache as she wrote of trying to keep from her neighbors the family secret that "there is any thing between the brothers but brotherly love"—she feared it was already known in some families in Fredonia. "My dear Sam," she maundered on, "dont say light things about your brother it grieves your mother"—and at that point she had to stop to get a wet cloth for her head. "I dont know any thing that would give me more pleasure than to see my only two sons have a [brothery?] like brothers should have. . . . Now my dear son write to him and tell him to finish his book and send it to you and you will take it to Boston and have it published dont send It. take it yourself."[5]

Even before he received this pained appeal, Sam seems to have gotten word of his mother's angst, for two days before she set pen to paper he had written Pamela that "Ma forces me to reveal what I have concealed for a couple of months." He described his largesse toward his brother, explaining it in the same terms he had used with Orion and asserting that "it is not *my* money he is receiving, but *his own*—and fairly and honestly earned."[6] The letter arrived in Fredonia the morning after Jane had mailed hers. When her daughter handed it to her the old lady was not only appeased, she was elated almost beyond words. "My dear Sam," she rejoiced, "your letter your letter your confession proved a noble kind heart a generous good heart. . . . Thank the lord my prayers are answered. my pen cannot tell you how happy I am."[7]

In Fredonia some entrepreneurs had started a watch factory and were selling stock. Hoping to get Mark Twain to invest, they engaged Charles L. Webster, husband of Pamela's daughter Annie, to go to Hartford and talk to him. Webster, twenty-eight, had been trained as a civil engineer but now was a real estate salesman with prospects in local politics.[8] After Sam had visited Fredonia in the fall of 1879, he told Pamela he "achieved a higher opinion than ever of Charley, and his energy, capacity, and industry."[9]

Webster's mission was successful: Not only did he get his uncle to subscribe for five thousand dollars, Sam also put his nephew to work looking into some of his own affairs.[10] By the end of three weeks Sam had persuaded him to go to New York and take charge of his Kaolatype business, the company based on the process he had told Orion about. Pamela wrote to Orion and Mollie that Webster planned to leave his family in Fredonia and visit them every few weeks. "Mollie," added Jane, "I wish we could persuade Orion to move here and work like Charlie does. Orion could find plenty to do here. Orion hurry and finish the book. Osgood and co. are printing Sams. Boston co."[11]

Orion, who needed no urging, continued to write, sending increments to Sam. "If you can strike out, add to, or alter it enough to enable you to make out of it what I owe you," he said, "I shall be satisfied. If you can after that make out of it enough also to pay the government and widow McKee, I shall be glad."[12]

On January 18, 1882, Orion wrote his brother: "At last! the manuscript for the Autobiography of a Crank is in the Express Office, and I hold the Express-man's receipt, promising to deliver it to you, and stating a valuation of a thousand dollars."[13] He had inserted the 2,523 pages into twenty envelopes, marking each with the pages it contained, and packed them all in a box. But the next day he began to wonder if the parcel had been delivered properly, for he had not addressed it himself but left that for the agent to do in the prescribed manner. "If you will see if the box contains my ms., and let me know," he beseeched Sam, "I will be relieved of uneasiness."[14]

He still hadn't heard the second day, so he wrote again: "It has occurred to me that you might be willing to dispel my terrors by telegraphing me if you find things all right. I have been assuming the total loss of my two years' work, and hoping I would take the small-pox and die—perhaps from habitually expecting the worst."[15] On the third day Sam wrote, and, although his letter is missing from the Mark Twain Papers, he seems to have laid Orion's fears to rest, for on the twenty-ninth the relieved author wrote, "Many thanks for your dispatch. It made me as easy as an old shoe."[16]

A month passed without further word from Sam. At last Orion could contain himself no longer. "I am anxious to learn your opinion of the autobiography," he pleaded, "though I do not know that you have yet had time to take it up."[17] We do not have Sam's reply, but he seems, in one way or another, to have reassured Orion, for the latter wrote: "All right. You are a splendid brother. I shall not worry another dogoned bit." He told Sam he was now going to write a play he called "The Tragedy of Jephthah's Sacrifice."[18] Jephthah was a biblical character who vowed to God that if he were victorious in a battle he would sacrifice by fire whomever came out of the doors of his house on his return. That person turned out to be his only child, a daughter.[19]

Writing his autobiography had forced Orion to call to mind many incidents of the life of his only child—and, of course, her sudden death. At that time he had written to Thomas Starr King (a prominent Unitarian minister and fundraiser for the U.S. Sanitary Commission in California, which may have been how Orion knew him): "We have yielded up all we had to increase the Church in heaven—unwillingly, it is true, but still the sacrif . . ." And then he had crossed out the last unfinished word and substituted "fact" before going on, "may be something in our favor."[20] It was not out of character for Orion to take Jennie's death on his conscience. He may, in fact, have convinced himself that there was some causal connection between his success in Nevada and Jennie's demise. Like Jephthah,, he had been in a sort of battle (with California) and, also like the biblical figure, he had won. Less than a year later his daughter died of a fiery fever. "The Tragedy of Jephthah's Sacrifice," then, seems to have been an exercise in self-reproach—but it was more than that as well. Orion appears also to have been brooding about another of his tribulations—the excommunication—and he drew on more than twenty reference sources, from the Holy Scriptures to *The Bible for Learners,* to amass ammunition for an attack on organized religion.[21] What he envisaged was a book that would combine the stage play and an intellectual barrage.

As his jubilance on completing his autobiography attests, writing it had been an ordeal. Albert Bigelow Paine observed that it was "just one long record of fleeting hope, futile effort, and humiliation. It is the story of a life of disappointment; of a man who has been defeated and beaten down and crushed by the world until he has nothing but confession left to surrender."[22] Reliving such traumas as the loss of Jennie and the expulsion from the church must have tested Orion's mettle to the limit. After sending the manuscript off, as the days and weeks passed and (apparently) no further word came, his terrors redoubled. Sam's verdict meant everything. Had what began as "a model autobiography" somehow gone astray? Had the "Confessions of a Life that was a Failure" turned out to be itself a failure?

A month after Sam's last known communication to him, Orion penned a letter to his brother that was as strange as anything Sam had ever written to him. Instead of opening with "My Dear Brother," as was his wont, it began "Dear Friend" and went on inexplicably to state: "An unforeseen providence struck the enclosed manuscript with a bolt of lightning this afternoon. I beseech you to finish, or procure to be finished, 'The Tragedy of Jephtha's Sacrifice,' and render or have rendered unto me such meed of honor and profit as may fairly fall to me in the premises—be it much or nothing." Orion went on to declare that he hoped "the abused theatre folks in Chicago" would sometime use the enclosed work onstage "to preach against the parsons" and then enumerated the many sources he had consulted in writing it. As he reached the bottom of the third page his handwriting became a scrawl. "My malice may outrun my discretion," he scribbled,

> like the bull against the locomotive; but the church tried to thrust me into hell; and now if I can help to pull down the imposition and let its officials rot in peace, I shall be returning good for evil, so com-

paratively merciful will be my offense. (over) Think of their making a deliberate attempt to subject me to everlasting torture worse than the paddling in Sing Sing! But I don't think the preacher and elders will rot. Poor devils who are turned out of church may hope that spiritualists can yet prove that we live after this life.

"But if you think my ms. worthless," the runaway screed concluded,

do me the favor to put it in the fire, and oblige

Yours Respectfully,
Orion Clemens.[23]

His anguished vituperation was ostensibly directed at the authorities who excommunicated him, but in such phrases as "like the bull against the locomotive" and "pull down the imposition" (not to mention the strange formality of the salutation and closing) lies a hint that it may also have been intended for the formidable man who had imposed the torture of writing his life story on him—and then left him turning in the wind.

Orion's letter was written on March 30, 1882. It is possible Sam hadn't finished reading the autobiography at that time. Early that month he had entertained Howells in Hartford, and then the two men had gone briefly to New York on family business of Howells's.[24] Shortly after that, Jane Clemens and Pamela Moffett arrived in Hartford for a visit with Sam and Livy that lasted several weeks.[25]

One wonders whether Orion's book was discussed when the family got together and, if so, whether Jane Clemens once again exhorted her younger son to "take it to Boston and have it published." Actually, Sam wouldn't have had to go to that much trouble, because he had taken the first step toward becoming a publisher himself. His contract with the Boston firm of James R. Osgood and Company for *The Prince and the Pauper* made him essentially that, for by its terms he agreed to supply all the money for the manufacture of the book and to pay Osgood a royalty of 7.5 percent for selling it, reversing the usual conditions.[26] But instead of telling Osgood the next book he wanted to bring out was his brother's autobiography, Twain sent him a minor potboiler of his own material, which was eventually published as *The Stolen White Elephant*.[27]

In 1906 Mark Twain recalled that

Orion wrote his autobiography and sent it to me. But great was my disappointment; and my vexation, too. In it he was constantly making a hero of himself, exactly as I should have done and am doing now, and he was constantly forgetting to put in the episodes which placed him in an unheroic light. I knew several incidents of his life which were distinctly and painfully unheroic, but when I came across them in his autobiography they had changed color. They had turned themselves inside out, and were things to be intemperately proud of. In my dissatisfaction I destroyed a considerable part of that autobiography.[28]

Of course Orion hadn't constantly made a hero of himself—that would have been utterly out of character—but he had apparently done something that Sam found just as unacceptable: He had, as Paine reported, "drifted off into theological byways; into discussions of his excommunication and [religious] infidelities."[29] What had been meant to be "The Autobiography of a Coward" or "Confessions of a Life that was a Failure" had become merely "The Autobiography of a Crank." In any case, Sam deemed the project a nonsuccess, and sooner or later, in one way or another, Orion became aware of that fact and slipped over the edge, thereby realizing his wife's and mother's worst fears.

Perhaps the Clemenses in Hartford didn't discuss Orion's work at all, for they had a more pressing matter to attend to, one that had its origins when Sam hired Charles Webster. Annie, who had been taking care of both her ailing mother Pamela and her seventy-eight-year-old grandmother Jane, had moved from Fredonia to New York City to be with her husband, but Jane Clemens had "put her foot down very decidedly" that she would not live in that city.[30] Where, then, was the Clemens matriarch to reside?

It seems natural that Sam and Livy might have offered her quarters in their spacious manor (which they had provided with a special room for her when it was built), but if they did there is no record of it.[31] In any case, Jane insisted that Pamela go to live with her son in California while she would join Orion and Mollie in Keokuk. In what could be interpreted as a snub of her younger son, she said that "her place [was] with Orion" and that she looked forward to his reading to her.[32] "Ma wants to board with you," wrote Sam to his brother, "and pay her board. She will pay you $20 a month (she wouldn't pay a cent more in heaven; she is obstinate on this point), and as long as she remains with you and is content I will add $25 a month to the sum Perkins already sends you."[33]

Orion and Mollie went to Fredonia to take Mrs. Clemens back to Keokuk, but at Pamela's suggestion they decided to remain there until fall, when she would have wound up her business affairs and could accompany them back to Iowa before continuing on to California.[34] Despite her refusal to live in New York City, Jane Clemens was willing to visit there, and in June she and Pamela (no doubt accompanied by Orion and Mollie) went there in a private railway car Sam had instructed Charles Webster to arrange for.

When the travelers returned to Fredonia, Orion struggled for balance. He tried to resume his law studies, but as he reread Blackstone he found his attention becoming "slow and sleepy." Then, against his better judgment, he "slunk back [as he confessed to Sam], like a flop-eared, droop-tailed hound, to fooling away time on my *tragedy.*"[35] This was the "ms writing" Mollie so dreaded; it made her husband go "far off." She urged him instead to "turn his mind to the law."[36]

While Orion was in New York he had apparently met Charles Webster for the first time. Orion was not as taken with Annie's husband as Sam had been, and when Pamela told him of Webster's behavior toward her while they were living together in Fredonia, he was shocked. Pamela had inherited an estate when her husband died, and Webster had given her advice about how to invest it. One of his recommendations was to buy stock in the watch company Sam had invested in—stock that had become "absolutely without market price."[37] After Webster later saw to it that she was reimbursed, Pamela told Sam that Orion "entirely misunderstood Charley and misconstrued his acts," but at the time, Orion heard his sister tell him "the history of a gentle and yielding woman subjected for a series of years to gross, persistent, and often violent tyranny. . . . With extraordinary courage and resolution she saved herself from what looks like a deliberate plan on Charlie's part to strip her of half her fortune."[38]

When Orion learned that Webster was also handling (or mishandling) some of his mother's affairs, he wrote sternly to him: "When Mr. Bailey found that the deed was made and the title warranted by my mother, he had a right to conclude that she received his money; wherefore he may sue either you or her, and this makes it my business." The long, closely reasoned letter was not unfriendly, but it was firm: "As you have made the difficulty it is only fair that you should mend it."[39]

Was this the Orion of old, the righteous whistle-blower on Bliss's dealings—or was it the new Orion, the one who had trouble maintaining a grip on reality? There was another parallel with Bliss. Just as Orion had offered to keep an eye on his former employer for Sam, he now sent a copy of this letter to his brother and suggested: "Possibly my simple presence in the office of the Kaolatype Company might be useful to Charlie by saving him from yielding to temptation, and to you by saving you from the results of such yielding."[40] Webster also sent Orion's letter to Sam, along with his assurance that "this is *entirely* gratuitous and without the least foundation for fact. Grandma is old and forgetful and Uncle O has imposed upon here [*sic*] and made her to believe that I have *deliberately* swindled her I suppose."[41]

When these communications reached Sam, who was hard at work on his Mississippi River book, he became furious with Orion. He sent a blistering letter (now lost) accusing him of intentionally cheating the family (conceivably in regard to the Tennessee land) and perhaps demanding that he apologize to Annie. Orion did apologize. "I foolishly and needlessly hurt Charley's feelings," he humbly wrote his niece, "for which I am very sorry. I now retract all I said, apologize to him, and ask his pardon." He dutifully sent a copy to Sam, and Sam wrote to Webster: "Orion is quiet again. It is a waste of time to bother about him and his performances."[42]

But the matter was not closed. After letting more than a week go by, Orion replied to Sam's accusation. "Now that you have had time to cool," he began,

I think you will admit that you did me injustice in your last letter. Admitting for the sake of argument, what I do not admit in fact, that I intentionally cheated you all, that ought not to preclude me from the privilege of preventing others from cheating you if I can. . . .

I repeat, I do not want Charlie to lose his place. He may possess Jay Gould's financial abilities; but if he does he has with them Jay Gould's Conscience. All I ask is that while you keep him you watch him or set me or somebody else to watch him. I wish you could come here and listen to Pamela's confidence.

He concluded that "If I cannot be *useful* to you in New York I prefer to go to Keokuk. I would *rather* go to Keokuk, so far as *my own* comfort is concerned."[43]

Whether Charles Webster was culpable or not, it does seem that the watch factory he had represented was a shady operation, and Orion presented a bill of particulars to Sam.[44] This time Sam took time out from his book to compose a "very savage article exposing that watch company" and sent Webster to Fredonia with it, telling him to read it to the proprietors and threaten to publish it if they did not make good the stock they had sold to Sam and Pamela (and possibly Jane). The result was that the company "squared my account very promptly," as Sam wrote to his mother, "and I think that Charlie got the rest of you out of that scrape very cleverly." While giving credit to Webster, the letter made clear Charlie was but a cat's-paw for the real hero of the piece.[45]

The proprietors bought back Pamela's stock for $1,900, to her total satisfaction.[46] As Orion, Mollie, Jane, and Pamela prepared to depart for Keokuk, Orion reported to his brother that "Charley has completely settled with Pamela, doing well by her. . . . She . . . is going off as easy and happy as an old shoe."[47] But after they arrived at their destination, Orion told his brother that "nevertheless, I continue to think that Charlie settled everything satisfactorily *because you made him*." To this Jane Clemens added: "I lived in Fredonia a long time. I say keep both eyes open and watch as well as prey [*sic*]."[48]

That summer Orion had suffered from "spells" during which he was so "far off" that Mollie and Pamela made him promise to give up "writing on his old hobby about religion" and "forever let it alone."[49] On the other hand, in *l'affaire Webster* he seems to have kept his wits about him and to have acted in a manner appropriate to the situation as it was presented to him. If he had slipped over the precipice he still had a fingerhold—tenuous though it might be—on reality.

From Keokuk Orion continued to assail Sam with projects, and at one point he asked his brother, "Won't you please send me back the ms of my autobiography?" explaining that "I want to destroy all but about 100 pages."[50] Samuel seems to have ignored the plea. Orion was no doubt sincere when he promised Mollie and Pamela he would stop writing about religion, but when he got into a theological discussion with the editor of the *Keokuk Constitution,* Dr. George encouraged him to put his ideas into a lecture, for which he said he would assemble an audience. "I have not made up my mind to its delivery," Orion wrote to Sam, explaining that it had to do with (among other things) Jesus' teaching that sexual abstinence was a requirement for entering the kingdom of heaven. "This will give me time to hear from you, or to conclude by your silence that I am at liberty to take such course as I may choose."[51]

Mollie must have been looking over her husband's shoulder, for she confided to Pamela, "while he let his writing alone, he was like another person. But I don't see there is a ray of hope left for me. . . . I would tell you all about him; but it would do you harm and him no good that I can see."[52] The implication was that Orion's behavior was more bizarre than anyone else in the family suspected.

When Sam received Orion's letter he was so upset it cost him a day. He drafted "a dozen" replies but tore them up before settling on one. "Your Dr. George is a fool," this one charged, "your lecture would destroy you, and me too. Try to guard yourself jealously against two things—lecturing and writing; for you cannot achieve even a respectable mediocrity in either." In the Clemens family tradition, he prepared an oath for Orion. It called for him to refrain for the remainder of 1883 and all of 1884 from making any proposition of a business or literary nature to his brother, from asking his advice about any such project, from submitting "any piece of writing to him for judgment or criticism," and from lecturing. "I do beg that you will sign the enclosed oath," demanded Sam, "and abide by it—then we shall have peace. You are as good and kind as you can be, but you have no more this-worldly faculty than a babe."[53]

On February 27, 1883, Orion obediently signed the pledge and returned it with an apology for causing his brother so much worry and loss of valuable time.[54]

19
Orion's Death

He was a man who would walk through the snow to buy wheat for the sparrows when the days were cold and bleak. That was a parable of his life and more need not be said.

The Reverend W. L. Byers, at Orion's memorial service

In 1886 Samuel, Olivia, their three daughters, and a governess set out from Quarry Farm for Keokuk, arriving on July second. Since the fourth fell on a Sunday that year, Independence Day was celebrated on the third, and Keokuk had planned a grand observance, made even more exalted by the anticipated presence of Mark Twain. The day dawned sweltering hot. After a morning parade down Main Street, the organizers sent a carriage to Orion's house to take him and Sam to Rand Park, high on a bluff overlooking the imposing river, where an immense crowd had gathered. Sam was dressed "in an entire suit of white duck," as the *Constitution* reported, "with a tall white hat, and on his appearance a murmur of 'There he is,' passed through the crowd, and people edged up to get a closer view of the great humorist."[1] The Clemens brothers duly delivered, the carriage turned back to fetch the rest of the family.[2]

After the Second Regiment band played "Robin Adair," the Honorable Gibson Browne, president of the day, called the meeting to order, and a prayer was offered by the Reverend R. C. McIlwain. This was followed by another musical rendition and the reading of the Declaration of Independence by Orion Clemens "in a clear and distinct manner."[3] The speaker of the day was the Honorable Thomas Hedge Jr. of Burlington, who held forth for thirty minutes and was heartily applauded. Former Keokuk resident Samuel L. Clemens was then introduced to more applause.[4] As was everyone else, Mark Twain was in high patriotic fervor. "You have heard the declaration of independence with its majestic ending," he declaimed, and then went on to recapitulate the events of the day. "All I have to do is to add the verdict, which is all that can be added, and that is, 'It is a successful day.'" Of course an address by Mark Twain wouldn't be complete without a dig. "When I was here thirty years ago there were 3,000 people here," he told the citizens of Keokuk, "and they drank 3,000 barrels of whisky a day. They drank it in public then."[5] The first time the Clemens brothers had appeared on a platform together was in Keokuk, and on the third of July 1886 they so appeared for the last time, also in Keokuk.

Sam and his family remained in the city four days. During that time the brothers discussed Orion's research for a game about the English monarchs Sam had invented.[6] On their last evening in Keokuk, Sam and his family were honored by Orion and Mollie with a reception. More than four hundred invitations were sent out, and such a large crowd showed up that many guests had to move about on the lawn (which, like the house, was decorated with Chinese lanterns). Inside, there were two greeting lines. In the front parlor Jane Clemens, Orion, and Pamela (who had made her separate way to Keokuk for the family reunion) welcomed guests, while in the library Sam (again clad in white), Livy, and Mollie held court. As Fred Lorch pointed out, it was a proud moment for Jane Clemens; for the first time in fifteen years she had all her children and most of her grandchildren with her.[7] (It is worth noting that she welcomed guests at Orion's side rather than with her famous visiting son.)

Six years earlier, when Orion and Mollie went to Hartford, Sam had taken his brother into his confidence and shown him not only the unfinished manuscript of *The Prince and the Pauper* but the risqué sketch "1601" as well. Since then, he had kept Orion posted on his contract negotiations for the novel, his progress on *Huckleberry Finn* (although he didn't mention the title or subject), and his role in the publication of General Grant's memoirs.[8] Now in Keokuk, although he surely realized Orion would want to know, he didn't share the fact that he was in the midst of a new novel, one concerning a Connecticut Yankee in the court of King Arthur.

What meaning life still held for Orion largely derived from the reflected glory of his celebrated brother. He must therefore have been deeply wounded when, four months after Sam and his family returned to Connecticut, he learned of the work only by chance. Although he tried to sound upbeat, his real feelings about what he surely saw as a deliberate slight glimmered through his next letter: "I was greatly surprised as well as pleased that you have written another book, and that extracts from it so amused and entertained a New York audience. It will dissipate the owlish statements that your humor is losing the richness of the Jumping Frog. When will your new book be published? . . . I imagine you have been at work on it a good while."[9] This letter seems to have gone unanswered.

Less than a month later, Orion finished dinner and went upstairs to his and Mollie's room. There he picked up a bottle of aqua ammonia (ammonia water, used in cleaning), tilted his head back, and poured the contents into his mouth. Mollie heard him rushing down the stairs, and so alarming was the clamor that she thought: "Ma has a fit, or the house is on fire—in either case I must be calm." She jumped up and opened the stair door and discovered Orion "as white as death," his mouth wide open. When she asked what was wrong, he managed to gasp: "Oh my God, I have taken poison."

Determining what the substance was, Mollie gave him olive oil and sent her kitchen helper for Dr. Jenkins. Then, bareheaded and coatless, she and Orion ran out into the falling snow. Spying a horse and buggy standing unhitched, Mollie commandeered the conveyance and drove her husband to the pharmacy four blocks away. There Orion was given what Mollie called "ascid." He was spitting blood freely. By that time Mrs. Jenkins had called the doctor to his office above the drugstore. On examining Orion he said he feared some of the ammonia had gone down the windpipe, where it would form a membrane or cause spasms, either of which would be very serious. At last things settled down a little and the patient seemed to be out of immediate danger. Dr. Jenkins sent him home and told him to remain indoors.

The pungent solution had wreaked havoc. "Imagine the skin burned off the mouth, tongue, pallet, and clear down farther than can be seen *raw*," Mollie wrote to Sam and Livy. Orion claimed he thought he had been taking cough medicine, but his wife pointed out that "his cough medicin was on our bureau behind the door and he took this bottle off our wash stand," adding meaningfully: "I dont know how or why."[10] Orion's conversation was now limited to nods and shakings of the head, and he was,

Mollie told Sam and Livy, "dreadfully nervous." "He groans all the time. He expectorates great quantities." Despite the danger to himself, Orion's main concern was his research for Sam's game. "I am grievously disappointed," he wrote his brother a day or two after the incident, "for I wholly lost yesterday, and may lose all this week from your work."[11]

For six days and nights Orion got no rest because of the pain.[12] Unable to eat, he grew thin.[13] The doctor, concerned about diphtheria, croup, and pneumonia, watched him very closely.[14]

By April the patient was well enough to put in four hours a day for Sam—who cautioned him, however, to "take it perfectly easy, there's no hurry. Vary your day with anything that will afford relaxation for the mind. The kings have waited 800 years—we'll not let them rush us now."[15]

In August of 1890 Jane Clemens suffered a stroke. Sam rushed to Keokuk and remained at her bedside for several days. The old woman seemed to get better, and then a telegram arrived, calling Sam back east on business. Two months later, on October 27, 1890, Mrs. Clemens died at the age of eighty-seven. Her body was taken to Hannibal for burial in Mount Olivet Cemetery, between her husband and her son Henry. Sam arrived on October 30, the day of the funeral, which took place in the afternoon, and probably began his return trip to Hartford that evening.[16] Two days later Orion wrote him, "You have nothing to regret toward Ma. You did all you could, and nobly and generously; but I feel that your praises are not deserved. I am stung with remorse. If I had her back I would recall and abolish every harsh and over-loud modulation of voice; I would talk and listen to her more; I would cheer her oftener with hopes of the impossible."[17]

In mid-1891 Samuel moved his family to Europe (partly to save on expenses), but in the spring of 1893 he returned to the United States and traveled to Chicago with his partner Fred Hall to check on the headway of the Paige typesetting machine, in which he had invested heavily. He telegraphed Orion to meet him there, saying he wanted to consult with him on a question of law.[18] While in Chicago Sam came down with a severe cold and was confined to his room in the Great Northern Hotel.[19] Hall later recalled "his sitting up in bed and smoking—contrary to the doctor's orders—and swapping yarns with friends who dropped in to see him."

When Orion arrived, Hall had the impression that the sixty-eight-year-old man had "no sense of humor, and was the simplest, best natured, most

impractical and delightfully naive man I ever met." Since Sam had probably primed him, these impressions may not have been entirely fresh—but
what Hall recorded next surely was: "The way in which he received Mr. S.
L. Clemens' remarks about himself, and biting sarcasms, was at once pitiful
and amusing."[20]

Samuel returned to Europe, but in September he arrived back in New
York. His financial circumstances were, as the official biographer pointed
out, at a lower ebb than they had ever been—"lower, even, than during
those mining days among the bleak Esmeralda hills. Then he had no one
but himself and was young. Now, at fifty-eight, he had precious lives dependent upon him, and he was weighed down with a vast burden of debt.
. . . What he was to do Clemens did not know."[21] In addition to his wife
and children, two other "precious lives" were Orion's and Mollie's, and it is
to Samuel's credit that not only did he not miss a single month's check to
his brother and sister-in-law, but he also shielded them from his worst
business troubles.

Orion seemed to suspect, nonetheless, that his brother's publishing house,
Charles L. Webster & Co., was foundering. "I am afraid you are worrying
and working beyond your strength," he wrote Sam in December, and the
following month, after thanking his brother for his monthly fifty dollars,
he enclosed some manuscript he said he hoped would "pay your publishing
business." The fragment that survives hardly seems likely to have benefited
the business—but perhaps its significance lies elsewhere. This is the passage quoted in chapter 1 in which Orion described how John Marshall
Clemens had surrendered to his creditors all his assets, even offering "his
cow, and the knives and forks from his table."[22]

On April 18, 1894, the publishing house executed assignment papers
and closed its doors.[23] The following year Mark Twain set off with his wife
and daughter Clara on a speaking tour that would take them around the
world. When he reached Vancouver he issued a public statement to the
effect that he was not lecturing for his own benefit but for his creditors. "A
merchant who has given up all he has," declared the humorist, "may take
advantage of the rules of insolvency and start free again for himself; but I
am not a business man, and honor is a harder master than the law. It cannot compromise for less than a hundred cents on the dollar." He did not
enjoy the hardships of lecturing, said the fifty-nine-year-old man, and had

it not been for "the imperious moral necessity" of paying his debts he would never have undertaken this journey at his time of life. He could have supported himself comfortably by his pen, he asserted, "but writing is too slow for the demands I have to meet. Therefore I have begun to lecture my way around the world."[24]

He was, in other words, offering his creditors the equivalent of "his cow, and the knives and forks from his table." Henry Rogers (the Standard Oil Company millionaire who helped Mark Twain in his financial plight) and Olivia Clemens have both been credited with persuading Clemens to pay his debts dollar for dollar, but Orion's subtle reminder of how a Clemens comports himself in the face of bankruptcy—even to the point, if necessary, of working himself to death—may also have figured in the decision.

One year later, having worked their way through Australia, India, and South Africa, Sam, Olivia, and Clara arrived in England, where they took a house in Guildford, Surrey, for a month. On August 18, 1896, Susy Clemens, who had remained in Hartford, died of cerebrospinal meningitis, apparently the same disease that had claimed Jennie Clemens in Nevada in 1864. Sam thought he might go mad with grief.[25] He wrote to Orion and Mollie:

There is nothing to say. The bolt has fallen, and we with it—in pride, spirit, ambition, the zest of life.

We shall live here a few months, while I do some writing. We that are left are together, and all well—at least fairly well; and not apparently near to death—which is regretable [*sic*].[26]

Mark Twain's lecture tour had been successful, but it hadn't wiped out all his debts. Orion forwarded an offer from a prosperous Keokuk citizen to help him financially. Sam wrote back, "I beg you that you will give him my most cordial thanks. . . . But I cherish the feeling that all in good time I shall work out of debt by my own exertions. I have had this feeling from the first, and have never seen any reason to change it."[27]

It is difficult to escape the impression that he was posturing, for about the time he expressed these high-sounding sentiments to Orion, he also wrote: "I have grown so tired of being in debt that often I think I could part with my skin and my teeth to get out. I know that the custom is to wait till a man is dead and then gather up money for a monument for him, when he can't enjoy it; but if friends want to advance money for the monument now, my creditors will think that the more rational course, and so shall I."[28]

This was a draft of what was probably meant to be a letter to James Gordon Bennett of the *New York Herald* accepting his offer to sponsor a subscription fund for Mark Twain's relief. Whether that particular letter was sent we don't know, but we do know by Clemens's own testimony that he gave Bennett "my word that if it was ever put before the public I would stand by it and not repudiate it."[29] The campaign was announced in the *Herald* on June 1, 1897. When Henry Rogers and Olivia got word of it they both were opposed, and Olivia finally prevailed on her husband to stop the scheme and return the money.[30]

As it turned out, the amount collected was embarrassingly small, less than three thousand dollars.[31] In order to "reverse things and give me a handsome boom," Sam asked Henry Rogers ("if your conscience will let you") to "collect $40,000 privately for me from yourself, then pay it back to yourself, and have somebody tell the press it was collected [from the public] but that by Mrs. Clemens's desire I asked that it be returned to the givers and that it was done," adding, "nobody will ever be the wiser." Apparently even Rogers's challenged sense of right and wrong balked at such patent chicanery.[32]

Mark Twain had always been generous with his time and money in causes he considered worthy, but in terms of bold, magnanimous—even heroic— gestures, his world lecture tour surpassed anything he had done before. It was a milestone, and, as Greg W. Zacharias has pointed out, it not only gave his career a boost when it needed it most, it also helped to establish Twain as "an embodiment of national virtues."[33] Like Tom Driscoll in *Pudd'nhead Wilson,* Clemens may even have "imagined that his character had undergone a pretty radical change." But now, having moved across the world stage, the poor man was tired. He had originally intended to complete the tour in the States, but (as he told Frank Fuller) "I am not strong enough for the work and am too old."[34] When friends offered to help, it is understandable he accepted. What a pity, then, that after the subscription was terminated he reverted to his old ways and asked Rogers to connive with him. The ethical lapse was reminiscent of the Hopkins massacre hoax and the Sanitary Fund flour sack debacle. As the author of *Pudd'nhead Wilson* observed about Tom Driscoll and his newfound self-esteem: "But that was because he did not know himself."

In July Orion had another birthday. As he looked back over his life he felt sad. "I have made so many mistakes and caused so much trouble to others," he wrote to Pamela, "that I find no satisfaction in the past. Happily 72 years does not threaten a long continuance of my system of wreckage."[35] For her part, Mollie found she had to devote a good deal of attention to her husband.[36]

On November 30, 1897, Sam turned sixty-two. Orion wrote to congratulate him on "a life full of honor, with the promise of a happy future" and on the success of the recently published *Following the Equator*. "Few have so much cause for congratulation," he exulted. He told his brother of his latest literary project, a biography of Judas of Galilee that would probe the mystery of the Essene sect known as the society of the Dead Sea, and he proposed himself as a model for a "fool character" in a comic novel he wanted Sam to write.[37]

On the evening of Friday, December 10, 1897, Orion and Mollie entertained guests, and Mollie noted that Orion was especially bright and jolly. The following morning he got up at the usual hour of six and went downstairs to build a fire in the kitchen stove.[38] As he waited for the room to warm, he sat at the table and jotted down some notes on a brief for a case that was pending before the supreme court (presumably the Iowa court). Ordinarily, when the fire was going well he rapped on the ceiling to signal Mollie, but this morning his wife heard nothing. After waiting a while, she tapped on the bedroom floor. There was no response.

She tried again. Still no answer. She got up and went downstairs. There she found her husband seated at the kitchen table, his head bowed, hands hanging at his sides. She went to him and saw that he was dead. "The suddenness of the shock almost prostrated the bereaved wife," reported the *Gate City*. Pulling herself together, she hastened to the neighbors, who accompanied her home. Word spread, and soon other friends began showing up to lend support.[39]

Mollie sent a cablegram to Sam and Livy in Vienna, and at nine-thirty that evening, local time, they replied with a wire of sympathy. Half an hour later Sam wrote his sister-in-law a letter, "in the wintry mid-afternoon of the heaviest day you have known since we saw Jenny escape from this life thirty-three years ago, and were then too ignorant to rejoice at it."

"We all grieve for you," he continued,

our sympathy goes out to you from experienced hearts, and with it our love; and with Orion, and for Orion I rejoice. He has received life's best gift.

He was good—all good, and sound; there was nothing bad in him, nothing base, nor any unkindness. It was unjust that such a man, against whom no offense could be charged, should have been sentenced to live 72 years. It was beautiful, the patience with which he bore it.[40]

Years later Sam would speak of Orion's "long and troubled and pathetic and unprofitable life," but for the moment, and for Mollie's reading, he confined himself to his brother's goodness and beauty and patience.[41]

Newspapers from Muscatine, Iowa, to St. Louis, Missouri, and as far away as Buffalo, New York, noted Orion's death.[42] The *Keokuk Gate City* observed, "He was a most persistent and ardent worker in anything he undertook to do, a fact which will be attested to by those of the bar who have met him in the active practice of that profession."[43]

On Monday morning the Keokuk bar met in the district court room for the purpose of taking formal action on Orion's death. After a committee had submitted resolutions for consideration, the Honorable John E. Craig spoke on behalf of one of them. "He had filled high offices," he said of Orion, referring to his duties in Nevada Territory, "and while others came away from their offices, probably better financially than Mr. Clemens, he was contented with the self satisfaction of work well done. He was a man truly great and as a public officer he was recognized as a man of high character. His life should be looked up to by all."[44]

The Honorable D. F. Miller admitted that Orion "did not take hold of the work of a lawyer with the ease of one who had been a life long practitioner," but insisted that he was "courageous to a fault, even in trying a case, and when we say he was a good lawyer, we give him the highest praise and say as much as we shall ever have the honor to have said of us."[45]

Orion's colleagues passed two resolutions, one stating that they would always remember him as "a genial, pleasant, companionable friend" and the other that "we render to his widow the heartfelt sympathy of every member of this bar." At the suggestion of Judge Bank the members formed a double line at the courthouse door and marched to the Clemens residence, where "each in turn took his last look on the face of their departed brother lawyer."[46]

Private services were conducted at the Congregational Church by the Reverend W. L. Byers, an old friend. "He was a man," said the minister, "who would walk through the snow to buy wheat for the sparrows when the days were cold and bleak. That was a parable of his life and more need not be said."[47] That evening the church men's club, which Orion had helped organize, passed a resolution that spoke of "one . . . whose life has been to us and to all his friends a remarkable example of upright, honest character; whose cheerful, gentle manliness has endeared him to us in no ordinary degree."[48]

Orion's body was taken to Hannibal, and he was interred in Mount Olivet Cemetery alongside his mother, father, and brother Henry.[49] As Orion's birthday letter to Sam showed, even to the end of his life he was seeking the truth that had eluded him for so long; maybe the society of the Dead Sea would reveal it at last. This search was typical of him, and it probably exasperated his brother as much as ever. Orion was aware that Sam used him in his writings, and once again he offered himself as a target for ridicule; that too was characteristic.

Orion's life was not just "a remarkable example of upright, honest character." It was also proof that a person could overcome at least some of the errors of parents, church, and society. Even more important, it demonstrated the possibility of personal change. Sam never forgave his brother for playing the despot in the Hannibal printshop, but the fact is, Orion underwent a transformation after that. When he went to Nevada and found himself faced with a governmental crisis he alone could handle, somehow he found the inner resources to rise to the occasion. The boy for whom those Tennessee mountaineers had foreseen a shining future had come surprisingly close to attaining it. If after that his career went into a decline that lasted the rest of his life, he never returned to being the tyrant he had earlier been. He had become incapable of lording it over anyone. Instead of an Andrew Johnson, a Napoleon, or a Benjamin Franklin, Orion had become more like St. Francis of Assisi, a man who would make a special trip through the snow rather than let the sparrows go hungry.

If someone hadn't insisted in 1847 on autopsying the body of John Marshall Clemens the story of his two sons might have been vastly different. As it was, the main burden of the father's impropriety (if that is what it was) fell on Orion, and ever since the examination he had struggled to maintain his mental balance. In the West he seemed to overcome the ghost, but when Jennie died he must have realized he would never be free of it. The religion that had sustained him during those years began to show cracks, which in time grew to alarming proportions. In his travail he was not helped by Sam, who added to his burden when he assigned him the task of writing a painfully candid but distorted autobiography. When Sam rejected that work, Orion went over the edge. It is all the more remarkable, then, that throughout his long ordeal he somehow managed to retain his sense of humor, his openheartedness, and his essential goodness.

Judged by some standards, his life was a failure—"long and troubled and pathetic and unprofitable"—but as the outpouring of affection and esteem showed, not by everyone's measure. It was probably not what Orion had become that annoyed Sam so much as the fact he had shown growth was indeed possible. The author of *Puddn'head Wilson* wrote: "In several ways his opinions were totally changed, and would never go back to what they were before, but the main structure of his character was not changed, and could not be changed."[50] Ostensibly Sam was speaking of Tom Driscoll, but the words might as well have applied to himself.

20
Orion's Legacy

When he gets a notion into his head . . . the Devil can't get it out
again.

Sam characterizing Orion

If he got a notion in his head once, there warn't no getting it out
again.

Huck characterizing Jim

In 1906 a forty-four-year-old midwestern author named Albert Bigelow
Paine approached Mark Twain with the idea of writing his biography. Twain
consented, gave Paine a room in his house to work in, allowed him to go
through manuscripts and letters, and let him refer to the parts of Orion's
autobiography he hadn't destroyed.[1] Paine was also allowed to listen as
Clemens dictated sections of his autobiography to stenographer/typist
Josephine Hobby.[2] Paine was free to use the resulting texts, ask questions,
and suggest topics.

Twain seems to have granted Paine's request with little reflection, but
after the biographer's research was under way he became concerned about
what might turn up. "I find that Sam Moffett has been lending old letters
of mine to Mr. Paine without first submitting them to me for approval or
the reverse," he wrote to Howells in 1908, "and so I've stopped it. I don't
like to have those privacies exposed in such a way to even my biographer."
He bade his old friend not to comply if Paine asked him for letters and
added that "I must warn Twichell, too," rationalizing that "a man should
be dead before his private foolishnesses are risked in print."[3] Accordingly,
Howells returned "a huge mass" of Twain's letters to him.[4] Paine, who stood
in awe of Twain, seems to have raised no objection to these restrictions.

In addition to limiting the information that reached him, Twain seems
to have misled his biographer, for in the *Biography* Paine separates by nearly
two years Orion's veto of Herman Camp's offer for the Tennessee land and

Sam's putting a pistol to his head.[5] Had Paine been allowed to see Sam's 1865 letters to Orion he would have realized at least part of his mistake, but these documents were withheld ("There is not a line that has survived [from 1865]," Paine wrote in the collection of the letters he edited, published in 1917).[6] Had he connected those two events he would have had a striking illustration of how important Orion was in Sam's life. Paine never met his subject's elder brother, who had died nearly ten years before the biographer approached Twain, and so he was entirely dependent on what the humorist said about Orion, on his fragmentary autobiography, and on whatever other information Twain chose to make available.

As encyclopedic as the multivolume *Mark Twain: A Biography* is, it omits a number of topics that are critical to the relationship between Sam and Orion. There is no mention, for instance, of John Marshall Clemens's autopsy. Paine may not have seen the part of Orion's personal history that described that curious affair (it was probably in the "considerable part of that autobiography" Sam destroyed), but he does seem to have seen Howells's letter referring to it[7] and he presumably had access to the manuscript of "Villagers of 1840–3," which mentions it. Paine reported in the *Biography* that Sam's abrupt departure from Hannibal in 1853 was occasioned by tension between him and Orion, and he tells of Sam returning months later with a gun, but he makes no connection between the two events and fails to mention the strange game of hide-and-seek that took place in the interim.

We have no idea how much the biographer may have learned about the Sagebrush War and Sam's jealous reaction to Orion's triumph in it; we know only that those signal matters are not touched on in the *Biography*— nor is Jennie's death, a hinge in Orion's life. Sam's frantic plea to his brother to "strike a bargain" is not mentioned; since Twain seems to have withheld all the 1865 letters, Paine probably knew nothing about that episode, so vital to his undertaking. Mark Twain's preoccupation with Orion as a literary model, as shown, for instance, in his letters to Howells, receives no reference; those letters were probably in the "huge mass" Howells sent back to Twain. Paine doesn't mention in the *Biography* Twain's 1901 confession about buying a gun and traveling twelve hundred miles to kill a man, even though he included the letter to Joseph Twichell in which the admission was made when he compiled *Mark Twain's Letters.*

These events and others, had they been dealt with in the book, might have made clear Orion's deep and abiding effect on his brother. As it was, Paine, following the party line established by Twain in his autobiographical dictations, wrote of Orion near the beginning of the *Biography:* "Full of whims and fancies, unstable, indeterminate, he was swayed by every passing emotion and influence," and then proceeded, as Orion reappeared here and there, to perpetuate the image of a nitwit, albeit a well-meaning one.[8] Years after the *Biography* was published, when Paine compiled the correspondence, he acknowledged that "following the life of Mark Twain, whether through his letters or along the sequence of detailed occurrence, we are never more than a little while, or a little distance, from his brother Orion," but he failed to carry that thought through to its full import.[9]

Together, Twain in his *Autobiography* and Paine in his *Biography* set the tone for how Orion would be treated by future biographers and historians. In fairness it must be admitted that Orion himself, by agreeing to write his autobiography in the manner Sam stipulated, became a party to his own denigration. Still, he seems not to have followed his brother's rules religiously; one cannot help but feel that had Paine been more diligent and independent he might have written a more accurate biography, for even though Twain had destroyed much of the autobiography, what remained must have contained some hint, at least, that the myth of Orion the nonentity was just that.

Understandably, most subsequent writers have followed Twain and Paine's lead in portraying Orion—but there have been exceptions. Fred W. Lorch warned in 1929 that "it would be unsafe to rely upon Sam's estimate of Orion," pointing out that the humorist "made no real pretense to accuracy" and citing his "ever vivid imagination" and "capricious memory." Furthermore, Lorch asserted, during Orion's late years Sam could not have known him well, since the brothers had little direct contact. "Orion was not ridiculous," judged Lorch, who interviewed persons who had known him. "Somehow his more peculiar characteristics have come to be accepted as wholly indicative of the kind of man he really was."[10] In 1934 Minnie M. Brashear went even further. She judged that "as the whole record now appears—in [Twain's] description of Orion in his *Autobiography,* supplemented by his letters about him, especially those to William Dean Howells—it sounds too much like sport at the expense of a helpless creature." In Orion's defense she pointed out that he "was notable for his industry and integrity, and he was the main support of the Clemens family for over ten years." Brashear concluded by offering: "It is probably not an exaggeration to say that the greatest single influence in Mark Twain's life was his older brother, lasting through the publication of *Roughing It*."[11]

Twain's destruction of portions of Orion's manuscript probably took place in 1880, after Howells pleaded with him to "strike out" some of the most "intimate" passages. Today only a few pages of Orion's autobiography survive in the Mark Twain Papers. What happened to the part the humorist didn't destroy? When Dixon Wecter wrote *Sam Clemens of Hannibal*, around 1950, he stated that "a private but apparently trustworthy source asserts that most of Orion's narrative (save for a few scattered sheets in MTP) was lost before Mark Twain's death, when Paine's suitcase was stolen in the Grand Central Station—although Paine in fear of Mark's anger never confessed the loss."[12] Wecter's source may have been Isabel V. Lyon, Clemens's former secretary, who was at that time in her late seventies.[13] On July 11, 1907, Miss Lyon noted in her journal that she had run across "Tino" (her nickname for Paine) in New York. "He dropped into my cab and told me of the calamity that had befallen him. He'd lost his big new handbag in G. C. Station—with nearly all his clothes in it, photos of the King [Clemens], ms. of his own, and oh, everything; even the Orion letters he was carrying up to Elmira to read."[14] Note that it was "the Orion letters" that were lost—not his "autobiography" or his "manuscript"—so Miss Lyon's recollection forty years after the fact may have been in error.

In the *Biography* Paine wrote that "a quantity of Orion's manuscript has been lost and destroyed, but enough fragments of it remain to show its fidelity to the original plan" and "Fortunately the earliest of these chapters were preserved, and . . . furnished much of the childhood details for this biography."[15] The biographer even quoted directly from Orion's work at several points, such as on pages 24, 44, and 85 of the *Biography*. It seems, then, that a considerable portion of Orion's work was still on hand when Paine wrote *Mark Twain: A Biography*. In *The Boys' Life of Mark Twain* he stated that he "spent four years in collecting the material for the biography and two years in writing it."[16] If that chronology can be taken literally, the years 1906 to 1910 were occupied with researching the book and 1910 to 1912 with writing it (it was copyrighted in 1912). That suggests Wecter's source was wrong in asserting that "most of Orion's narrative . . . was lost before Mark Twain's death [in 1910]." It seems, then, that Orion's autobiography was not lost in Grand Central Station in July 1907—which is unfortunate, for if it had been, there would still remain the possibility, however slight, that someday it might resurface.

If it (or what was left of it) was in Paine's possession as late as, say, 1912, what happened to it subsequently? In April 1927 Fred W. Lorch, who was writing an article about Mark Twain's experiences in Iowa, wrote to Paine, who was then custodian of the Mark Twain Papers, and asked to see "Orion's autobiographical papers."[17] Paine replied: "Orion's memoirs are deep in the dusty obscurity of a safe deposit vault, and would, I think be of no use to you if you had them." In the fall of that year the persistent Lorch tried again, only to receive this reply:

> There is no hope of your seeing those odds and ends of Orion's Autobiography. It was M. T.'s wish that all should be destroyed, and most of them were burned. Some fragments may remain, but I am not sure, and in any case it is certain that the trustees would not dig them out. . . . Mrs. Gabrilowitsch (Clara Clemens) and myself are Mark Twain's literary executors. Knowing his feelings in the matter, our own feeling, and the feeling of the trustees, I am sure that permission to borrow, or to examine, any remaining fragments of Orion's record, supposing any still exists, would be quite out of the question.[18]

Between April and October 1927, then, the papers (or "most of them") had apparently gone from the "dusty obscurity of a safe deposit vault" to ashes. Had Paine actually destroyed them during that period (perhaps as a result of Lorch's inquiry), or had he merely changed his story to turn away the importunate researcher? Unfortunately, we probably have to take Paine at his word that those "odds and ends of Orion's *Autobiography . . . were* burned."

Such was the sad tale of how Mark Twain propagated—even from the grave—the impression that Orion Clemens was a laughable nincompoop who had negligible impact on his famous brother. The great humorist did such a good job of clouding the issue that Orion became virtually the invisible man of Mark Twain studies. Not only were the facts of the brothers' lifelong interaction obscured, but Orion's full influence on Mark Twain's fiction was missed. Franklin R. Rogers, in *Mark Twain's Satires and Burlesques,* identified a number of characters in the minor stories who owe their existence to Orion, but I believe Orion's impact goes further and

deeper. (In what follows we enter the treacherous waters of literary interpretation, so I should emphasize that these are my opinions only and that
others will no doubt disagree.)

Recurring themes in several novels can be traced to the saga of Orion
and Samuel. As we have seen, one is that of two innocents thrown together
by fate and borne by a snug conveyance into unknown territory, in the
process discovering their fellowship. That is what I believe happened to
Orion and Samuel as they traveled from St. Louis to Carson City, and
Mark Twain covered that journey (as well as many other incidents) in *Roughing It*. An observer who is independently acquainted with the events and
personalities that book claims to portray might expect Orion to loom large,
but he emerges as a mere pasteboard character, hardly more than a piece of
stage scenery. In *The Gilded Age* Washington and Clay Hawkins find themselves on a steamboat making its way up the Mississippi to a new home and
learn they can be friends as well as accidental brothers.[19] After showing us
this comradely pastoral, Mark Twain proceeds to explore the comedic possibilities in Orion's character and to hint at the relationship he and Orion
began to assume at the time this novel was written, that of benefactor and
beneficiary ("help him along all you can, Clay").

In *Huckleberry Finn* Mark Twain's genius came up with a surprising new
contrivance: a callow white youth and a black slave who is his superior in
every way save caste. In placing these two unlikely companions (whose age
difference might be about ten years) on a raft and setting them adrift on
the Mississippi, the author gave us the most true-to-life and moving rendition of his repeated motif. Even though they were members of the same
household, the boy and the slave seem not to have known each other well,
but as they float languidly down the majestic river, encountering adventures along the way, they make up for that failing. Huck grudgingly admits
at one point that Jim "was right; he was most always right; he had an uncommon level head for a nigger," but on another occasion he remarks: "I
never see such a nigger. If he got a notion in his head once, there warn't no
getting it out again."[20] This disparaging observation sounds surprisingly
like one Sam made about his elder brother in 1856: "But you know what
Orion is," he wrote to Henry. "When he gets a notion into his head, and
more especially if it is an erroneous one, the Devil can't get it out again."[21]
Twain's divergent impulses toward Orion are reflected in Huck's alternat-
ing acceptance and rejection of the slave, and the fascination the reader

finds in watching these two interact may owe much to the sinuous bond between Sam and Orion.

If in laying down the guidelines for Orion's autobiography Sam effectively barred him from ever claiming credit for his younger brother's moral enlightenment, in the passage in *Huckleberry Finn* (written three years later) wherein Huck resolves, "I'll *go* to hell" to save Jim,[22] Mark Twain seems symbolically to acknowledge his debt—for if it weren't for Jim's friendship and ennobling influence, Huck probably would have remained as callow and benighted as ever. Mark Twain was able to envision through Huck's eyes what it might be like to accept Orion as a brother, but in the end he failed to pursue to their logical conclusion the implications of the boy's insight. In the final chapter, Tom Sawyer's news of Miss Watson's manumission of the slave and his forty-dollar prize for Jim no more compensated him for what had been done to him than Sam's twenty-five dollar raise and Orion's "free papers" (as Mollie called them) did Orion justice. Mark Twain saw where we wanted to go, but Sam Clemens couldn't find a way to get there.

Another repeated topic in Twain's fiction is the exchange of estates. In *The Prince and the Pauper* Tom Canty trades places with Edward, Prince of Wales, who then becomes a "forlorn and friendless prince" striving to win his way back to his rightful throne. As Mark Twain wrote that novel, he was holding court in his palatial mansion in Hartford, while in far-off Keokuk, Orion, whom Samuel had "banished," was living near the poverty line and longing to return to Connecticut. As Tom Canty, Mark Twain allowed himself to usurp the throne, while in the flamboyant persona of Miles Hendon he swept to the rescue of the wronged prince. Nor (truth to tell) did he need to depart very far from the facts of his life to do so, for, as we have seen, virtually every wrong he did Orion was matched with a compensating act of charity. In *Those Extraordinary Twins* Luigi and Angelo Capello alternate control of their shared body every seven days, and in the unfinished novel "Which Was It?" the former slave Jasper becomes George Harrison's overlord.

Perhaps the most important pattern that owes something to Orion is that of the pariah who turns out to be right. As we have seen, Orion may have become the goat of the Clemens family because of his "premature" aversion to slavery, only to be vindicated in the end. In *Pudd'nhead Wilson* David Wilson earns his sobriquet by making a wry comment about killing half a dog that goes over the heads of his bucolic listeners. "Well," Tom Driscoll taunts the lawyer and tinkerer in chapter 11, "how does the law come on? Had a case yet?" Pudd'nhead has to admit he has, in fact, never had a client, but asserts that he has kept up his studies "all these years" just in case. Later the villagers recognize Wilson's worth and ask him to run for mayor, and by the end of the novel he has not only won the election but has given Driscoll his comeuppance by proving him both a murderer and an impostor.

The renegade who is vindicated in the end also shows up in the *Mysterious Stranger Manuscripts* and *Huckleberry Finn*. The stranger who appears inexplicably at the door of Heinrich Stein's printshop is taken for a fool and a milksop, but later he is seen to be independent, fascinating, courageous, and powerful.[23] Jim is only a slave, the lowest of the low, yet he emerges as *Huckleberry Finn*'s most glorious character.

In "No. 44, The Mysterious Stranger" Emil Schwarz, August Feldner's "Duplicate" and feared rival, seeks August's help in becoming free from the bonds of flesh. "Say you will be my friend, as well as brother!" he pleads, "for brothers indeed we are; the same womb was mother to us both, I live by you, I perish when you die—brother, be my friend!"[24] August is powerfully stirred by Schwarz's speech. He "jumped up and seized him by both hands and wrung them passionately, declaring that with all my heart and soul I would plead for him with the magician."[25] From the time he was a young boy and tried to sit on Orion's boot to the writing of the passage above near the end of his life, Samuel Clemens was next to obsessed with his big brother. On the one hand, he seemed truly to love and respect him, not only as a close family member but as a person who strove tirelessly for a goodness Sam could only shake his head at. On the other hand, from the earliest days the younger sibling had a ravening hunger to best this estimable person, a drive that persisted even after Orion had ceased to be a legitimate rival. Orion's ceaseless questioning of conventional wisdom, epitomized by his reversal concerning slavery, deeply unsettled his younger brother. The anguish Sam felt when he realized what had become of Orion in his old age—what he himself had in a measure done to him—fully matched his chronic chagrin at his heterodoxy.

Sam's admiration found its most direct and sincere expression in the letter to Orion in which he spoke of his brother "tower[ing] head and shoulders above any of the small-fry preachers of my experience!" Unfortunately, his negative thoughts were more frequently stated, as when he ridiculed Orion in letters to his younger brother, Henry, to his mother, Jane, to his friend Howells—and to Orion himself.

Throughout his life Samuel yearned for a normal relationship with his brother. During the stagecoach trip to Nevada Territory he thought he had found it, and later, when the two "governors" considered their prospects so favorable they invited their mother to come live with them, he may have believed it had arrived again. Twice in his fiction Mark Twain seemed on the verge of doing right by Orion—when Huck decided to "go to hell" to save Jim, and when August Feldner and Emil Schwarz agreed to ignore their differences and part amicably.

By the same token, Orion twice came close to changing the course of the relationship by simply standing up to his abusive brother—when, after Jervis Langdon offered to buy the Tennessee property, he heatedly wrote to Sam, "Neither you nor Ma nor Pamela know anything about the land" and again when he declared accusingly, "I think you will admit that you did me injustice" after Sam accused him of cheating the family. If Orion had followed through on either of those overtures, things might have turned out differently. As it was, neither brother capitalized on his opportunities, and so both shared a degree of blame for the fact that as the last surviving member of John Marshall Clemens's family went to join Halley's Comet in wandering "forlorn among the empty eternities," he carried with him, unresolved, the excruciating ambivalence toward his elder brother that had colored his life and that left an indelible mark on American literature.

Notes

ABBREVIATIONS

BL   Bancroft Library, University of California, Berkeley.

CHS   Connecticut Historical Society, Hartford.

CU-MARK   Mark Twain Papers, Bancroft Library, University of California, Berkeley.

KPL   Keokuk Public Library, Keokuk, Iowa.

MPL   Musser Public Library, Muscatine, Iowa.

NHS   Nevada Historical Society, Reno.

NSLA   Nevada State Legislative Archives, Carson City.

SHSM   State Historical Society of Missouri, Columbia.

VDL   Vermont Department of Libraries, Montpelier.

PREFACE

1. Wecter, *Sam Clemens of Hannibal,* 231.
2. Paine, *Mark Twain: A Biography,* 4:1592.
3. Ibid., 1:93; *Mark Twain's Letters,* 1:195.
4. *Mark Twain's Letters,* 1:262.

CHAPTER 1

1. Webster, *Mark Twain, Business Man,* 45.
2. Paine, *Mark Twain: A Biography,* 1:6.
3. Paine, *Mark Twain's Autobiography,* 1:3, 4.

4. Paine, *Mark Twain: A Biography,* 1:1–2.

5. Ibid., 42.

6. Ibid., 15.

7. Ibid., 17.

8. Ibid.

9. Paine, *Mark Twain's Autobiography,* 2:272.

10. Holcomb, *History of Marion County,* 203–5, 246.

11. See Wecter, *Sam Clemens of Hannibal,* 74.

12. Holcomb, *History of Marion County,* 256–58.

13. Paine, *Mark Twain: A Biography,* 1:5.

14. Webster, *Mark Twain, Business Man,* 44.

15. Paine, *Mark Twain: A Biography,* 1:5; Webster, *Mark Twain, Business Man,* 9; Wecter, *Sam Clemens of Hannibal,* 29.

16. Paine, *Mark Twain's Autobiography,* 2:268.

17. Brashear, *Mark Twain,* 88.

18. Varble, *Jane Clemens,* 112.

19. Orion to Sam, Nov. 30, 1897, CU-MARK.

20. Paine, *Mark Twain: A Biography,* 1:9.

21. Webster, *Mark Twain, Business Man,* 42.

22. Orion and Jane Clemens to Sam, Sept. 27, 1888, CU-MARK.

23. Paine, *Mark Twain: A Biography,* 1:12.

24. Ibid., 13.

25. Ibid., 2:677 n. 1.

26. Ibid., 1:19.

27. Henderson and Gregory, "Judge John Marshall Clemens," 25, 27.

28. Wecter, *Sam Clemens of Hannibal,* 56.

29. Paine, *Mark Twain: A Biography,* 1:27.

30. Wecter, *Sam Clemens of Hannibal,* 227.

31. Paine, *Mark Twain: A Biography,* 1:85.

32. Orion and Mollie to Olivia Clemens, Dec. 6 and 7, 1879, CU-MARK.

33. Orion and Jane Clemens to Sam, Sept. 27, 1888, CU-MARK.

34. Paine, *Mark Twain: A Biography,* 1:28.

35. "Ex-Mayor J. B. Brown" in "Hannibal's Tribute to Samuel L. Clemens," *Hannibal Morning Journal,* Apr. 26, 1910, SHSM.

36. Paine, *Mark Twain: A Biography,* 1:41.

37. See Wecter, *Sam Clemens of Hannibal,* 68.

38. Orion to Sam, Jan. 6, 1894, CU-MARK.

39. Paine, *Mark Twain: A Biography,* 1:41.

40. Wecter, *Sam Clemens of Hannibal,* 75.

41. Paine, *Mark Twain: A Biography,* 1:43.

42. John Marshall Clemens to Jane Clemens and family, Jan. 5, 1842, CU-MARK.

43. Wecter, *Sam Clemens of Hannibal,* 75.

44. John Marshall Clemens to Pamelia G. Hancock, Mar. 16, 1842, CU-MARK.
45. Wecter, *Sam Clemens of Hannibal*, 220.
46. Paine, *Mark Twain: A Biography*, 1:44.
47. Ibid.
48. Blair, *Mark Twain's Hannibal*, 40, continued in Rogers, *Mark Twain's Satires and Burlesques*, 200.
49. Rogers, *Mark Twain's Satires and Burlesques*, 203.
50. Orion to Sam, Jan. 7, 1861, CU-MARK.
51. *Roughing It*, 574. When citing *Roughing It*, if I give a page number I refer to editorially interlarded material in the edition described in the bibliography; if I give a chapter number I refer to Mark Twain's words, which can be found in any edition.
52. Paine, *Mark Twain: A Biography*, 1:54–55.

CHAPTER 2

1. John Marshall Clemens to Pamela Clemens, May 5, 1845, CU-MARK.
2. Wecter, *Sam Clemens of Hannibal*, 112–13.
3. Ibid., 115.
4. Paine, *Mark Twain: A Biography*, 1:73.
5. See Wecter, *Sam Clemens of Hannibal*, 114.
6. Paine, *Mark Twain: A Biography*, 1:73.
7. Blair, *Mark Twain and Huck Finn*, 40.
8. Paine, *Mark Twain: A Biography*, 1:74–75.
9. Blair, *Mark Twain and Huck Finn*, 40.
10. Wecter, *Sam Clemens of Hannibal*, 116.
11. *Mark Twain–Howells Letters*, 1:315.
12. Wecter, *Sam Clemens of Hannibal*, 117.
13. *Mark Twain's Letters*, 1:116 n. 11; see also Webster, *Mark Twain, Business Man*, 58.
14. Wecter, *Sam Clemens of Hannibal*, 15, 20.
15. *Encyclopedia Americana*, 26:183–85; *Encyclopaedia Britannica*, 984–85; Quetel, *History of Syphilis*, 131.
16. Interview with and private communication from Dr. Risse, Nov. 1997.
17. Pickard and Buley, *Midwest Pioneer*, 105.
18. *Dictionary of American Medical Biography*, 254–55.
19. See Walker, *Mark Twain's Travels*, 144, and Clemens, *A Tramp Abroad*, chap. 23.
20. Quetel, *History of Syphilis*, 3.
21. *New Yorker*, June 26–July 13, 1995, 129–30.
22. *Huckleberry Finn*, chap. 9. Because Mark Twain's works are available in a variety of editions, in quoting or referring to specific passages I have generally cited chapter numbers only, following the example of a number of other writers.

23. Ibid., chap. 5.
24. Ibid., chap. 7.
25. Paine, *Mark Twain: A Biography*, 1:30; Wecter, *Sam Clemens of Hannibal*, 91.
26. *Mark Twain's Letters*, 1:86 n. 2.
27. Paine, *Mark Twain: A Biography*, 1:74.
28. Tuckey, *Mark Twain's "Which Was the Dream?"* 194–95.
29. Ibid., 201–2.
30. Paine, *Mark Twain: A Biography*, 4:1591.
31. Ibid., 1:75.
32. Wecter, *Sam Clemens of Hannibal*, 121.
33. Ibid., 152.
34. See ibid., 294 n. 5.
35. Ibid., 121.
36. Clemens, "Chapters from My Autobiography," 117–18.
37. Rogers, *Mark Twain's Satires and Burlesques*, 158–60.
38. See Wecter, *Sam Clemens of Hannibal*, 239.
39. Ibid., 121.
40. Rogers, *Mark Twain's Satires and Burlesques*, 136.
41. Ibid., 137, 148.
42. Ibid., 138.

CHAPTER 3

1. Edward Bates to Orion, Mar. 8, 1848, quoted in Orion to Sam, Jan. 7, 1861, CU-MARK.
2. Webster, *Mark Twain, Business Man*, 15–16.
3. Paine, *Mark Twain: A Biography*, 1:84.
4. Wecter, *Sam Clemens of Hannibal*, 226.
5. Ibid., 225.
6. *Hannibal Western Union*, Oct. 10, 1850, SHSM.
7. Paine, *Mark Twain: A Biography*, 1:85.
8. *Hannibal Western Union*, Nov. 14, 1850, SHSM.
9. *Hannibal Western Union*, Nov. 21, 1850, SHSM.
10. *Hannibal Western Union*, Jan. 9, 1851, SHSM.
11. Wecter, *Sam Clemens of Hannibal*, 201–2.
12. Ibid., 235–36, 241.
13. *Hannibal Western Union*, Jan. 23, 1851, SHSM.
14. Paine, *Mark Twain: A Biography*, 1:46.
15. Ibid., 79–80; Paine, *Boys' Life*, 44.
16. Neider, *Autobiography of Mark Twain*, 24.
17. Paine, *Mark Twain: A Biography*, 1:85.
18. Hornberger, *Mark Twain's Letters to Will Bowen*, 27.
19. Wecter, *Sam Clemens of Hannibal*, 235.

20. Ibid., 227.
21. Webster, *Mark Twain, Business Man,* 87.
22. Paine, *Mark Twain: A Biography,* 4:1591.
23. Wecter, *Sam Clemens of Hannibal,* 234.
24. Paine, *Mark Twain's Autobiography,* 2:285.
25. Wecter, *Sam Clemens of Hannibal,* 239.
26. Ibid., 240.
27. Branch, *Literary Apprenticeship,* 278; *Webster's American Biographies,* 1142.
28. Wecter, *Sam Clemens of Hannibal,* 240.
29. Ibid., 241.
30. Ibid., 233.
31. Clemens, *Sketches,* 110–13.
32. Brashear, *Mark Twain,* 115.
33. Paine, *Mark Twain: A Biography,* 1:90.
34. Brashear, *Mark Twain,* 114–15.
35. Ibid., 119.
36. Ibid., 115.
37. Clemens, *Sketches,* 113.
38. *Mark Twain's Letters,* 1:2.
39. Paine, *Mark Twain: A Biography,* 1:92–93.
40. Gibson, *Mark Twain's "Mysterious Stranger" Manuscripts,* 251, 254–55.
41. Paine, *Mark Twain: A Biography,* 1:93.
42. *Mark Twain's Letters,* 1:2; Paine, *Mark Twain: A Biography,* 1:94.
43. *Mark Twain's Letters,* 1:2. Readers seeking further information about Hannibal should consult two excellent sources: *Lighting Out for the Territory* by Shelley Fisher Fishkin and *Dangerous Waters* by Ron Powers.
44. Wecter, *Sam Clemens of Hannibal,* 263–64.
45. Paine, *Mark Twain: A Biography,* 1:92.
46. Ibid.
47. Ibid.
48. *Hannibal Journal,* Aug. 11, 1853, SHSM.
49. Paine, *Mark Twain: A Biography,* 1:92.
50. *Mark Twain's Letters,* 1:3.
51. Rogers, *Mark Twain's Satires and Burlesques,* 200.
52. *Mark Twain's Letters,* 1:15 n. 5.
53. Ibid., 18 n. 3.
54. See ibid., 19.
55. Brashear, *Mark Twain,* 104.
56. *Mark Twain's Letters,* 1:15 n. 5.
57. "Introduction," *Muscatine Journal,* Sept. 30, 1853, MPL.
58. Lorch, "Lecture Trips," 415.
59. Lorch, "Orion Clemens Number," 362.
60. Wecter, *Sam Clemens of Hannibal,* 232–33.

61. *Muscatine Journal,* Nov. 4, 1853, MPL.
62. "Freedom of the Press," *Muscatine Journal,* Jan. 13, 1854, MPL.
63. "Whig Meeting," *Muscatine Journal,* July 22, 1854, MPL.
64. "Address of the Whig Central Committee of Muscatine County TO THE VOTERS OF MUSCATINE COUNTY," signed by J. A. Mills, Orion Clemens, and Asa Gregg, *Muscatine Tri-Weekly Journal,* Aug. 4, 1854, MPL.
65. *Muscatine Weekly Journal,* Aug. 5, 1854, MPL.
66. "A Scrap of Curious History," in *What Is Man?* 182.
67. Webster, *Mark Twain, Business Man,* 64.

CHAPTER 4

1. *Mark Twain's Letters,* 1:19–24.
2. Paine, *Mark Twain: A Biography,* 1:99.
3. See Gribben, *Mark Twain's Library,* 1:241–43.
4. Rogers, *Mark Twain's Satires and Burlesques,* 200.
5. Franklin, *Autobiography,* 26.
6. Ibid., 28.
7. Paine, *Mark Twain's Autobiography,* 2:287.
8. Franklin, *Autobiography,* 101.
9. Ibid., 128.
10. Ibid., 105.
11. Ibid., 37.
12. *Mark Twain's Letters,* 1:4.
13. Ibid., 28–29.
14. Ibid., 33.
15. Ibid., 471.
16. Ibid., 45.
17. Clemens, "Samuel Langhorne Clemens."
18. Paine, *Mark Twain: A Biography,* 1:101–2.
19. *Mark Twain's Letters,* 1:45.
20. Ibid.
21. Paine, *Mark Twain: A Biography,* 1:102.
22. Paine, *Mark Twain's Letters,* 2:714.
23. Ibid., 713.
24. Paine, *Mark Twain: A Biography,* 1:102.
25. Paine, *Mark Twain's Autobiography,* 2:288.
26. Clemens, *Letters from the Earth,* 224.
27. Paine, *Mark Twain's Letters,* 1:31.
28. Ibid., 2:714.
29. Rogers, *Mark Twain's Satires and Burlesques,* 333.
30. Ibid., 335–36.
31. Ibid., 339.

32. Ibid., 339–40.
33. Ibid., 315.
34. Ibid., 340.
35. Ibid., 340–41.
36. Ibid., 342–43.
37. Ibid., 343.
38. Ibid., 364–65, 378, 427.
39. Ibid., 422.
40. Paine, *Mark Twain's Letters*, 1:419.
41. *Muscatine Daily Journal,* May 17, 1882, MPL.
42. *Muscatine Daily Journal,* May 19, 1882, MPL.

CHAPTER 5

1. *Mark Twain's Letters,* 1:66.
2. *Mark Twain's Letters,* 1:46; Paine, *Mark Twain: A Biography,* 1:103.
3. Sattlemeyer, "Did Sam Clemens Take the Abolitonists for a Ride?" 294.
4. Ibid., 297.
5. Blair, *Mark Twain's Hannibal,* 48.
6. Paine, *Mark Twain: A Biography,* 1:104.
7. *Mark Twain's Letters,* 1:58; Webster, *Mark Twain, Business Man,* 25.
8. Paine, *Mark Twain: A Biography,* 1:104.
9. *Mark Twain's Letters,* 1:58.
10. Lorch, "Lecture Trips," 420.
11. Ibid., 421.
12. Ibid., 420.
13. Paine, *Mark Twain's Autobiography,* 2:290; Lorch, "Lecture Trips," 419.
14. *Mark Twain's Letters,* 1:65 n. 2.
15. Ibid., 63.
16. Lorch, "Orion Clemens Number," 387.
17. Ibid., 365–66.
18. *Mark Twain's Letters,* 1:67 n. 3, 68 n. 7.
19. Ibid., 66.
20. Paine, *Mark Twain: A Biography,* 1:110.
21. *Mark Twain's Letters,* 1:70.
22. Ibid.
23. Webster, *Mark Twain, Business Man,* 33.
24. Lorch, "Orion Clemens Number," 388.
25. Ibid., 361.
26. Ibid., 358.
27. Mack, "Orion Clemens," 68.
28. *Mark Twain's Letters,* 1:77.
29. Ibid., 79 n. 11; Lorch, "Orion Clemens Number," 359.

30. *Roughing It,* 772–74.
31. Lorch, "Orion Clemens Number," 358.
32. Webster, *Mark Twain, Business Man,* 36; *Mark Twain's Letters,* 1:86 n. 2.
33. *Mark Twain's Letters,* 1:86 n. 2.
34. Ibid., 382.
35. Paine, *Mark Twain: A Biography,* 1:143.
36. Ibid., 142.
37. Ibid., 142–44.
38. Ibid., 4:1592.
39. "ORION CLEMENS . . . Short Sketch of His Life," *Keokuk Gate City,* Dec. 12, 1897, KPL.
40. *Mark Twain's Letters,* 1:98 n. 1, and appendix D.
41. Paine, *Mark Twain: A Biography,* 1:145.
42. Paine, *Mark Twain's Letters,* 1:42.
43. Ibid.
44. Paine, *Mark Twain: A Biography,* 1:151.
45. See illustration in *Mark Twain's Letters,* 1:402, top.
46. Lorch, "Orion Clemens Number," 359.
47. See *Mark Twain's Letters,* 1:111.
48. *Roughing It,* 574.
49. *Mark Twain's Letters,* 1:96–97.

CHAPTER 6

1. Varble, *Jane Clemens,* 244; *Webster's American Biographies,* 74.
2. Mack, *Mark Twain in Nevada,* 48.
3. "ORION CLEMENS . . . Short Sketch of His Life," *Keokuk Gate City,* Dec. 12, 1897, KPL.
4. *Memphis People's Messenger,* Dec. 16, 1897, SHSM.
5. Webster, *Mark Twain, Business Man,* 47.
6. *Mark Twain's Letters,* 1:114 n. 9.
7. *Roughing It,* 574.
8. Lorch, "Orion Clemens Number," 359.
9. *Roughing It,* chap. 1.
10. *Life on the Mississippi,* chap. 14.
11. See *Mark Twain's Letters,* 1:115, 403.
12. See Wecter, *Sam Clemens of Hannibal,* 128.
13. See Paine, *Mark Twain: A Biography,* 1:168.
14. *Mark Twain's Letters,* 1:121.
15. Ibid.
16. Paine, *Boys' Life,* 103; *Mark Twain, Collected Tales,* 863.
17. *Mark Twain's Letters,* 1:121.
18. Neider, *Autobiography of Mark Twain,* 102.

19. Webster, *Mark Twain, Business Man,* 60.

20. Ibid., 62.

21. Ibid., 60.

22. *Mark Twain's Letters,* 1:121; Paine, *Mark Twain: A Biography,* 1:164.

23. Paine, *Mark Twain: A Biography,* 1:164–69.

24. Miller, "Samuel L. and Orion Clemens," 2.

25. Ibid., 1.

26. Mack, *Mark Twain in Nevada,* 48–49.

27. Ibid., 49.

28. Tuckey, *Mark Twain's "Which Was the Dream?"* 160.

29. Paine, *Mark Twain: A Biography,* 1:168.

30. Ibid., 170.

31. Ibid., 171.

32. *Roughing It,* chap. 1.

33. Miller, "Samuel L. and Orion Clemens," 2, emphasis in original.

34. Paine, *Mark Twain's Letters,* 1:52.

35. TERR 0070, C 96, NSLA.

36. Lorch, "Orion Clemens Number," 359.

37. *Mark Twain's Letters,* 1:122.

38. Mack, "Orion Clemens," 70.

39. *Roughing It,* chap. 2.

40. Ibid.; passages from *Roughing It* are quoted not as veridical descriptions of what happened but mainly to show how Orion and Samuel's trip lodged in the latter's memory and imagination.

41. Ibid., chap. 3.

42. Ibid., chap. 13.

43. Library of America edition of *Roughing It,* annotation on page 606, kindly sent by Kent Rasmussen.

44. *Muscatine Weekly Journal,* Nov. 11, 1854, MPL.

45. Rogers, *Pattern for Mark Twain's "Roughing It,"* 46.

46. Ibid., 47–48.

47. *Roughing It,* chap. 17.

48. Ibid., chap. 18.

49. Ibid., chap. 21.

CHAPTER 7

1. *Roughing It,* chap. 21.

2. Mack, "Orion Clemens," 73.

3. Neider, *Autobiography of Mark Twain,* 103.

4. Bancroft, *History of Nevada,* 76; Mack, "Orion Clemens," 73.

5. Orion to Comptroller Whittlesey, Sept. 4, 1861, CU-MARK; Mack, "Orion Clemens," 73; *Mark Twain's Letters,* 1:146 n. 2.

6. *Roughing It,* 577.

7. Rogers, *Pattern for Mark Twain's "Roughing It,"* 55.

8. *Roughing It,* 772–74.

9. Paine, *Mark Twain: A Biography,* 1:177, 188; Mack, "Orion Clemens," 73.

10. Mack, "Orion Clemens," 73.

11. Ibid., 74; *Mark Twain's Letters,* 1:129 n. 3.

12. Mack, "Orion Clemens," 74; *Roughing It,* chap. 25.

13. *Roughing It,* 25.

14. Mack, "Orion Clemens," 76–77; *Mark Twain's Letters,* 1:179 illustration.

15. Orion to Hodge and Wood, Dec. 3, 1861, CU-MARK.

16. *Mark Twain's Letters,* 1:176.

17. *Roughing It,* chap. 12, 25; Paine, *Mark Twain: A Biography,* 1:177–78.

18. *Mark Twain's Letters,* 1:129 n. 3.

19. Mack, "Orion Clemens," 78.

20. Miller, "Samuel L. and Orion Clemens," 3.

21. Marsh, *Letters from Nevada Territory,* 51–53, 57.

22. Ibid., 59.

23. Ibid., 205–6.

24. *Roughing It,* chap. 22.

25. *Mark Twain's Letters,* 1:323.

26. Webster, *Mark Twain, Business Man,* 63.

27. Paine, *Mark Twain's Autobiography,* 2:307; *Mark Twain's Letters,* 1:183 n. 5.

28. *Roughing It,* chap. 25.

29. Paine, *Mark Twain: A Biography,* 1:189.

30. *Mark Twain's Letters,* 1:184 n. 5.

31. Orion to Whittlesey, Dec. 21, 1861, CU-MARK; Mack, "Orion Clemens," 83; Miller, "Samuel L. and Orion Clemens," 3.

32. Mollie to Orion, Nov. 17 and 18, 1861, CU-MARK; *Mark Twain's Letters,* 1:146 n. 6.

33. *Mark Twain's Letters,* 1:161 n. 1.

34. Ibid., 145.

35. Ibid., 147–48.

36. Mack, "Orion Clemens," 82.

37. Paine, *Mark Twain: A Biography,* 1:189.

38. Mack, "Orion Clemens," 82–83.

39. Paine, *Mark Twain: A Biography,* 1:189.

40. Ibid.

41. *Mark Twain's Letters,* 1:159.

42. *Life on the Mississippi,* chap. 14.

43. Clemens, *Connecticut Yankee,* chap. 6.

44. Ibid., chap. 8.

45. Clemens, *Mark Twain's Speeches,* 169.

46. *Mark Twain's Letters,* 1:159–61.

47. Ibid., 168 n. 7.
48. Paine, *Mark Twain: A Biography,* 1:193.
49. *Mark Twain's Letters,* 1:186.
50. *Mark Twain's Notebooks and Journals,* 1:62.
51. Mack, *Mark Twain in Nevada,* 156.
52. *Mark Twain's Letters,* 1:189 n. 12.
53. Ibid., 186–87.
54. Ibid., 189–90.
55. Ibid., 194–95.
56. Paine, *Mark Twain: A Biography,* 1:194.
57. *Mark Twain's Letters,* 1:229.
58. Ibid.
59. Ibid., 231.
60. *Roughing It,* chap. 42.
61. Paine, *Mark Twain's Autobiography,* 2:309.
62. Mack, *Mark Twain in Nevada,* 220–21; Mack, "Orion Clemens," 90.
63. Miller, "Samuel L. and Orion Clemens," 4–5.
64. Paine, *Mark Twain's Autobiography,* 2:307–8.
65. *Mark Twain's Letters,* 1:146 n. 6; Mack, "Orion Clemens," 90.
66. Mack, "Orion Clemens," 90.
67. Paine, *Mark Twain: A Biography,* 1:218.
68. Marsh, *Letters from Nevada Territory,* 408.
69. Unpublished proceedings of the Second Session of the House, 232, 235, NSLA.
70. Paine, *Mark Twain's Autobiography,* 2:307–8.
71. Paine, *Mark Twain: A Biography,* 1:220.
72. Ibid., 221.
73. Paine, *Mark Twain's Autobiography,* 2:309.
74. *Mark Twain's Letters,* 1:246 n. 1.
75. Paine, *Mark Twain: A Biography,* 1:222.

CHAPTER 8

1. Unpublished proceedings of the Second Territorial Legislature, passim, NSLA.
2. Orion to Second Auditor for U.S. Treasurer, Feb. 3, 1863, CU-MARK.
3. Angel, *History of Nevada,* 563; Mack, *Nevada,* 399.
4. Mack, *Nevada,* 394.
5. Marsh, *Letters from Nevada Territory,* 432–33.
6. Mack, *Nevada,* 399.
7. Angel, *History of Nevada,* 100–101; Orion to Governor Leland Stanford, Feb. 21, 1863, CU-MARK.
8. Mack, *Nevada,* 403.

9. Orion to William Hill Naileigh, Mar. 3, 1863, CU-MARK.

10. Bancroft, *History of Nevada,* 154, 165 n. 47.

11. TERR 0401, KK-6, NSLA.

12. Orion to William H. Naileigh, Mar. 3, 1863, CU-MARK.

13. TERR 0104, NSLA; Orion to William H. Seward, Mar. 18, 1863, CU-MARK.

14. Orion to Leland Stanford, Mar. 4 and 5, 1863, CU-MARK.

15. Angel, *History of Nevada,* 401, 100; Mack, *Nevada,* 397–98, 403.

16. Bancroft, *History of Nevada,* 154; Mack, *Nevada,* 403.

17. Mack, *Nevada,* 403.

18. Bancroft, *History of Nevada,* 154–55; Mack, *Nevada,* 403.

19. TLEGIS 0034, 167, NSLA.

20. Angel, *History of Nevada,* 101.

21. "Political Brokerage," *Virginia City Territorial Enterprise,* Mar. 23, 1863, Scrapbook 2:30, CU-MARK.

22. Leland Stanford's Mar. 30, 1863, message to the California legislature, unidentified clipping in Scrapbook 2:35, CU-MARK.

23. "The Boundary Question Again," *Virginia City Territorial Enterprise,* Apr. 3, 1863, clipping in Scrapbook 2:36, CU-MARK.

24. *Mark Twain's Letters,* 1:198–99 n. 8.

25. Ibid., 197.

26. Orion to General Wright, Apr. 6, 1863, CU-MARK.

27. Orion to Maj. C. McDermit, Apr. 20, 1863, CU-MARK.

28. "Personal," *Virginia City Daily Union,* Apr. 8, 1863, Scrapbook 1:43, CU-MARK.

29. *Virginia City Union,* Apr. 9, 1863, Scrapbook 2:38, CU-MARK.

30. Orion to Samuel Youngs, Apr. 9, 1863, CU-MARK.

31. Orion to Judge Robinson, Apr. 15, 1863, CU-MARK.

32. "The Boundary Question—Debate in the California Senate," unidentified newspaper clipping in Scrapbook 1:41, CU-MARK.

33. *Mark Twain's Letters,* 1:249 n. 5.

34. "To Orion Clemens," *Virginia City Daily Union,* Apr. 10, 1863, Scrapbook 2:38–39, CU-MARK.

35. "Another Junius," *Virginia City Territorial Enterprise,* Apr. 11, 1863, Scrapbook 2:39, CU-MARK.

36. *Mark Twain's Letters,* 1:247.

37. Ibid., 248.

38. Orion to Maj. C. McDermitz [*sic*], Apr. 20, 1863, CU-MARK.

39. Orion to General Wright, Apr. 27, 1863, CU-MARK.

40. Mack, *Nevada,* 403; Angel, *History of Nevada,* 402.

41. Mack, *Nevada,* 405.

42. "Mark Twain," *Virginia City Territorial Enterprise,* May 3, 1863, Scrapbook 2:43, CU-MARK.

43. Fatout, *Mark Twain in Virginia City,* 50–51.
44. *Mark Twain's Letters,* 1:253, 255.
45. Ibid., 256–57.
46. Ibid., 262.
47. Orion to Captain John Bryden, June 1863, CU-MARK.
48. Orion to Columbus Davis, June 10, 1863, Orion to Thomas B. Smithson, June 29, 1863, and Orion to General Wright, June 29, 1863, all CU-MARK.
49. Unidentified clipping, Scrapbook 2:42, CU-MARK.
50. "Removal of Judge Ladd for Disloyalty," *Virginia City Daily Union,* July 7, 1863, Scrapbook 2:42, CU-MARK.
51. Orion to J. Williams, July 23, 1863, CU-MARK.
52. "Advertisement," undated clipping from the *Reese River Reveille* in Scrap book 1:40, CU-MARK.
53. Orion to R. W. Taylor, Sept. 10, 1863, CU-MARK.

CHAPTER 9

1. *Mark Twain's Letters,* 1:262.
2. Ibid., 263–64.
3. Ibid., 264–65.
4. Ibid., 266.
5. Fatout, *Mark Twain in Virginia City,* 53.
6. Ibid., 100.
7. Paine, *Mark Twain: A Biography,* 1:229–30, 4:1598; Fatout, *Mark Twain in Virginia City,* 100.
8. Paine, *Mark Twain: A Biography,* 4:229–30.
9. Kaplan, *Mark Twain and His World,* 53.
10. Fatout, *Mark Twain in Virginia City,* 101.
11. Ibid., 102.
12. Ibid., 103.
13. Ibid.
14. Paine, *Mark Twain: A Biography,* 1:230–31.
15. Fatout, *Mark Twain in Virginia City,* 105.
16. Mack, "Orion Clemens," 88; Davis, *History of Nevada,* 193.
17. Branch, *Literary Apprenticeship,* 80.
18. Mack, "Orion Clemens," 88–89.
19. Paine, *Mark Twain: A Biography,* 1:239–40; Paine, *Mark Twain's Letters,* 1:94.
20. Fatout, *Mark Twain in Virginia City,* 130.
21. *Mark Twain's Letters,* 1:266.
22. "The Constitutional Convention," *Virginia Evening Bulletin,* Jan. 4, 1864, NHS.

23. *Mark Twain's Letters,* 1:267–68.

24. Fatout, *Mark Twain in Virginia City,* 150.

25. Paine, *Mark Twain's Letters,* 1:95.

26. Mack, "Orion Clemens," 89.

27. *Mark Twain's Letters,* 1:271.

28. Angel, *History of Nevada,* 102.

29. Ibid., 101.

30. Davis, *History of Nevada,* 209.

31. Mack, "Orion Clemens," 96.

32. Mack, *Nevada,* 253.

33. Angel, *History of Nevada,* 215.

34. Mack, *Mark Twain in Nevada,* 276.

35. *Mark Twain's Letters,* 1:272 n. 1; Mack, "Orion Clemens," 89–90.

36. *Mark Twain's Letters,* 1:272.

37. Mack, "Orion Clemens," 93.

38. Paine, *Mark Twain: A Biography,* 1:247.

39. Orion to Thomas Starr King, Feb. 26, 1864, CU-MARK.

40. Mack, *Mark Twain in Nevada,* 276.

41. Orion to Thomas Starr King, Feb. 26, 1864, CU-MARK; Mack, *Mark Twain in Nevada,* 277–78.

42. Mollie's Journal, KPL.

43. Smith, *Mark Twain of the "Enterprise,"* 151.

44. Jane Clemens to Orion, Mollie, and Sam, Mar. 6, 1864, CU-MARK.

45. Orion and Mollie to Sam and Livy, Jan. 16, 1881, CU-MARK.

46. Fatout, *Mark Twain in Virginia City,* 150.

47. *Mark Twain's Letters,* 1:275–76.

48. Ibid., 275.

49. Pamela to Sam, Mar. 6, 1864, CU-MARK.

50. *Mark Twain's Letters,* 1:284 n. 4; Fatout, *Mark Twain in Virginia City,* 186–87.

51. See Mollie to Orion, Nov. 17 and 18, 1861, CU-MARK.

52. See *Mark Twain's Letters,* 1:282.

53. Marsh, *Letters from Nevada Territory,* 496; *Mark Twain's Letters,* 1:298 n. 1.

54. Smith, *Mark Twain of the "Enterprise,"* 179, 181.

55. Mack, *Nevada,* 279; *Mark Twain's Letters,* 1:282.

56. *Mark Twain's Letters,* 1:282.

57. Ibid., 286 n. 14.

58. Fatout, *Mark Twain in Virginia City,* 188.

59. Ibid.

60. *Mark Twain's Letters,* 1:574.

61. Fatout, *Mark Twain in Virginia City,* 192.

62. *Mark Twain's Letters,* 1:289 n. 2.

63. Ibid.

64. Ibid.
65. Ibid.
66. Ibid., 283.
67. Ibid.
68. Undated clipping in Scrapbook 1:67, CU-MARK.
69. *Mark Twain's Letters,* 1:287 n. 18.
70. Ibid., 289 n. 3.
71. Ibid., 290 n. 3, 291 n. 2.
72. Ibid., 290.
73. Ibid., 292.
74. Ibid., 295 n. 3.
75. Ibid., 296 n. 3.
76. See ibid., 296.
77. Ibid., 296, 297 n. 2.
78. Ibid., 297–98.
79. Ibid., 299.
80. Ibid., 301.
81. Ibid., 302.

CHAPTER 10

1. Mack, *Nevada,* 256–57; *Reese River Reveille,* Oct. 13, 1864, Library, University of California, Berkeley.
2. *Virginia City Daily Union,* Oct. 11, 1864, Scrapbook 5:81, CU-MARK.
3. Paine, *Mark Twain's Autobiography,* 2:318.
4. Ibid.
5. *Gold Hill Daily News,* Oct. 10, 1864, NHS.
6. *Gold Hill Evening News,* Oct. 11, 1864, NHS.
7. *Gold Hill Evening News,* Oct. 13, 1864, NHS.
8. *Gold Hill Evening News,* Oct. 11, 1864, NHS.
9. *Gold Hill Evening News,* Oct. 13, 1864, NHS.
10. *Mark Twain's Letters,* 1:316.
11. Ibid., 318.
12. *Gold Hill Daily News,* Dec. 8, 1864, NHS; Angel, *History of Nevada,* 87.
13. Bancroft, *History of Nevada,* 186–87; Paine, *Mark Twain's Autobiography,* 2:318–19.
14. SUPCT-0414, p. 11, NSLA.
15. Angel, *History of Nevada,* 88.
16. *Mark Twain's Letters,* 1:324.
17. Ibid., 322–23.
18. Branch and Hirst, *Early Tales and Sketches,* 2:269; published as "Jim Smiley and His Jumping Frog" in the *New York Saturday Press,* Nov. 18, 1865.
19. *Mark Twain's Letters,* 1:322.

20. Orion to Miss Wood, Oct. 3, 1858, CU-MARK.

21. *Mark Twain's Letters,* 1:117.

22. Ibid., 324; Clemens's brackets.

23. "Union Campaign Meetings," *Carson Daily Appeal,* Nov. 2, 1865, and "The Union Meeting Tonight," *Carson Daily Appeal,* Nov. 3, 1865, both NHS.

24. "The Union Meeting Last Night," *Carson Daily Appeal,* Nov. 7, 1865, NHS.

25. "The Results in Carson," *Carson Daily Appeal,* Nov. 8, 1865, NHS.

26. *Mark Twain's Letters,* 1:327 n. 1.

27. Ibid., 326.

28. Ibid.

29. Ibid.

30. *San Francisco Daily Evening Bulletin,* Dec. 19, 1865.

31. Monton, *Winegrowing in Eastern America,* 169; Longworth is also mentioned on pages 26 and 31.

32. Paine, *Mark Twain's Autobiography,* 1:88.

33. Maritime arrival report, *New York Times,* Jan. 13, 1866.

34. *Mark Twain's Letters,* 1:343.

35. Paine, *Mark Twain's Autobiography,* 2:320.

36. Ibid., 319.

37. Ibid., 320–21.

38. Taper, *Mark Twain's San Francisco,* 195–96.

39. Paine, *Mark Twain: A Biography,* 4:1591.

40. *Gold Hill Daily News,* Jan. 22, 1866, BL.

41. *Mark Twain's Letters,* 3:218 n. 8.

42. *Gold Hill Daily News,* Jan. 22 and 29, Feb. 12 and 19, 1866, BL.

43. See "Death of Alfred Barstow," *San Francisco Call,* Mar. 14, 1895, 14.

44. Branch, *Clemens of the Call,* 314 n. 1.

45. *Mark Twain's Letters,* 1:313–14 n. 3.

46. Paine, *Mark Twain: A Biography,* 1:264.

47. Scharnhorst, "Mark Twain's Imbroglio," 686–91.

48. Gribben, *Mark Twain's Library,* 1:425–26; *Mark Twain's Letters,* 1:326 n. 6.

49. For a fuller discussion of Samuel's San Francisco crisis, including Bret Harte's possible role in pulling him out of his suicidal funk and helping him get a new lease on life, see Fanning, "One Story Mark Twain *Wouldn't* Tell," 38–47.

CHAPTER 11

1. *Journal of the Assembly during the Second Session of the Legislature of the State of Nevada,* 291–92, Special Collections Department, Library, University of Nevada, Reno.

2. Ibid.; "Letter of Resignation from Hon. Orion Clemens," *Carson City Daily Appeal,* Feb. 27, 1866, Scrapbook 6:78, CU-MARK.

3. Stedman and Gould, *Life and Letters of Edmund Clarence Stedman*, 2:275.

4. *Mark Twain's Letters*, 1:338.

5. Ibid., 333.

6. Ibid.

7. Ibid., 342.

8. Mollie's Journal, KPL.

9. Orion to Jane Clemens and Pamela Moffett, Mar. 19 and 20, 1866, CU-MARK.

10. Orion to Mollie, June 7, 1866, CU-MARK; Branch and Hirst, *Early Tales and Sketches*, 2:542; *Mark Twain's Letters*, 1:342 n. 1.

11. *Mark Twain's Letters*, 1:339.

12. Ibid., 341.

13. Ibid., 341, 343 n. 4.

14. Ibid., 343.

15. Orion to Mollie, June 7, 1866, CU-MARK.

16. Ibid.; Orion to Mollie, June 13, 1866, CU-MARK; *Mark Twain's Letters*, 1:342 n. 1.

17. Orion to J. A. Byers, July 12, 1866, CU-MARK.

18. *Mark Twain's Letters*, 1:152 n. 12, 2:11 n. 1.

19. Ibid., 1:342 n. 1.

20. Ibid.

21. Paine, *Mark Twain's Autobiography*, 2:322.

22. Mack, "Orion Clemens," 95–96.

23. *Mark Twain's Notebooks and Journals*, 1:163.

24. *Mark Twain's Letters*, 1:353.

25. Varble, *Jane Clemens*, 272.

26. *Mark Twain's Letters*, 1:367.

27. Ibid., 355 n. 6.

28. *Roughing It*, chap. 78.

29. *Mark Twain's Letters*, 1:342 n. 1.

30. Ibid., 361.

31. Paine, *Mark Twain: A Biography*, 1:291.

32. *Mark Twain's Letters*, 1:361–62.

33. See Branch, *Literary Apprenticeship*, 188.

34. *Mark Twain's Letters*, 1:280 n. 11, 365.

35. Ibid., 2:11 n. 1.

36. Ibid., 59 n. 5.

37. Orion Clemens, "Letter from St. Louis," Oct. 15, 1866; *Mark Twain's Letters*, 2:59 n. 5.

38. Orion Clemens, "Letter from St. Louis," Dec. 22, 1866.

39. Orion Clemens, "Letter from Tennessee," Dec. 28, 1866.

40. Orion Clemens, "Letter from Tennessee," Mar. 11, 1867.

41. Ibid.

42. Orion Clemens, "Letter from St. Louis," Mar. 11, 1867.

CHAPTER 12

1. *Mark Twain's Letters,* 2:1–2.
2. Ibid., 11 n. 2.
3. Walker, *Mark Twain's Travels,* 101; *Mark Twain's Notebooks and Journals,* 1:301.
4. *Mark Twain's Letters,* 2:11 n. 2.
5. Walker, *Mark Twain's Travels,* 121.
6. Ibid., 121, 126.
7. Paine, *Mark Twain: A Biography,* 1:308–9.
8. *Mark Twain's Letters,* 2:19 n. 3.
9. Ibid., 59 n. 5.
10. Ibid., 57.
11. Ibid., 12 n. 3.
12. Ibid., 59 n. 5.
13. Ibid., 26 n. 7.
14. Ibid., 23 n. 1.
15. Orion to Mollie, May 14, 1867, CU-MARK.
16. *Mark Twain's Letters,* 2:59 n. 5.
17. Ibid., 50.
18. Ibid., 59 n. 5.
19. Ibid., 57–58.
20. Ibid., 78–79 n. 2.
21. Orion to Mollie, Sept. 6, 1867, CU-MARK.
22. Orion to Mollie, Sept. 18, 1867, CU-MARK.
23. Orion to Mollie, Oct. 31, 1867, CU-MARK.
24. Jane and Pamela to Orion, Nov. 17, 1867, CU-MARK.
25. *Mark Twain's Letters,* 2:220 n. 2.
26. Orion to Mollie, Nov. 26, 1867, CU-MARK.
27. *Mark Twain's Letters,* 2:106.
28. Ibid., 78.
29. Ibid., 179.
30. Orion to Mollie, Feb. 17, 1868, CU-MARK.
31. Orion to Mollie, Feb. 27, 1868, CU-MARK.
32. *Mark Twain's Letters,* 2:198 n. 1.
33. Ibid., n. 2.
34. Ibid., 197.
35. Ibid., 197–98.
36. Ibid., 120 n. 1, 163 n. 3.
37. Ibid., 160.
38. Neider, *Autobiography of Mark Twain,* 183.

39. *Mark Twain's Letters,* 2:249 n. 4.
40. Ibid., 251.
41. Ibid., 252.
42. Ibid., 345.
43. Paine, *Mark Twain's Autobiography,* 2:329; *Mark Twain's Letters,* 2:198 n. 2.
44. *Mark Twain's Letters,* 2:270.
45. Orion to Mollie, Oct. 30, 1868, CU-MARK.
46. *Mark Twain's Letters,* 2:252 n. 1, 257 n. 1.
47. Ibid., 1:84.
48. Ibid., 3:177.
49. Later published in *Packard's Monthly,* ibid., 228, 230 n. 3.
50. Ibid., 260.
51. Ibid., 271.
52. Ibid., 276.
53. Ibid., 280 n. 2.
54. Ibid., 277 n. 4.
55. Ibid., 310.
56. Ibid., 280.
57. Ibid., 281 n. 4, 287 n. 2.
58. Ibid., 310–13.
59. Ibid., 311–12.
60. Ibid., 2:244 n. 3, 1:428 n. 2.
61. Ibid., 4:182.
62. Ibid., 3:279 n. 1.
63. Letter of Nov. 4, 1880, ibid., 388–89 n. 2.
64. Ibid., 279.

CHAPTER 13

1. *Mark Twain's Letters,* 3:388 n. 1.
2. Ibid.
3. Ibid., 387.
4. Ibid., 393–94 n. 1.
5. Paine, *Mark Twain's Letters,* 1:166.
6. Ibid., 172.
7. *Mark Twain's Letters,* 3:430 n. 2, 433.
8. Paine, *Boys' Life,* 180.
9. *Mark Twain's Letters,* 4:115 n. 1.
10. Ibid., 3:294 n. 2, 440 n. 2.
11. Ibid., 388 n. 1.
12. Ibid., 4:130, 131 n. 3.
13. Webster, *Mark Twain, Business Man,* 114–15; *Mark Twain's Letters,* 4:151–52.

14. *Mark Twain's Letters,* 3:120.
15. Ibid., 4:47.
16. Webster, *Mark Twain, Business Man,* 114–15; *Mark Twain's Letters,* 4:151–52.
17. *Mark Twain's Letters,* 4:153 n. 6.
18. Ibid., 171.
19. Ibid., 175.
20. Ibid., 114, 138.
21. Ibid., 177–78.
22. Ibid., 186–87.
23. *Roughing It,* 809.
24. *Mark Twain's Letters,* 4:187.
25. Ibid., 187 n. 2, 372; *Roughing It,* 822, 842.
26. *Mark Twain's Letters,* 4:230, 231 n. 6.
27. Ibid., 372, including n. 1.
28. Ibid., 348–49, including n. 4.
29. See ibid., 218.
30. Ibid., 219.
31. Ibid.
32. Ibid., 220.
33. Ibid., 196, 212.
34. Ibid., 218, 219.
35. Ibid., 221.
36. Ibid., 220–22.
37. Ibid., 223.
38. Ibid., 172 n. 4.
39. Ibid., 229–30.
40. Ibid., 245.
41. Ibid., 275.
42. Ibid., 298.
43. Ibid., 297 n. 3.
44. Ibid., 275, 297.
45. Ibid., 320 n. 1.
46. Ibid., 352–53 n. 1.
47. Ibid., xxviii.
48. Ibid., 353 n. 1.
49. Ibid., 351–52.
50. *Roughing It,* 780–81.
51. Ibid.
52. *Mark Twain's Letters,* 4:365 n. 5.
53. Ibid., 342, 345–46 n. 7.
54. Ibid., 365 n. 5.
55. Ibid., 364 n. 2.

56. Ibid., 364–65.
57. Ibid., 368, 377, 378, 379 n. 1.
58. Probably Thomas Wallace Knox; see Gribben, *Mark Twain's Library*, 386.
59. *Mark Twain's Letters*, 4:379 n. 1.
60. Ibid., 387 n. 1.
61. Ibid., 386.

CHAPTER 14

1. *Geer's Hartford City Directory*, n.p.
2. *Mark Twain's Letters*, 4:395.
3. Ibid., 354 n. 1, 396, including n. 3.
4. Ibid., 365, 367, 391, 405.
5. Ibid., 405, 411.
6. Ibid., 410.
7. Ibid., 432 n. 1, 431.
8. Ibid., 423.
9. Ibid., 424 n. 2.
10. Ibid., 431, 432 n. 5.
11. *Roughing It*, chap. 62.
12. Ibid., 859.
13. *American Publisher*, July 1871, 4, Library of Congress and CU-MARK.
14. Orion to Sam, July 4, 1871, CU-MARK.
15. *Mark Twain's Letters*, 4:445 n. 2.
16. Ibid., 451.
17. Ibid., 443–44.
18. Ibid., 444.
19. Ibid., 457.
20. Ibid., 462–63.
21. Ibid., 457.
22. Paine, *Mark Twain: A Biography*, 2:442–43, 435.
23. *Mark Twain's Letters*, 4:462 n. 1.
24. Ibid., 472 n. 1.
25. Ibid., 520.
26. Orion to SLC, May 17, 1872, CU-MARK.
27. "MORAL COURAGE," *American Publisher*, Oct. 1871, 4, CU-MARK.
28. *Roughing It*, 877.
29. *Mark Twain's Letters*, 5:55.
30. Ibid.
31. Ibid., 4:179, 565–66.
32. Hill, *Mark Twain's Letters to His Publishers*, 70–71.
33. *Roughing It*, 878.
34. *Mark Twain's Letters*, 5:59.

35. Hill, *Mark Twain's Letters to His Publishers*, 70–71.
36. *Roughing It*, 879.
37. *Mark Twain's Letters*, 5:87.
38. Ibid., 88 n. 6.
39. Ibid., 88–89 n. 6.
40. *Roughing It*, 879.
41. Hill, *Mark Twain's Letters to His Publishers*, 69, 75 n. 3.
42. Paine, *Mark Twain's Autobiography*, 2:231.
43. Wecter, *Mark Twain to Mrs. Fairbanks*, 162; Paine, *Mark Twain: A Biography*, 2:457; Paine, *Mark Twain's Letters*, 1:196.
44. Orion to Mollie, July 26, 1872, CU-MARK.
45. Orion to Sam, Aug. 2, 1872, CU-MARK.
46. *Mark Twain's Letters*, 5:143–44.
47. Paine, *Mark Twain's Autobiography*, 2:323.
48. *Mark Twain's Letters*, 5:179, 188.
49. Schuyler Colfax to Orion, Feb. 15, 1873, and Sam to Jane Clemens, May 10, 1874, both CU-MARK.
50. Webster, *Mark Twain, Business Man*, 122–23.
51. Paine, *Mark Twain's Autobiography*, 2:323.
52. Paine, *Mark Twain: A Biography*, 2:477.
53. Olivia to Mrs. Jervis Langdon, Jan. 19, 1873, CU-MARK.
54. Clemens, *Gilded Age*, chap. 4.
55. Ibid.
56. *Roughing It*, chap. 3.
57. Ibid.
58. Clemens, *Gilded Age*, chap. 4.
59. Alan Gribben, in a private communication, incisively points out that this episode additionally implies a "*three*-way guilt circle," since it surely also goes back to the author's involvement in his brother Henry's death— "Henry," as Gribben observes, "who would *never* wear a wedding ring."

CHAPTER 15

1. Scrapbook 6, CU-MARK.
2. Schuyler Colfax to Orion, Feb. 15, 1873, CU-MARK.
3. Orion to Mollie, July 26, 1872, CU-MARK.
4. Orion to Sam, Feb. 23, 1882, CU-MARK; Paine, *Mark Twain's Autobiography*, 2:323; "THE GLOBE. What the Press Say of It," *Rutland Globe*, July 4, 1873, VDL; "The Little Institution around the Corner," *Rutland Daily Herald*, July 2, 1873, VDL.
5. Paine, *Mark Twain's Autobiography*, 2:323.
6. Orion to Sam, Apr. 27, [1874], 47503, CU-MARK.
7. Orion to Mollie, Nov. 23, 1873, CU-MARK.

8. Orion to Sam, Mar. 23, 1880, and Orion to Sam, May 19, 1880, both CU-MARK.

9. *Hartford Courant,* Apr. 18, 1873, CHS; *Mark Twain's Letters,* 5:363 n. 1.

10. *Mark Twain's Letters,* 5:364 n. 3.

11. Ibid., 363 n. 1; "Independent Journalism," *Rutland Daily Globe,* May 7, 1873, VDL.

12. Sam to Orion, May 5, 1873, *Mark Twain's Letters,* 5:363.

13. *Rutland Daily Globe,* May 13, 1873, VDL.

14. "The Little Institution around the Corner," *Rutland Daily Herald,* July 2, 1873, VDL.

15. "Independence," *Rutland Globe,* July 4, 1873, VDL.

16. "The Little Institution around the Corner."

17. "The Ill-Liberal Organ," *Rutland Daily Herald,* July 14, 1873, VDL.

18. "Minor Items," *Rutland Daily Herald,* Monday, July 21, 1873, VDL.

19. Orion to Mollie, July 21, 1873, CU-MARK; see *Mark Twain's Letters,* 5:364 n. 1.

20. See Mollie to Orion, Oct. 30, 1873, CU-MARK.

21. Mollie to Orion, Oct. 26, 1873, CU-MARK.

22. Orion to Mollie, Oct. 31, 1873, CU-MARK.

23. Orion to Sam, Apr. 27, [1874], 47503, CU-MARK.

24. Orion to Sam, Feb. 23, 1882, CU-MARK.

25. "Dixon's Pencils," *Rutland Daily Globe,* May 12, 1873, VDL.

26. Olivia to Mollie, June 23, 1873, CU-MARK; Mack, "Orion Clemens," 98; Webster, *Mark Twain, Business Man,* 123; "Hartford and Vicinity," *Hartford Evening Post,* Jan. 29, 1873, 2, CHS.

27. *Roughing It,* 797.

28. Hill, *Mark Twain's Letters to His Publishers,* 75.

29. *Mark Twain, Collected Tales,* 970.

30. Orion to Mollie, Oct. 23, 1873, CU-MARK.

31. Orion to Mollie, Oct. 16 to 19, 1873, CU-MARK.

32. Mollie to Orion, Oct. 18 to 22, 1873, CU-MARK.

33. Orion to Mollie, Oct. 19, 1873, CU-MARK.

34. Orion to Mollie, Oct. 23, 1873, CU-MARK.

35. Mollie to Orion, Oct. 26, 1873, CU-MARK.

36. Paine, *Mark Twain: A Biography,* 2:495.

37. Ibid.

38. See Orion to Mollie, Nov. 23, 1873, CU-MARK.

39. See Orion to Mollie, Oct. 28, Nov. 3 and 5, 1873, all CU-MARK.

40. Orion to Mollie, Nov. 7, 1873, 2nd of 2, CU-MARK.

41. *Mark Twain–Howells Letters,* 1:254.

42. *Mark Twain's Letters,* 5:470.

43. Ibid., 471 n. 1.

44. Paine, *Mark Twain: A Biography,* 2:490; *Mark Twain, Collected Tales,* 970–71.

45. Orion to Mollie, Nov. 18, 1873, CU-MARK.

46. Jane Clemens to Orion, Nov. 23, 1873, CU-MARK.

47. Orion to Mollie, Nov. 18, 1873, CU-MARK.

48. Orion to Mollie, Dec. 4, 1873, CU-MARK.

49. Orion to Mollie, Dec. 14, 1873, CU-MARK.

50. Orion to Jane Clemens and Pamela Moffett, Dec. 30, 1873, 47167, misfiled, I believe, at CU-MARK as Dec. 30, 1878.

51. *Mark Twain's Letters,* 6:26–27.

52. Jane Clemens to Sam and Olivia, Feb. 4, 1874, CU-MARK.

53. Orion to Sam, Apr. 25, 1874, CU-MARK.

54. See Mollie to P. J. Lomax, Apr. 23, 1874, CU-MARK.

55. Mollie to Jane Clemens, Apr. 25, 1874, CU-MARK.

56. Orion to Sam, Apr. 25, 1874, CU-MARK.

57. Ibid.

58. Ibid.

59. Mollie to Jane Clemens, Apr. 25, 1874, CU-MARK.

60. Orion to Sam, Apr. 27, [1874], CU-MARK.

61. *Mark Twain's Letters,* 6:141.

62. Ibid., 143.

63. *Mark Twain–Howells Letters,* 1:16–17.

64. Jane Clemens to Sam, Jan. 12, 1881, CU-MARK.

CHAPTER 16

1. Orion to Mollie, May 14 and 15, 1875, CU-MARK.

2. Orion to Sam, June 9, 1875, CU-MARK.

3. Orion to Sam, Jan. 21, 1876, CU-MARK.

4. *Mark Twain's Letters,* 1:86 n. 2.

5. Wecter, *Sam Clemens of Hannibal,* 293 n. 32; Jane Clemens to Robards, Aug. 5, 1876, CU-MARK.

6. Orion to Sam, June 28, 1876, CU-MARK.

7. Ibid.

8. Ibid.

9. Lorch, "Orion Clemens Number," 375.

10. Orion to the Rev. Dr. W. G. Craig, Oct. 20, 1877, CU-MARK.

11. Orion to Sam, Feb. 26 and 27, 1878, CU-MARK.

12. Jane to Samuel and Olivia, Jan. 12, 1881, CU-MARK.

13. Orion to Sam, Oct. 29, 1877, CU-MARK.

14. Mollie to Sam and Olivia, Nov. 1, 1877, CU-MARK.

15. Orion to Sam, Nov. 17, 1877, CU-MARK.

16. Orion to Howells, Nov. 26, 1877, CU-MARK.

17. Orion to Sam, Dec. 3 and 9, 1877, CU-MARK.

18. Orion to Sam, Dec. 15, 1877, CU-MARK.

19. Sam to Orion, Dec. 19, 1877, CU-MARK. These previously unpublished words by Mark Twain are © 2003 by Richard A. Watson and Chase Global Private Bank as Trustees of the Mark Twain Foundation, which reserves all reproduction or dramatization rights in every medium. Quotation is made with the permission of the University of California Press and Robert H. Hirst, General Editor of the Mark Twain Project. Subsequent quotations from previously unpublished words by Mark Twain are also © 2003 and are designated by an asterisk (*) in their citation.
20. Orion to Sam, Jan. 24, 1878, CU-MARK.
21. Ibid.
22. Orion to Sam, Feb. 5 and 8, 1878, CU-MARK.
23. Paine, *Mark Twain's Letters,* 1:319.
24. Sam to Orion, Feb. 21, 1878, CU-MARK.*
25. Sam to Jane Clemens, Feb. 23, 1878, CU-MARK.*
26. Orion to Sam, Mar. 17 and 18, 1878, CU-MARK.
27. Orion to Jane Clemens and Pamela Moffett, Mar. 30 and 31, 1878, CU-MARK.
28. Paine, *Mark Twain's Letters,* 1:322–24.
29. *Mark Twain–Howells Letters,* 1:253.
30. *Webster's American Biographies,* 531.
31. *Mark Twain–Howells Letters,* 1:257.
32. Sam to Orion, Feb. 9, 1879, NN-B, #12332, CU-MARK.*
33. *Mark Twain–Howells Letters,* 1:253.
34. Ibid., 256.
35. Ibid.
36. Ibid., 257.
37. Lorch, "Orion Clemens Number," 375.
38. Ibid., 376.
39. *Keokuk Daily Constitution,* May 12, 1879, KPL.
40. Wood, "'Mark Twain's' Elder Brother," n.p.
41. *Keokuk Daily Constitution,* Mar. 12, 1879, KPL.
42. Wood, "'Mark Twain's' Elder Brother," n.p.
43. "Mark Twain's Brother: Why He Has Been Excommunicated from the Presbyterian Church," *New York Times,* June 1, 1879, p. 10, col. 6.
44. Lorch, "Orion Clemens Number," 380.
45. Webster, *Mark Twain, Business Man,* 138.
46. Sam to Orion, May 29, 1879, CU-MARK.*
47. *Mark Twain's Notebooks and Journals,* 2:309.

CHAPTER 17

1. Sam to Pamela Moffett, Sept. 15, 1879, CU-MARK.
2. Orion to Sam, Sept. 17, 1879, CU-MARK.

3. See Orion to Sam, Oct. 6, 1879, CU-MARK.

4. Ibid.

5. Paine, *Mark Twain's Letters,* 1:370–73.

6. Sam to Orion, Nov. 14, 1879, CU-MARK.*

7. Orion to Sam, Nov. 18, 1879, CU-MARK.

8. See Orion to Sam, Feb. 29, 1880, CU-MARK.

9. Orion to Sam, May 28, 1881, CU-MARK.

10. Webster, *Mark Twain, Business Man,* 142–43.

11. Ibid., 142–44.

12. Blair, *Mark Twain and Huck Finn,* 223.

13. Paine, *Mark Twain: A Biography,* 2:561; Rogers, *Mark Twain's Satires and Burlesques,* 135.

14. Orion to Sam, Feb. 29 and Mar. 1, 1880, CU-MARK.

15. Orion to Sam, Mar. 3, 1880, CU-MARK.

16. Orion to Sam, Mar. 26, 1880, and Orion to Sam, Mar. 27, 1880, both CU-MARK.

17. *Mark Twain–Howells Letters,* 1:298.

18. Webster, *Mark Twain, Business Man,* 145.

19. See Orion to Sam, Apr. 8, 1880, CU-MARK.

20. Sam to Orion, Apr. 4, 1880, CU-MARK.

21. Orion to Sam, Apr. 8, 1880, CU-MARK.

22. Webster, *Mark Twain, Business Man,* 146.

23. Jane Clemens to Orion, Apr. 25, 1880, CU-MARK.

24. Pamela Moffett to Orion, Apr. 27, 1880, CU-MARK.

25. Paine, *Mark Twain's Letters,* 1:378, but published version lacks "own" and the comma.

26. Sam to Orion, May 6, 1880, CU-MARK.

27. Paine, *Mark Twain: A Biography,* 2:675.

28. Jane Clemens to Orion, May 6, 1880, CU-MARK.

29. Sam to Orion, May 12, 1880, CU-MARK.*

30. Pamela Moffett and Jane Clemens to Sam and Olivia, May 13, 1880, CU-MARK.

31. Sam to Jane Clemens and Pamela Moffett, May 14, 1880, CU-MARK.*

32. Orion to Sam, May 15, 1880, CU-MARK.

33. Orion to Sam, May 18, 1880, CU-MARK.

34. Ibid.

35. Orion to Sam, May 19, 1880, CU-MARK.

36. Orion to Sam, June 3, 1880, CU-MARK.

37. *Mark Twain–Howells Letters,* 1:312–13.

38. Ibid., 313.

39. Howells to Sam, June 14, 1880, CU-MARK; reprinted with changes in *Mark Twain–Howells Letters,* 1:315.

40. See Sam to Orion, June 15, 1880, and Orion to Sam, June 26, 1880, both CU-MARK.

41. Jane Clemens to Orion and Mollie, July 4 and 5, 1880, CU-MARK.

42. Orion and Mollie to Sam, July 26, 1880, CU-MARK.

43. Sam to Orion, May 6, 1880,* and Orion to Sam, May 12, 1880, both CU-MARK.

44. Hill, *Mark Twain's Letters to His Publishers,* 125–26.

45. *Mark Twain's Letters,* 4:461.

46. Orion to Sam, May 19, 1880, CU-MARK.

CHAPTER 18

1. Mollie to Sam and Olivia, Nov. 21, 1880, CU-MARK.

2. Orion to Sam, Dec. 2, 1880, CU-MARK.

3. See Orion to Sam, Nov. 4, 1880, CU-MARK.

4. Orion to Sam, Dec. 2, 1880, CU-MARK.

5. Jane Clemens to Sam and Livy, Jan. 12, 1881, CU-MARK.

6. Sam to Pamela Moffett, Jan. 10, 1881, CU-MARK.*

7. Jane Clemens to Sam and Olivia, Jan. 13, 1881, CU-MARK.

8. Blair, *Mark Twain and Huck Finn,* 265.

9. Webster, *Mark Twain, Business Man,* 139.

10. Paine, *Mark Twain: A Biography,* 2:727.

11. Pamela Moffett to Orion and Mollie, Mar. 19, 1881, and Pamela Moffett and Jane Clemens to Orion and Mollie, Apr. 17, 1881, both CU-MARK.

12. Orion to Sam, May 28, 1881, CU-MARK; widow McKee has not been identified.

13. Orion to Sam, Jan. 18, 1882, CU-MARK.

14. Orion to Sam, Jan. 19, 1882, CU-MARK.

15. Orion to Sam, Jan. 20, 1882, CU-MARK.

16. Orion to Sam, Jan. 29, 1882, CU-MARK.

17. Orion to Sam, Feb. 23, 1882, CU-MARK.

18. Orion to Sam, Mar. 3, 1882, CU-MARK.

19. Judges 11:30–39.

20. Orion to Thomas Starr King, Feb. 26, 1864, CU-MARK.

21. Orion to Sam, Mar. 30, 1882, CU-MARK.

22. Paine, *Mark Twain: A Biography,* 2:676–77.

23. Orion to Sam, Mar. 30, 1882, CU-MARK.

24. *Mark Twain–Howells Letters,* 1:392 n. 1, 393.

25. Ibid., 393.

26. Paine, *Mark Twain: A Biography,* 2:707.

27. *Mark Twain–Howells Letters,* 1:397–98.

28. Clemens, "Chapters from My Autobiography," 344.

29. Paine, *Mark Twain: A Biography,* 2:676.

30. Pamela Moffett to Orion and Mollie, May 9, 1881, CU-MARK.

31. Sam to Orion, Sept. 21, 1874, CU-MARK.

32. Pamela Moffett to Orion and Mollie, Mar. 27, 1882, CU-MARK.

33. Paine, *Mark Twain: A Biography,* 2:791–92.

34. Orion to Sam, June 7, 1882, CU-MARK.

35. Orion to Sam, June 29, 1882, CU-MARK.

36. Orion and Mollie to Samuel Moffett and Pamela Moffett, Feb. 18, 1883, CU-MARK.

37. Orion to Sam, Aug. 4 and 5, 1882, CU-MARK.

38. Pamela Moffett to Sam, Aug. 30, 1882, and Orion to Sam, Aug. 4 and 5, 1882, all CU-MARK.

39. Orion to Charles Webster, July 11, 1882, CU-MARK.

40. Orion to Sam, July 12, 1882, CU-MARK.

41. Webster to Sam, July 17, 1882, CU-MARK.

42. Webster, *Mark Twain, Business Man,* 191.

43. Orion to Sam, Aug. 4 and 5, 1882, CU-MARK.

44. Orion and Mollie to Sam and Olivia, Aug. 25, 1882, CU-MARK.

45. Sam to Jane Clemens, Oct. 9, 1882, CU-MARK.*

46. Pamela Moffett to Sam, Aug. 30, 1882, and Pamela Moffett to Sam, Sept. 13, 1882, both CU-MARK.

47. Orion to Sam, Aug. 29, 1882, CU-MARK.

48. Orion and Jane Clemens to Sam, Sept. 8, 1882, CU-MARK; it seems safe to say that she intended no irony by her misspelling.

49. Orion and Mollie to Samuel Moffett and Pamela Moffett, Feb. 18, 1883, CU-MARK.

50. Orion to Sam, Feb. 15, 1883, CU-MARK.

51. Ibid.

52. Orion and Mollie to Samuel Moffett and Pamela Moffett, Feb. 18, 1883, CU-MARK.

53. Sam to Orion, Feb. 22, 1883, CU-MARK.*

54. Orion to Sam, Feb. 27, 1883, CU-MARK.

CHAPTER 19

1. *Keokuk Weekly Constitution,* July 7, 1886, KPL.

2. Pamela Moffett to Samuel Moffett, July 2 and 3, 1886, CU-MARK.

3. Lorch, "Mark Twain in Iowa," 537.

4. *Keokuk Weekly Constitution,* July 7, 1886, KPL.

5. Ibid.

6. Orion to Sam, June 18, 1888, CU-MARK.

7. Lorch, "Mark Twain in Iowa," 540.

8. Webster, *Mark Twain, Business Man,* 147–48, 305; Paine, *Mark Twain's Letters,* 1:434.

9. Orion to Sam, Nov. 24, 1886, CU-MARK.

10. Orion and Mollie to Sam and Olivia, Dec. 19 and 20, 1886, CU-MARK.

11. Ibid.

12. Mollie to Sam and Olivia, Feb. 3, 1887, CU-MARK.

13. Orion and Mollie to Sam and Olivia, Dec. 29 and 30, 1886, CU-MARK.

14. Orion and Mollie to Sam and Olivia, Dec. 19 and 20, 1886, CU-MARK.

15. Orion to Sam, Apr. 27, 1887, and Sam to Orion, May 5, 1887, both CU-MARK.*

16. *Mark Twain's Notebooks and Journals,* 3:592 n. 67.

17. Orion to Sam, Nov. 1, 1890, CU-MARK.

18. Orion to Pamela Moffett, Apr. 20, 1893, CU-MARK.

19. Paine, *Mark Twain: A Biography,* 3:965.

20. Frederick J. Hall to Albert Bigelow Paine, Jan. 14, 1909, CU-MARK.

21. Paine, *Mark Twain: A Biography,* 3:969.

22. Orion to Sam, Jan. 6, 1894, CU-MARK.

23. Paine, *Mark Twain: A Biography,* 3:984.

24. Zacharias, "Henry Rogers," 5.

25. Wecter, *Love Letters,* 323.

26. Sam to Orion and Mollie, Sept. 14, 1896, CU-MARK.*

27. Sam to Orion, Mar. 28, 1897, CU-MARK.*

28. Leary, *Mark Twain's Correspondence with Henry Huttleston Rogers,* 284 n. 1.

29. Ibid., 283.

30. Ibid., 287 n. 2.

31. Ibid., 285 n. 1.

32. Ibid., 286.

33. Zacharias, "Henry Rogers," 6.

34. Leary, *Mark Twain's Correspondence with Henry Huttleston Rogers,* 288 n. 4.

35. Orion to Pamela, Aug. 8, 1897, CU-MARK.

36. Mollie to unknown, Aug. 18, 1896, CU-MARK.

37. Orion to Sam, Nov. 30, 1897, CU-MARK.

38. Pamela to Samuel E. Moffett, Dec. 15, 1897, CU-MARK.

39. *Keokuk Gate City,* Dec. 12, 1897, KPL.

40. Lorch, "Orion Clemens Number," 386.

41. Paine, *Mark Twain's Autobiography,* 2:331–32.

42. Lorch, "Orion Clemens Number," 385; Pamela to Samuel Moffett, Dec. 15, 1897, CU-MARK.

43. *Keokuk Gate City,* Dec. 12, 1897, KPL.

44. Ibid.

45. Ibid.

46. Ibid.

47. *Keokuk Gate City,* Dec. 14, 1897, KPL.
48. Ibid.
49. Pamela to Samuel Moffett, Dec. 15, 1897, CU-MARK.
50. Clemens, *Puddn'head Wilson,* chap. 10.

CHAPTER 20

1. Paine, *Mark Twain: A Biography,* 2:676, 677 n. 1.
2. *Mark Twain, Collected Tales,* 993–94.
3. *Mark Twain–Howells Letters,* 2:828.
4. Ibid., 830.
5. Paine, *Mark Twain: A Biography,* 1:263, 291.
6. Paine, *Mark Twain's Letters,* 1:101.
7. See Paine, *Mark Twain: A Biography,* 2:676.
8. Ibid., 1:28, passim.
9. *Mark Twain's Letters,* 1:352.
10. Lorch, "Orion Clemens Number," 382, 353–54.
11. Brashear, *Mark Twain,* 105–6.
12. Wecter, *Sam Clemens of Hannibal,* 282 n. 31.
13. Rasmussen, *Mark Twain A to Z,* 297.
14. IVL Journal, July 11, 1907, CU-MARK; Barbara Schmidt found an advertisement Paine placed in the *New York Times* of July 12, 1907, offering a reward for the return of his property (Schmidt, "Paine in the Lost and Found," 32).
15. Paine, *Mark Twain: A Biography,* 2:676, 677 n. 1.
16. Paine, *Boys' Life,* 366.
17. Lorch, "Lecture Trips," 409.
18. Ibid., 409 n. 2.
19. *The Gilded Age,* chap. 4.
20. *Huckleberry Finn,* chap. 14.
21. *Mark Twain's Letters,* 1:66.
22. *Huckleberry Finn,* chap. 31.
23. Gibson, *Mark Twain's "Mysterious Stranger" Manuscripts,* 239, 318.
24. Ibid., 369.
25. Ibid., 370.

Bibliography

MANUSCRIPT SOURCES

Bancroft Library, University of California, Berkeley.
Connecticut Historical Society, Hartford.
Keokuk Public Library, Keokuk, Iowa.
Mark Twain Papers, Bancroft Library, University of California, Berkeley.
Musser Public Library, Muscatine, Iowa.
Nevada Historical Society, Reno.
Nevada State Legislative Archives, Carson City.
State Historical Society of Missouri, Columbia.
University of California, San Francisco.
University of Nevada, Reno.
Vermont Department of Libraries, Montpelier.

BOOKS AND ARTICLES

Angel, Myron, ed. *History of Nevada.* Oakland: Thompson and West, 1881.
Bancroft, Hubert Howe. *History of Nevada, Colorado, and Wyoming.* San Francisco: History Company, 1890.
Bates, Edward. *Diary, 1859–1866.* Edited by Howard K. Beale. Washington, D.C.: American Historical Association, 1932.
Blair, Walter. *Mark Twain and Huck Finn.* Berkeley: University of California Press, 1960.
————, ed. *Mark Twain's Hannibal, Huck and Tom.* Berkeley: University of California Press, 1969.

Branch, Edgar Marquess. *Clemens of the Call: Mark Twain in San Francisco.* Berkeley: University of California Press, 1969.

———. *The Literary Apprenticeship of Mark Twain.* New York: Russell and Russell, 1966.

Branch, Edgar Marquess, and Robert H. Hirst, eds. *Early Tales and Sketches.* Vol. 1, *1851–1864.* Berkeley: University of California Press, 1979.

———. *Early Tales and Sketches.* Vol. 2, *1864–1865.* Berkeley: University of California Press, 1981.

Brashear, Minnie M. *Mark Twain, Son of Missouri.* Chapel Hill: University of North Carolina Press, 1934.

Clemens, Orion. "JIM." *American Publisher,* July 1871.

———. "Letter from St. Louis." Oct. 15, 1866, signed "Missouri." *San Francisco Times,* Nov. 10, 1866. Scrapbook 4, 37–38. Mark Twain Papers, Bancroft Library, University of California, Berkeley.

———. "Letter from St. Louis." Dec. 2, 1866, signed "C." *San Francisco Times,* Dec. 28, 1866. Mark Twain Papers, Bancroft Library, University of California, Berkeley.

———. "Letter from St. Louis." Dec. 22, 1866, signed "Cumberland." *San Francisco Times,* Jan. 19, 1867. Mark Twain Papers, Bancroft Library, University of California, Berkeley.

———. "Letter from St. Louis." Mar. 11, 1867. *San Francisco Times.* Mark Twain Papers, Bancroft Library, University of California, Berkeley.

———. "Letter from St. Louis." Apr. 25, 1867, signed "Conrad Crozier." *San Francisco Times,* May 22, 1867. Mark Twain Papers, Bancroft Library, University of California, Berkeley.

———. "Letter from Tennessee." Dated Dec. 28, 1866, signed "Cumberland." *San Francisco Times,* Jan. 26, 1867. Clipping in Scrapbook 4, 38. Mark Twain Papers, Bancroft Library, University of California, Berkeley.

———. "Letter from Tennessee." Mar. 11, 1867. *San Francisco Times.* Mark Twain Papers, Bancroft Library, University of California, Berkeley.

Clemens, Orion (attributed). "Saved by a Slave." Signed "Leon Treulon." *New York Weekly,* Apr. 18, 1867.

Clemens, Samuel Langhorne (*see also* Mark Twain). *Adventures of Huckleberry Finn.* New York: Charles L. Webster and Co., 1885.

———. "Chapters from My Autobiography." *North American Review,* Jan. 18, 1907.

———. *A Connecticut Yankee in King Arthur's Court.* New York: Charles L. Webster and Co., 1889.

———. *Letters from the Earth.* Edited by Bernard DeVoto. New York: Harper and Row, 1962.

———. *Life on the Mississippi.* Boston: James R. Osgood and Co., 1883.

———. *Mark Twain's Speeches.* Introduction by William Dean Howells. New York: Harper and Brothers, 1910.

———. *The Prince and the Pauper.* New York: Charles L. Webster and Co., 1884.

———. *Pudd'nhead Wilson and Those Extraordinary Twins.* Hartford: American Publishing, 1899.

———. *Roughing It.* Edited by Harriet Elinor Smith and Edgar Marquess Branch. Berkeley: University of California Press, 1993.

———. "Samuel Langhorne Clemens," autobiographical sketch. MS of 14 pages, Henry W. and Albert A. Berg Collection, New York Public Library, Astor, Lenox and Tilden Foundations, New York City, 1899.

———. *Sketches, New and Old.* Hartford: American Publishing, 1875.

———. *A Tramp Abroad.* Hartford: American Publishing, 1880.

———. *What Is Man? And Other Essays.* New York: Harper and Brothers, 1917.

Clemens, Samuel Langhorne (with Charles Dudley Warner). *The Gilded Age: A Tale of To-day.* Hartford: American Publishing, 1873.

Davis, Sam P., ed. *The History of Nevada.* Reno: Elms Publishing, 1913.

DeVoto, Bernard, ed. *Mark Twain in Eruption.* New York: Harper and Brothers, 1940.

Dictionary of American Medical Biography. New York: Appleton and Co., 1928.

Encyclopaedia Britannica. 1910.

Encyclopedia Americana. Danbury, Conn.: Grolier Inc., 1994.

Evans, Albert [Amigo, pseud.]. "Our San Francisco Correspondence: A Brilliant Idea." *Gold Hill (Nev.) Daily News,* Jan. 22, 1866, 2.

———. "Our San Francisco Correspondence: The Police." *Gold Hill (Nev.) Daily News,* Jan. 29, 1866, 2.

———. "Our San Francisco Correspondence: Nothing Personal." *Gold Hill (Nev.) Daily News,* Feb. 12, 1866, 2.

———. "Our San Francisco Correspondence: Mark Twain." *Gold Hill (Nev.) Daily News,* Feb. 19, 1866, 2.

Fanning, Philip Ashley. "One Story Mark Twain *Wouldn't* Tell." *The Californians* 12, no. 1 (January–February 1995): 38–47.

Fatout, Paul. *Mark Twain in Virginia City.* Bloomington: Indiana University Press, 1964.

Franklin, Benjamin. *Autobiography.* Boston: Whittlemore, Niles, and Hall, 1857.

Geer's Hartford City Directory for 1871–1872. Hartford: Hartford Steam Printing, 1871.

Gibson, William, ed. *Mark Twain's "Mysterious Stranger" Manuscripts.* Berkeley: University of California Press, 1969.

Gribben, Alan. *Mark Twain's Library: A Reconstruction.* 2 vols. Boston: G. K. Hall, 1980.

———. "Those Other Thematic Patterns in Mark Twain's Writings." *Studies in American Fiction* 13 (1985): 185–200.

Henderson, Roswell P., and Ralph Gregory. "Judge John Marshall Clemens." *Bulletin of the Missouri Historical Society,* October 1964.

Hill, Hamlin. *Mark Twain, God's Fool.* New York: Harper and Row, 1973.

———, ed. *Mark Twain's Letters to His Publishers, 1867–1894.* Berkeley: University of California Press, 1967.

Holcomb, R. I. *History of Marion County, Missouri.* St. Louis: E. F. Perkins, 1884.

Hornberger, Theodore, ed. *Mark Twain's Letters to Will Bowen.* Austin: University of Texas Press, 1941.

Journal of the Assembly during the Second Session of the Legislature of the State of Nevada. Carson City: John Church, 1866.

Kaplan, Justin, ed. *Mark Twain and His World.* New York: Simon and Schuster, 1974.

Leary, Lewis, ed. *Mark Twain's Correspondence with Henry Huttleston Rogers, 1893–1909.* Berkeley: University of California Press, 1969.

Lorch, Fred W. "Lecture Trips and Visits of Mark Twain in Iowa." *Iowa Journal of History and Politics* 27, no. 4 (1929): 408–56.

———. "Mark Twain in Iowa." *Iowa Journal of History and Politics* 27, no. 3 (1929): 507–42.

———. "Orion Clemens Number." *Palimpsest* no. 10 (1929): 353–88.

Mack, Effie Mona. *Mark Twain in Nevada.* New York: Scribner, 1947.

———. *Nevada: A History of the State from the Earliest Times through the Civil War.* Glendale: Arthur H. Clark, 1936.

———. "Orion Clemens, 1825–1897." *Nevada Historical Society Quarterly* 4 (July–December 1961): 63–109.

Mark Twain, Collected Tales, Sketches, Speeches, and Essays, 1852–1890. New York: Library of America, 1992.

Mark Twain–Howells Letters: The Correspondence of Samuel L. Clemens and William Dean Howells, 1872–1910. 2 vols. Edited by Henry Nash Smith and William M. Gibson. Cambridge: Belknap Press of Harvard University Press, 1960.

Mark Twain's Letters. Vol. 1, *1853–1866.* Edited by Edgar Marquess Branch, Michael B. Frank, Kenneth M. Sanderson, Harriet Elinor Smith, Lin Salamo, and Richard Bucci. Berkeley: University of California Press, 1988.

Mark Twain's Letters. Vol. 2, *1867–1868.* Edited by Harriet Elinor Smith, Richard Bucci, and Lin Salamo. Berkeley: University of California Press, 1990.

Mark Twain's Letters. Vol. 3, *1869.* Edited by Victor Fischer, Michael B. Frank, and Dahlia Armon. Berkeley: University of California Press, 1992.

Mark Twain's Letters. Vol. 4, *1870–1871.* Edited by Victor Fischer, Michael B. Frank, and Lin Salamo. Berkeley: University of California Press, 1995.

Mark Twain's Letters. Vol. 5, *1872–1873.* Edited by Lin Salamo and Harriet Elinor Smith. Berkeley: University of California Press, 1997.

Mark Twain's Letters. Vol. 6, *1874–1875.* Edited by Michael B. Frank and Harriet Elinor Smith. Berkeley: University of California Press, 2002.

Mark Twain's Notebooks and Journals. Vol. 1, *1855–1873.* Edited by Frederick Anderson, Michael B. Frank, and Kenneth M. Sanderson. Berkeley: University of California Press, 1975.

Mark Twain's Notebooks and Journals. Vol. 2, *1877–1883.* Edited by Frederick Anderson, Lin Salamo, and Bernard L. Stein. Berkeley: University of California Press, 1975.

Mark Twain's Notebooks and Journals. Vol. 3, *1883–1891.* Edited by Frederick Anderson, Robert Pack Browning, Michael B. Frank, and Lin Salamo. Berkeley: University of California Press, 1979.

Marsh, Andrew J. *Letters from Nevada Territory, 1861–1862.* Edited by William C. Miller, Russell W. McDonald, and Ann Rollins. [Reno]: Legislative Counsel Bureau, State of Nevada, 1972.

Miller, William C. "Samuel L. and Orion Clemens vs. Mark Twain and His Biographers (1861–1862)." *Mark Twain Journal* 16 (Summer 1973): 1–9.

Monton, Lucie T. *Winegrowing in Eastern America.* Ithaca: Cornell University Press, 1985.

Neider, Charles, ed. *The Autobiography of Mark Twain.* New York: Harper and Brothers, 1959.

Paine, Albert Bigelow. *The Boys' Life of Mark Twain.* Edited by Walter Barnes. New York: Harper and Brothers, 1915.

———. *Mark Twain: A Biography.* 4 vols. New York: Harper and Brothers, 1912.

———, ed. *Mark Twain's Autobiography.* 2 vols. New York: Harper and Brothers, 1924.

———. *Mark Twain's Letters.* 2 vols. New York: Harper and Brothers, 1917.

Pickard, Madge E., and R. Carlyle Buley. *The Midwest Pioneer: His Ills, Cures, and Doctors.* New York: Henry Schuman, 1946.

Quetel, Claude. *History of Syphilis.* Translated by Judith Braddock and Brian Pike. Baltimore: Johns Hopkins University Press, 1990.

Rasmussen, R. Kent. *Mark Twain A to Z: The Essential Reference to His Life and Writings.* New York: Facts on File, 1995.

Rogers, Franklin R. *The Pattern for Mark Twain's "Roughing It": Letters from Nevada by Samuel and Orion Clemens, 1861–1862.* Berkeley: University of California Press, 1961.

———, ed. *Mark Twain's Satires and Burlesques.* Berkeley: University of California Press, 1967.

Sattlemeyer, Robert. "Did Sam Clemens Take the Abolitionists for a Ride?" *New England Quarterly* 68, no. 2 (1995): 294–99.

Scharnhorst, Gary. "Mark Twain's Imbroglio with the San Francisco Police: Three Lost Texts." *American Literature* 62 (December 1990): 686–91.

Schmidt, Barbara. "Paine in the Lost and Found." *Mark Twain Journal* 31, no. 2 (1993): 32.

Smith, Henry Nash, ed., with Frederick Anderson. *Mark Twain of the Enterprise.* Berkeley: University of California Press, 1957.

Stedman, Laura, and George M. Gould. *Life and Letters of Edmund Clarence Stedman.* 2 vols. New York: Moffat, Yard, and Co., 1910.

Taper, Bernard, ed. *Mark Twain's San Francisco.* New York: McGraw Hill, 1963.

Tuckey, John S., ed. *Mark Twain's "Which Was the Dream?" and Other Symbolic Writings of the Later Years.* Berkeley: University of California Press, 1967.

Twain, Mark (*see also* Clemens, Samuel Langhorne). *Roughing It.* Edited by Harriet Elinor Smith and Edgar Marquess Branch. Berkeley: University of California Press, 1993.

Varble, Rachel M. *Jane Clemens: The Story of Mark Twain's Mother.* Garden City, N.Y.: Doubleday, 1964.

Walker, Franklin, ed. *Mark Twain's Travels with Mr. Brown, Being Heretofore Uncollected Sketches Written by Mark Twain for the San Francisco Alta California in 1866 and 1867, etc.* New York: Knopf, 1940.

Webster, Samuel Charles, ed. *Mark Twain, Business Man.* Boston: Little, Brown, 1946.

Webster's American Biographies. Edited by Charles Van Doren and Robert McHenry. Springfield, Mass.: Merriam-Webster, 1984.

Wecter, Dixon. *Sam Clemens of Hannibal.* Boston: Houghton Mifflin, 1952.

———, ed. *The Love Letters of Mark Twain.* New York: Harper and Brothers, 1947.

———. *Mark Twain to Mrs. Fairbanks.* San Marino, Calif.: Huntington Library, 1949.

Wood, Rich'd B. B. "'Mark Twain's' Elder Brother, His Trial for Heresy." Typescript. Keokuk Public Library, "taken from THE DAILY GATE CITY sometime around the year 1880."

Zacharias, Greg W. "Henry Rogers, Public Relations, and the Recovery of Mark Twain's 'Character.'" *Mark Twain Journal* 31, no. 1 (1993).

Index

About the Author

Philip Ashley Fanning is an independent scholar living in San Francisco.